MARXISM AND THE U.S.A.

MARXISM AND THE U.S.A.

Alan Woods

AAKAR

MARXISM AND THE U.S.A.
Alan Woods

Published in agreement with Wellred Books, England
for publication and sale only in the Indian Subcontinent
(India, Pakistan, Bangladesh, Nepal, Maldives,
Bhutan & Sri Lanka)

First Published in India, 2009

ISBN 978-81-89833-58-9 (Pb)

Published by
AAKAR BOOKS
28 E Pocket IV, Mayur Vihar Phase I, Delhi-110 091
Phone : 011-2279 5505 Telefax : 011-2279 5641
aakarbooks@gmail.com; www.aakarbooks.com

Printed at
Arpit Printographers
arpitprinto@yahoo.com

About the Author

Alan Woods was born in Swansea, South Wales, in 1944 into a working-class family with a strong left wing tradition. At the age of 16 he joined the Young Socialists and became a Marxist. He studied Russian in Sussex University and later in Sofia (Bulgaria) and the Moscow State University (MGU).

In the course of nearly forty-five years of active participation in revolutionary politics, he has acquired a wide experience of the international Labor movement. Alan was actively involved in the Marxist movement in Spain, where he personally participated in the underground struggle against the Franco dictatorship. He has also been actively involved in the revolutionary movement in Latin America, Russia and Pakistan. He speaks several languages, including Spanish, French, German and Russian. Alan Woods is the author of many articles, books and pamphlets covering a huge spectrum of issues: politics, history, economics, world affairs, the antiwar movement, philosophy, science, history, art and literature and the class struggle. His articles on the war in Iraq and Venezuela have earned him a wide audience worldwide, mainly through the popular website *In Defence of Marxism* (www.marxist.com).

He is the author a number of books including: *Ireland: Republicanism and Revolution, The Venezuelan Revolution: A*

Marxist Perspective, Bolshevism – the Road to Revolution, and *Lenin and Trotsky: What They Really Stood For* and *Reason in Revolt: Marxist Philosophy and Modern Science,* the last two written in conjunction with Ted Grant. In particular, *Reason in Revolt* has been hailed as a major contribution to Marxist theory. Among its admirers is President Chavez of Venezuela. *Reason in Revolt* has been translated into many languages, including Turkish, Greek and Urdu and has also been published in the U.S.A.

Also due for publication is *Marxism and the National Question.* He is presently working on two important new books: *The History of Philosophy* and *Marxism and Art.* He is currently the editor of the Marxist journal *Socialist Appeal,* published in London, and also of the *In Defence of Marxism* website (www.marxist.com), which is followed by many labor activists and students of Marxism around the world.

In addition to his literary work, Alan travels extensively, lecturing on Marxism in many parts, including Pakistan, Russia and different countries in Latin America, where he has established a considerable recognition as an able defender and popularizer of Marxist ideas. He is now 60 years of age, is married, and lives in London.

Contents

Introduction

The present work began life as a draft introduction to the American edition of *Reason in Revolt*. Starting out from the idea that most Americans have been prejudiced against Marxism as an alien ("foreign") ideology, I started to explain that the history of the United States contains a great revolutionary tradition, beginning with the War of Independence that set up the U.S.A. in the first place. However, on delving more deeply into the subject, it became clear that it was much too extensive to be satisfactorily contained in the Introduction to a book. I therefore put it to one side and wrote another one, the content of which was mainly of a scientific character.

Later on I showed a copy of the original draft to an American friend, who suggested that, suitably expanded, it could be published separately, and he very kindly furnished me with some interesting additional information. As a result, I felt obliged to introduce some more material on matters such as the American Revolution, the Civil War and the history of trade unionism in the U.S.A.

The subject is fascinating, and unfortunately very poorly known in Europe, where it has become a fashionable (and quite erroneous) idea that the U.S.A., as the bastion of world imperialism (which Gore Vidal, the greatest living American writer, describes as "the Empire"), never produced anything of interest to socialists and revolutionaries. Actually, the reverse is true, as I hope I have shown in this long essay. Part of my intention was to combat the kind of senseless anti-Americanism that one encounters all too frequently in left circles. Marxists are internationalists and do not take up a negative stance in relation to the people of any country. We stand for the unity of all working people against oppression and exploitation. What we oppose is not Americans, but American capitalism and American imperialism.

The American people and above all the American working class have a great revolutionary tradition. On the basis of great historical events they are destined to rediscover these traditions and to stand once more in the front line of the world revolution, as they did in 1776 and 1860. The future of the entire world depends ultimately on this perspective. And although today it may seem very far off, it is not so incredible as one might think. Let us recall that before 1917 tsarist Russia was the bastion of world reaction, as the U.S.A. is today. Many people were convinced that the idea of socialist revolution in Russia was a crazy delusion on the part of Lenin and Trotsky. Yes, they were completely convinced, and completely wrong.

The rapacious greed of the big corporations and the ambitions of the ruling elite of "the Empire" are dragging the U.S.A. into one adventure after another. New nightmares can flow from such adventures. Fifty-eight thousand young Americans were killed in the quagmire of Vietnam. The aggressive policies of the Bush White House threaten many more casualties, American and others. Sooner or later this will impact back on the U.S.A., producing a general reaction against a system that could produce such monstrosities. The mass demonstration in Seattle and other U.S. cities have served notice on the establishment that the youth of America will not be prepared to remain silent forever.

CHAPTER ONE

The U.S.A. and the World

The terrible events of September 11, 2001 marked a turning point in the history of the United States and the whole world. Overnight, it became impossible for ordinary U.S. citizens to imagine that what was happening in the outside world was no concern of theirs. A general sense of insecurity and apprehension seized the national psychology. Suddenly, the world became a hostile and dangerous place. Ever since September 11, Americans have been trying to make sense of the kind of world that could produce such horrors.

Many people have been asking themselves: what have we done that there should be such hatred against us? Of course, ordinary Americans have done nothing to deserve this kind of thing. And we regard it as a criminal act to kill innocent civilians, of whatever nation, to make a political point. What is not in doubt, however, is that the actions of the United States in the world - its government, its big corporations and its armed forces - have aroused feelings of deep antipathy and resentment, and it would be as well for Americans to try to understand why this is so.

For much of its history, isolationism has played a central role in the politics of the U.S.A. But the fact is that in the modern world no country can cut adrift from the rest of the world, no matter how big and powerful. Nowadays, the most decisive phenomenon of our times is precisely this:

the crushing domination of the world market. It is often known by the latest buzzword, globalization. But in fact it is not new. Already over 150 years ago in that most contemporary of all works, *The Communist Manifesto*, Marx and Engels predicted that the capitalist system, beginning as a series of national states, would create a world market.

The participation of the U.S.A. in world economy and world politics has grown almost continuously for the last century. All attempts to pull America into a state of self-imposed isolation have failed, and will inevitably fail, as George W. Bush has found out very quickly. The United States has inherited the role that was previously held by Great Britain –that of the world's policeman. But whereas Britain's dominant role in the world took place at a time when the capitalist system was still in its ascending phase, America now finds itself ruling over a world that is mortally sick. The sickness is the product of the fact that capitalism on a world scale is in a state of irreversible decline. This expresses itself in a series of convulsions that are increasingly of a violent character. The terrible cataclysm of September 11 was only one manifestation of this.

Anti-Americanism is, unfortunately, widespread. I say unfortunately because the present writer holds no ill feelings towards the people of the U.S.A. or any other country. As a Marxist, I am opposed to nationalism and chauvinist attitudes that sow hatred and conflicts between different peoples. But that does not mean that one can condone the actions of particular governments, companies and armed forces that are pursuing actions that are harmful to the rest of the world. It just means that it is wrong to confuse the ruling class of any country with the workers and poor people of that country.

The phenomenon of anti-Americanism is strongest in poor countries in Asia, Africa, Latin America and the Middle East. The reasons for this are related to the exploitation of the resources of these countries by voracious U.S. multinational corporations, backed by the U.S. military and the CIA, leading to the impoverishment of their people, the destruction of the environment, the destabilization of their currencies, their economies, and even their governments. Such actions are not designed to promote love and respect for the U.S.A. in the world at large.

A couple of years ago *The Economist* concluded that the prices of raw materials were at their lowest level for 150 years –that is, since records began. The situation has varied somewhat since, but it has not changed the position of millions of workers and peasants of the Third World who are being forced to work for slave wages by big U.S. corporations. One American golfer, Tiger Woods, for instance, earns more than the entire workforce of Nike in Indonesia.

The ruthless conduct of these big corporations is shown by the Bhopal tragedy in 1984, when 40,000 men, women and children were killed one night by the poisonous fumes from a Union Carbide plant situated too close to their homes. A recent report reveals that the area remains dangerously polluted to this day. This case is unusual only inasmuch as it hit the headlines.

The super-exploitation of what is known as the Third World by rapacious corporations is what causes a backlash in Africa, Asia, the Middle East, and Latin America which may sometimes take the form of a rejection of all things American, but which is at bottom an expression of anti-imperialism. The best way to put an end to the poverty and starvation in the Third World is to fight for the expropriation of the big corporations that are the enemies of working people everywhere – beginning with the workers of the U.S.A., as we shall show.

CHAPTER TWO

Europe and America

Anti-Americanism is not confined to poor countries. Some Europeans have somewhat negative attitudes to America. They resent the subordinate role they have been compelled to accept on the world stage, and they fear the consequences of the colossal economic and military domination of the transatlantic giant. Behind the polite façade of diplomacy between the "allies" lies an uneasy and contradictory relationship, which manifests itself in periodic trade conflicts and diplomatic rows. On a different level, many Europeans resent what they see as the intrusion of an alien culture, brash and commercialized, which threatens to devalue and undermine their cultural identity. Behind the cultural resentments of the European intellectuals lies a deep-seated feeling of inferiority that seeks to hide behind a kind of cultural snobbishness. This feeling has a material basis, and in fact reflects the real state of affairs.

It is a simple fact that the history of the last hundred years is the history of the decline of Europe and the rise of the U.S.A. As the Russian Revolutionary Leon Trotsky predicted, the Mediterranean (which in the Latin tongue signifies "the cen-ter of the world") has become an unimportant lake. The center of world history has passed first to the Atlantic and finally to the Pacific – two mighty oceans, straddled by a colossus – the United States. The real relationship between Europe and America is summed up by the relationship between George W. Bush and Tony Blair. It is the relationship of the master and his lackey. And like a good English lackey, Mr. Blair does his level best to imitate the style and manners of his master, notwithstanding which, no one in his right mind can mistake the real relation between the two.

The airs of superiority that until recently were adopted by members of the British Establishment with regard to the values and culture of America are particularly comical. They resemble the airs and graces of the penniless English aristocrats in the 19th century in the presence of the wealthy bourgeois upstarts, a phenomenon well documented in the novels of Jane Austen and others. These airs and graces, of course, did not stop them from marrying off their daughters to the sons of the upstart money-grubbers at the earliest opportunity.

The negative attitude of Europeans towards American culture is the product of a misunderstanding. They are thinking of the *made in the U.S.A.* "cultural exports" that flood the markets of the world with bad music that makes you deaf, overpriced "designer clothes" produced by slave labor in the Third World that makes you indig-nant and cholesterol-clogged fast food produced by slave labor in the high street that makes you obese. It is the kind of cheap and nasty commercialism that is the hallmark of capitalism in the period of its senile decay. That such monstrosities produce a feeling of revulsion in all thinking and feeling human beings is perfectly natural.

However, the concept of culture, above all in the modern world, is far broader than pop music, Coca-Cola and McDonald's. It also includes such things as computers, the Internet, and many other aspects of science and technology. On this level, it is impossible to deny the impressive achievements of the U.S.A. Moreover, it is precisely these scientific advances that are laying the foundations for an unprecedented cultural revolution, once they are correctly harnessed by a planned socialist economy on a world scale.

The present writer has no time for crude anti-Americanism. I am profoundly convinced that the colossal potential of the United States is destined to play a decisive role in the future socialist world order. But it must also be admitted that at the present moment in world history, the role of the U.S.A. on a world scale does not reflect its real potential for good, but only the rapacious greed of the big multinational companies that own America and control its actions in their own selfish interests. This author is a fervent admirer of the real America, and an implacable opponent of the other America, the America of the big banks and monopolies, the enemy of freedom and progress everywhere.

CHAPTER THREE

An "Un-American" Idea?

In order to understand the ideas of Marxism, it is first necessary to approach them without prejudice. This is difficult, because until now, the great majority of Americans have only heard of Marxism in connection with that monstrous caricature that was Stalinist Russia. Marxism ("communism") is therefore associated in the minds of many people with an alien regime, a totalitarian state where the lives of men and women are dominated by an all-powerful bureaucracy, and where individual initiative and freedom are stifled and negated. The collapse of the U.S.S.R. apparently proves the inadequacy of socialism, and the superiority of the free market economy. What more needs to be said?

Well, there is a great deal more to be said. The monstrous bureaucratic regime of the U.S.S.R. had nothing to do with the ideas of Marx and Lenin, who advocated a democratic socialist society, where men and women would be free to determine their own lives, in a way that they do not do in the U.S.A. or any other country today. This subject was very well explained in a marvelous book written by my friend and lifelong comrade Ted Grant (*Russia, from Revolution to Counter-Revolution*). The fall of Stalinism in Russia did not signify the failure of socialism, but only a bureaucratic caricature thereof. It certainly did not signify the end of Marxism, which today is more relevant than ever before. It is my contention that only Marxism, with its scientific methodology, can furnish us with the necessary analytical tools whereby we can understand the processes that are unfolding on a world scale – and in the U.S.A.

Whatever one thinks about Marxism, it has clearly had an enormous impact on the whole course of human history Today it is impossible for any man or woman to claim to be properly educated, unless they have taken the trouble to understand at least the basic ideas of Marxism. This goes as much for those who are opposed to socialism as those who are for it. A serious barrier that confronts the American reader who approaches Marxism is the thought that this is a foreign import that has no place in the history, culture and traditions of the United States. Although the infamous House Un-American Activities Committee and the late Senator Joseph McCarthy are now bad memories of the past, yet the psychological legacy remains, that "communism and revolution are not for us".

Actually, this is a serious misunderstanding of American history, which is not difficult to dispel. In fact, communism has far more ancient roots in America than capitalism. The latter has only existed for less than two centuries. But long before the first Europeans set foot on the soil of the New World (as they called it), Native Americans had been living in a communist society for thousands of years. The Native Americans did not understand private property (at least, not in our modern sense of the word). The state and money did not exist. There were neither police nor prisons. The idea of wage labor and capital was so alien to them that they could never be properly integrated in the new capitalist society that destroyed their old way of life, expropriated their ancestral common lands and reduced them to an appalling state of misery and degradation – all in the name of Christian civilization.

This new way of life called capitalism, with its greed, absence of solidarity, and morality of the jungle – was really an alien system, imported from foreign lands. It can be argued – quite correctly – that this is precisely what made possible the opening up of America, the colossal development of industry, agriculture, science and technology that have made the U.S.A. into the greatest economic power the world has ever seen. And since Marxism maintains that the key to all human progress lies in the development of the productive sources, this represented progress on a gigantic scale. Indeed, that is true. But there has been a price to pay for the progress that results from the anarchy of capitalism and the blind play of market forces. With the passing of time, an increasing number of people – not necessarily socialists – are becoming aware of the threat posed to the human species by the systematic destruction of the environment – the air we breathe, the water we drink, the food we eat. This apprehension is not lessened, but rather increased, by the remarkable progress of science and technology, which have advanced far more rapidly in the U.S.A. than in any other country in the world.

Before the Europeans arrived, America was a land of unspoiled prairies, pristine forests and crystalline cascades and lakes. It was a land in which men and women could breathe freely. To the original inhabitants of America, the land was sacred and nature was respected:

"As the ecological patterns of this large geographic area varied enormously, each native group adjusted its lifestyle to benefit from the available resources. Such patterns reflected not so much economic prudence as a spiritual relationship with nature. Regardless of regional variations, the native peoples viewed the world as a balanced system in which all creation, animate and inanimate, existed harmoniously. Thus the biological world of edible plants or fish or game remained intimately attached to a spirit world.

Humanity was but one part of that system. The acquisition of food, clothing, or shelter therefore depended upon maintaining spiritual relations with the rest of creation. From this perspective, the idea of owning parcels of land, bits of creation, was unthinkable." (P.N. Carroll and D.W. Noble, *The Free and the Unfree, a New History of the United States*, pp. 27-8.)

How things have changed! The big companies that now dominate America have no concern for the environment – our common heritage. All is reduced to a question of profit for a few (a concept the Native Americans would have found incomprehensible). The advent of genetically modified crops undoubtedly contains the potential for important advances, but under the present system poses a deadly threat to the future of humanity.

There was a time when films about the "Wild West" inevitably presented Native Americans as bloodthirsty savages, and the white men as the bearers of civilization, destined to take over their lands and consign them to reservations where they would learn the benefits of Christian charity. Nowadays, this is no longer considered acceptable. Native Americans are presented in a more positive light. Yet in practice, the average American knows little about their culture and way of life. Actually, the man who did more than anyone else to write about the society and civilization of these peoples was the great American anthropologist, Lewis Henry Morgan. His famous book *Ancient Society* represented a revolutionary new departure in the study of anthropology and ancient history. He gave the first scientific explanation of the gens or clan as the basic unit of human society in prehistory:

"The simplest and lowest form of the council was that of the gens. It was a democratic assembly because every adult male and female member had a voice upon all questions brought before it. It elected and deposed its sachem and chiefs, it elected Keepers of the Faith, it condoned or avenged the murder of a gentilis, and it adopted persons into the gens. [...]

"All the members of an Iroquois gens were personally free, and they were bound to defend each other's freedom; they were equal in privileges and in personal rights, the sachem and chiefs claiming no superiority, and they were a brotherhood bound together by ties of kin. Liberty, equality and fraternity, though never formulated, were cardinal principles of the gens." (Lewis Henry Morgan, *Ancient Society*, p. 85.)

And again: "A powerful popular element pervaded the whole organization and influenced its action. It is seen in the right of the gentes to elect and depose their sachems and chiefs, in the right of the people to be heard in council through orators of their own selection, and in the voluntary system in the military service. In this and the next succeeding ethnical period democratic principles were the vital element of gentile society." (Morgan, *Ancient Society*, p. 144.)

Morgan's work was read with great interest by Marx and Engels and played an important role in developing their ideas about ancient societies. Morgan's writings about the Iroquois and other tribes were absolutely central to Engels' book *The Origins of the Family, State and Private Property* – one of the seminal works of Marxism. This, in turn, was the basis of Lenin's celebrated book *The State and Revolution*, which was written in 1917 and presents the genuine Leninist model of a socialist democracy, in which the old oppressive bureaucratic state would be dis-solved and replaced by a direct democracy, based on:

- Free elections with right of recall of all officials.
- No official to receive a wage higher than that of a skilled worker.

- No standing army, but the armed people.
- Gradually, all the tasks of running the state to be done by everybody in turn (when everybody is a bureaucrat, nobody is a bureaucrat).

It is quite ironic that the source of some of the most basic writings of Marxism turns out to be – the United States. It is even more ironic that the democratic constitution that Lenin and Trotsky introduced into the young Soviet Republic after November 1917 had its roots in the writings of Lewis Morgan and is, in essence, a return to the old communist order of the Native Americans, though obviously on the higher foundations made possible by modern industry, science and technology. So, in a way, one could argue that it was Russia that imported an old American idea, and not vice-versa!

CHAPTER FOUR

Genocide of the first Americans

It is impossible to read today the accounts of the first contacts between Europeans and Native Americans without a profound sense of sadness. In every case the newcomers were greeted with the hospitality that was a sacred obligation for the people the haughty strangers regarded as "savages". Columbus wrote: "Of anything they have, if you ask them for it, they never say no." His journal is full of examples of the generosity of the unsuspecting natives, who were about to be enslaved and exterminated as a reward. "They ought to be good servants and of good skill," Columbus concluded.

The European colonization of the Americas had a devastating effect on the lives and cultures of the Native Americans. In the 15th to 19th centuries, their populations were decimated, by the privations of displacement, by disease, and in many cases by warfare with and enslavement by European settlers. The latter liked to portray their treatment of the Native Americans as the result of an admirable civilizing and humanitarian mission (just as the imperialists of our own period describe their missions in Iraq and elsewhere). They were bringing Christianity and Civilization to a bunch of ignorant savages and naked heathens. In practice, however, their motives were simple greed and insatiable lust for gold and land.

A contemporary account describes the response of the most Christian Spaniards when the Aztec emperor distributed presents of gold among them:

"The Spanish burst into smiles; their eyes shone with pleasure... They picked up the gold and fingered it like monkeys; they seemed to be transported by joy, as if their hearts were illumined and made new." (Quoted in P.N. Carroll and D.W. Noble, op. cit., pp. 40.)

The first Native American group encountered by Columbus, the 250,000 Arawaks of Haiti, were enslaved and brutally treated. By the year 1550 only 500 were still alive and the entire people was totally extinct before 1650. This set the tone for the treatment of the First Americans for the next 400 years. When the Native Americans realized they were being expropriated and robbed, they reacted with predictable violence. A long and bloody conflict was born.

Here is a typical report of a Captain John Mason, who came across a Native American fort early one morning while the inhabitants were still asleep. Having blocked the exits, he then ordered his men to set fire to the wigwams:

"The captain also said: 'We must burn them', ... (and immediately stepping into the Wigwam where he had been before,) brought out a Fire-Brand and putting it into the Matts with which they were covered, set the Wigwams on fire ... and when it was thoroughly kindled, the Indians ran as Men most dreadfully Amazed. And indeed such a dreadful Terror did the Almighty let fall upon their Spirits, that they would fly from us and into the very Flames, where many of them perished. And when the Fort was thoroughly Fired, Command was given, that all should fall off and surround the Fort; which was readily attended by all; ... The Fire was kindled on the North East Side to windward; which did swiftly over-run the Fort, to the extreme Amazement of the Enemy, and great Rejoycing of ourselves.

Some of them climbing to the Top of the Palisade; others of them running into the very Flames; many of them gathering to windward, lay pelting at us with their Arrows; and we repayed them with our small Shot; Others of the Stoutest issued forth as we did guess, to the Number of Forty, who perished by the Sword. ...

"And thus in little more than one Hour's space was their impregnable Fort with themselves utterly destroyed, to the Number of Six or Seven Hundred, as some of themselves confessed. There were only Seven taken Captive and about Seven escaped. ...

"Of the English, there were two Slain outright, and about twenty wounded." (Quoted in Leo Huberman, *We the People*, pp. 26-7.)

This amounted to outright genocide. Although there were honourable exceptions, most Europeans felt free to rob and kill the "primitive" people they found in their path. Europeans also brought diseases against which the Native Americans had no immunity. Usually it was unintentional, but sometimes they intentionally spread disease among the native tribes. This is probably the earliest example of germ warfare in history

Illnesses like chicken pox and measles, though rarely a cause of death among Europeans, often proved fatal to Native Americans. More deadly diseases such as smallpox caused the most terrible devastation in Native American populations. Nobody knows the exact percentage of the total Native American population killed in this way, but it is known that waves of disease often destroyed entire villages. Some historians believe that up to 80 per cent of some Indian populations may have died as a result of European-derived diseases:

"Sir Jeffrey Amherst – for whom Amherst College is named – had a plan for exter-minating the Indians. He was commander in chief of the British forces in America in the

1760s, while the French and Indian War was going on. With all deference to historical perspective, the viewpoint of the age, and so on, his plan makes one more or less ashamed of the human race. His idea was to kill the Indians by spreading smallpox among them – and to spread it he proposed giving them blankets inoculated with the disease. The blankets were to be given as presents, accompanied by smiles and expressions of goodwill." (W.E. Woodward, *A New American History*, p. 106.)

In other words, the advent of "civilization" (read: capitalism) was disastrous for the Native Americans. Their tribal lands were plundered. They were killed like animals or herded into so-called reservations where they suffered a slow death from hunger, disease, alcohol abuse or simple despair. Proud and ancient cultures were annihilated as the alien culture of Christianity was foisted on a defeated people. Having robbed them of their lands, the conquerors now proceeded to rob them of their soul.

The treatment of the Native peoples, along with the enslavement of the black Africans, constitutes a blot on the history of the U.S.A. But the Europeans have no reason to feel in any way morally superior in comparison to Americans. This bloody barbarism constitutes a definite stage in capitalism, which Marx called the Primitive Accumulation of capital. In every country it bore the same hallmarks. In England we had the Enclosure Acts that robbed the peasants of their land and reduced them to beggary and starvation in their own country.

Marx pointed out that capitalism first came onto the stage of history dripping blood from every pore. The genesis of the capitalist system is the systematic expropriation of the property of the peasants, the Native Americans, the Scottish clans and the peoples of the enslaved colonies, and, in Marx's words, this history "is written in the annals of mankind in letters of blood and fire":

"The spoliation of the church's property, the fraudulent alienation of the State domains, the robbery of the common lands, the usurpation of feudal and clan property, and its transformation into modern private property under circumstances of reckless terrorism, were just so many idyllic methods of primitive accumulation. They conquered the field for capitalistic agriculture, made the soil part and parcel of capital, and created for the town industries the necessary supply of a 'free' and outlawed proletariat."

Capitalism always destroys every older social system with which it enters into contact. This destructive task has always been accomplished with the utmost barbarity and ruthlessness. In Scotland we had the so-called Highland Clearances, which deprived the free peasants of the Highlands of their ancestral lands and broke up the ancient clan system. Starving men, women and children were driven off their land like beasts and the estates turned into hunting preserves for the English aristocrats. To this day the North of Scotland is a wilderness. Many of the expropriated Scottish peasants were forced to emigrate to the United States and Canada.

The difference in the United States lies in the racial component. The First Americans were seen as inferior beings, not fully human, who could be conquered, enslaved, plundered or killed without any qualms of conscience. In the early days a bounty was paid for the scalp of every Native American man, woman or child handed in to the authorities. The first reported case of white men scalping Native Americans took place in New Hampshire colony on February 20, 1725. In spite of the movies, the Native Americans probably learned scalping from the Europeans and not vice-versa.

CHAPTER FIVE

"Custer's Last Stand"

In the 19th century, the westward expansion of the United States led to a colossal increase in the numbers of Native Americans expelled from vast areas of their territory. Whole peoples were forced into marginal lands in areas farther and farther west, or simply by massacring them. The mask of hypocrisy was always available to salve the consciousness of the Christian businessmen and politicians involved in this plunder. Numerous treaties were entered into during this period, but later violated or simply abrogated. When the natives resisted, it was reported at the time as the "Indian Wars". In fact, these wars had an entirely one-sided character.

This portrayal of the Native Americans as "savages" was perpetrated by countless novels, stories and above all the cinema, where the white settlers were habitually portrayed as the victims, while the "Indians" were portrayed as bloodthirsty aggressors. The "Injun fighter" was always the hero. In turn these movie images fed racist prejudice that re-emerged time and time again in the bloody history of American imperialism. After all, racism is only the distilled essence of imperialism.

Among the military engagements of the "Indian Wars" one stands out as an example not only of the bravery of the Native Americans but also of their grasp of military tactics and strategy. I refer to the famous Native American victory at the Battle of the Little Bighorn in 1876. This episode has been subjected to an incredible campaign of falsification. It has entered the annals of Western history as "Custer's last Stand" and has acquired virtually the status of a myth. At the time the press published prints of the gallant general surrounded by his faithful troopers, valiantly defending the flag until the last man was cut down by the "murdering redskins". This myth was later popularized in various Hollywood films, depicting Custer and his men as great heroes.

The achievements of the U.S. cinema industry are well known and justly celebrated. But the American film directors have to this day shown themselves to be incapable of producing a single honest film about the Vietnam War. Some films have appeared that are quite good, cinematographically speaking. They at least attempt to show the Vietnam War as a barbaric war – although, generally speaking, the U.S. soldiers are presented as the main victims of this barbarity.

This is a one-sided view, to put it mildly. The people of Vietnam suffered invasion by a foreign army; were killed by the hundreds of thousands by bullets, napalm, shrapnel, and chemical weapons ("defoliants"). Yet even in supposedly anti-war films they rarely appear as real human beings – usually they appear only as "collateral damage". The Vietnamese fighters who took on the might of the U.S. military are never presented as what they truly were -heroic resistance fighters -but rather, as a shadowy and depersonalized enemy. In place of the "murdering redskins" of the old John Wayne movies we have the Vietnamese "gooks" or the Iraqi "terrorists". We really have not advanced very far!

The truth about the Battle of the Little Bighorn was very different from the fictional accounts. Recent research of the battlefield has finally nailed the lie. There was no "Custer's Last Stand". The U.S. Cavalry was outmaneuvered and outfought by the Native American warriors, and cut down as they fled in panic. But this could not be admitted! How could the American public be informed that supposedly inferior "savages" had a better grasp of military science than an American general? How could they fight better than the crack troops of the Seventh Cavalry? In this way the lying propaganda of Custer's Last Stand was born. In one form or another it has been with us ever since.

The Native American victory at the Little Big Horn had to be avenged and was avenged with interest in the massacre at Wounded Knee in 1890. On January 31, 1876 the United States government ordered all remaining Native Americans to move into reservations or reserves. This was the end of a civilization. By the stroke of a bureaucrat's pen, the astonishing Prairie Culture that developed around the use of the horse for hunting, travel and trading was crushed underfoot.

Nowadays many people in the U.S.A. realize that the image of the Native Americans as primitive savages is a travesty and a falsification of history. These peoples were not savages, but nations with a culture and a complex civilization from which we can learn many things. There is a natural desire to make amends. Naturally, all the rights of the Native Americans must be upheld. But the clock cannot be put back 150 years. When a way of life and a culture has passed into history it can no more be revived than a dead person can be brought back to life. We must march onwards to a higher stage of human civilization, while preserving and absorbing all that is valuable from the past.

It is very sad that the good name of America has been besmirched for so long by the taint of racism. After all, American history is the history of a gigantic melting pot that has absorbed people from many different nations, religions and cultures. It is this rich ethnic mix in part that makes the American character so vital, energetic and outward going. Under socialism, the highest form of human civilization and culture, this stain will be erased once and for all, and the people of every ethnic background will have the possibility of a free development in conditions of complete liberty, equality and fraternity.

CHAPTER SIX

Forgotten Aspects of American History

In the 17th century, the Pilgrims began the task of taming the great American wilderness, displaying indomitable courage in the most difficult conditions. Who were they? They were political refugees fleeing from an oppressive regime in Britain. This regime was the result of the counter-revolution that took place after the death of Oliver Cromwell, when the English bourgeoisie compromised with reaction and invited Charles II back from France.

We must remember that at that time politics and religion were inextricably linked. Each different Church or sect represented not only differing interpretations of the Gospels, but a definite strand of political opinion, and, in the last analysis, the standpoint of a definite class or sub-class in society. Thus, the Catholics represented open feudal reaction, and the Episcopalians were a disguised version of the same. The Presbyterians represented the wealthy merchants of the City of London, inclined to compromise with the monarchy. The Independents, typified by Cromwell, represented the more radical wing of the petty bourgeoisie, and so on.

On the extreme left wing there was a mass of sects, ranging from revolutionary democrats to communists: Fifth

Monarchy men, Ranters, Seekers, Anabaptists, Quakers, and others were based in the lower levels of the petty bourgeoisie, the artisans and semi-proletarians, the fish-wives and apprentices – in short, the masses. The Levellers and particularly the Diggers openly questioned the right to hold private property even at this time. In all these groups we see a fierce attachment to democracy, a hatred for the rich and powerful (whom they regarded as the agents of Satan and the "sons of Belial") and an equally fierce attachment to equality. This was the spirit that inspired the English revolution of the 17th century.

The revolutionary masses believed that they would establish the kingdom of God on this earth. We now know that this was an illusion. The level of historical development at that time was not ripe for the establishment of a classless society. The real function of the English (and later the American) Civil War was to clear the decks for the development of capitalism. But this would never have been possible without the active involvement of the masses, who were inspired by a very different vision.

Having come to power by basing himself on the revolutionary semi-proletarian masses, Cromwell brutally suppressed the left wing, and thus prepared the way for the return of the hated monarchy and its attendant bishops. The remnants of the Puritan left wing found themselves subjected to civil and religious persecution. That is why the "Pilgrim Fathers" (as they came to be called) went to America to found communities based not only on religious freedom but also on principles of strict equality and democracy.

The one hundred and two souls who set sail on the Mayflower were not men and women of property but poor men and women from the lower classes of English society: small farmers, manual workers, artisans, weavers, carpenters, blacksmiths and the like. Only a few were schoolteachers. As members of a dissident religious sect (the Brownites or Separatists), they were oppressed by poverty and the extreme difficulty in making a living in Restoration England. Politically, they were what we would call nowadays left-wing revolutionaries. Many of them emigrated to Holland, the only country in Europe that upheld religious toleration. But some of the more daring decided to make the long and dangerous crossing of the Atlantic in search of social, political and religious freedom.

As Alexis de Tocqueville points out: "Puritanism was not merely a religious doctrine, but it corresponded in many points with the most absolute democratic and republican theories." (Alexis de Tocqueville, *Democracy in America,* p. 35.) But the Separatists were a more radical tendency than the run-of-the-mill Puritans. They advocated reform not only in religious but also in secular matters. This was enough for the authorities to regard them as dangerous subversives, much as the U.S. authorities regard Marxists today. Worse still, they believed in holding property in common and sharing the products of labor. *In short, the Pilgrims were Communists.*

The colony founded by these pioneers was based on a communal system. Whatever was produced was to go into a common fund and everyone was to be fed and clothed out of it. In other words, they based themselves on the communist principle: "from each according to his or her ability, to each according to his or her need." For the first seven years there was to be no private property in land. In the end it broke down, of course. It is impossible to construct a communist system on the basis of poverty and a low level of development of the productive forces. By 1623 the social differentiation was already so pronounced, and the objections to the communal system so general, that Governor Bradford abolished it and gave every family a plot of land.

However, even after that the Pilgrims organized their communities on extremely democratic and equalitarian lines: "In Connecticut the electoral body consisted, from its origin, of the whole number of citizens; and this is readily to be understood, when we recollect that this people enjoyed an almost perfect equality of fortune, and a still greater uniformity of opinions. In Connecticut, at this period, all the executive functionaries were elected, including the Governor of the State. The citizens above the age of sixteen were obliged to bear arms; they formed a national militia, which appointed its own officers, and was to hold itself at all times in readiness to march for the defense of the country." (Alexis de Tocqueville, *Democracy in America*, pp. 37-8.)

This model of popular democracy is not very different to the one implemented by the revolutionary people of Paris in the Commune of 1870, which in turn gave Marx the idea of what a workers' democracy (the "dictatorship of the proletariat") would look like. It was the model that Lenin cited in his book *The State and Revolution*, which formed the basis of the original soviet democracy of 1917 in Russia, before it was overthrown by the Stalinist political counterrevolution. But this historical parallel, for some reason, has never occurred to the official historians of the U.S.A.! According to these ladies and gentlemen the Pilgrims were only religious people, seeking the freedom to worship their God in their own way. Of course, this is partly true, but it does not convey the whole truth. These people were courageous revolutionaries fleeing from religious *and political* persecution in the Old World. They were very advanced in many ways. For example, they introduced compulsory public education, which they naturally justified in religious terms:

"It being one chief project of the old deluder Satan to keep men from the knowl-edge of the Scriptures [...] by persuading from the use of tongues, that learning may not be buried in the grave of our fathers, in the church and commonwealth, the Lord assisting our endeavors [...]" and so on.

If we look at the substance and not the religious form, this was an extremely advanced and enlightened reform. Schools were established in every village and town and the inhabitants were obliged to support them under pain of heavy fines. The municipal authorities were bound to enforce attendance at school and to impose fines on parents who failed to do so. It was at least two centuries before similar laws were passed in Europe.

These people practiced their own version of republican democracy at a time – let us not forget – when America was still under British rule and therefore formally a monarchy. They established a kind of regime of double power in which a republic and a citizen's democracy, complete with a people's militia, the election of all officials, and a general assembly of all the people, existed in every town and village. And this was at a time when Absolute Monarchies ruled the roost in all Europe and trampled the people's rights in the dust.

CHAPTER SEVEN

Class Struggle and Slavery

The class struggle existed from the beginning on American soil. The appearance of rich and poor had political consequences. The arrival of large numbers of poor people and indentured servants from England accentuated the differences. The existing landowners intended to become wealthy large landowners with estates worked by bonded labor. But the poor immigrants had other ideas and strove to get small plots of land to work for themselves. John Winthrop of Massachusetts expressed the attitude of the better-off colonists towards the newly arrived immigrants. He wrote of "the unwarrantableness [...] of referring matters of council or juricature to the body of the people, *quia* the best part is always the least, and of that the best part is always the lesser." Later he said that he favored a "mixt aristocracy".

Winthrop tried to restrict the number of voters. He had a law passed that limited the suffrage to church members. Then church membership was made exclusive. Political radicals could be expelled from the church and thus stripped of their political rights. Narrowness and intolerance began to take a hold. Under the guise of religious purity and Puritan rigor, there was an uninterrupted struggle going on between rich and poor, privileged and unprivileged.

As a matter of fact, the wages of English laborers were usually no more than what a slave owner paid for the food, lodging and clothes of a slave. The generally held view of that time was that wages should be no more than what was necessary to keep the workers alive and able to reproduce. The subsistence-level theory of wages already existed in practice long before it acquired a theoretical expression in the writings of the classical economists at the start of the 19th century. This held that it was absolutely necessary to keep the working class in a state of abject poverty. The problem was that there was nothing to prevent a free worker from setting out for the vast western frontier, which was not far away, and establishing himself as a small farmer.

The British Virginia Colony was based on the cultivation of tobacco and the ownership of slaves. Plantation agriculture depended on slavery and a variant of it: the system of indentured labor. An indentured servant was bound to serve for a specified number of years. Some were convicts. They were sent to the Colonies as a kinder alternative to the punishments meted out by English law at a time when the theft of one shilling was punishable by death and a man could be hanged for pulling down a fence or poaching or stealing a sheep. However, as there were few other choices available for a poor laborer, so most indentured servants renewed their contracts for as long as they could.

This led to the creation of the plantation owners' greatest fear: a permanent class of poor, discontented, and armed laborers. Their fears were realized with Bacon's Rebellion, a class revolt led by Nathaniel Bacon that succeeded in burning Jamestown to the ground in 1676. After this experience plantation owners sought to replace white indentured laborers with what they hoped would be a less rebellious form of labor – African slaves.

The introduction of slaves from Africa was the answer of the plantation owners to the annoying tendency of the free workers' efforts to improve their lot and fight against exploitation. Even before 1700 most of the slaves were in the Southern Colonies. But New England had its fair share. In Rhode Island in 1756 there were 35,939 whites and 5,697 black Africans. Most of the slaves in the colonies north of Virginia were house servants, but not all. One man in Philadelphia ran his iron foundry with thirty slaves. During the 18th century so active was the slave trade with the New England Colonies that the price of newly landed slaves fell to thirty pounds.

The number of black slaves increased enormously in South Carolina after the introduction of rice growing in 1696. From 1700 on the number of blacks always out-numbered the white population. On the eve of the American Revolution the proportion was two to one. The slave owners lived in terror of a slave uprising. The punishments for black slaves were barbaric in the extreme. They were often burned alive for offences for which whites were hanged. In 1739 there was a slave insurrection. It was brutally put down but not before 21 whites and 44 slaves were killed. As a result the assembly approved a draconic slave code. It became a penal offence to teach a slave to read and write. Slaves were not allowed to hold meetings, even church services, unless a white person was present. At the same time some concessions were made: the hours of work should not exceed fifteen, and Sunday should be a holiday.

The slave trade was an important and very profitable industry. The prosperity of towns like Liverpool was based upon it. In 1771 there were 107 slave ships from Liverpool on the African coast, and a further 60 or 70 from America. They were generously financed by wealthy corporations in the City of London and the British government actively supported and aided the slavers. Considerable fortunes were made from the slave trade, including that of the family of William Gladstone, the future leader of the British Liberal Party.

In the South the whole socio-economic system was based on slavery. The luxurious lifestyle of the landowners was entirely based on the labor of the slaves. George Washington, a big landowner, had numerous indentured servants. A letter to his agent in Baltimore dated 1774 states that four men convicts and a man and his wife had been purchased on his account for the sum of 110 pounds sterling. The four men had to serve for three years and the married couple four years. This works out at five and a half pounds per year for each one. Even Thomas Jefferson, the author of the Declaration of Independence, who wrote that "all men are created equal", owned more than 200 black slaves, whom he never freed, though others, including Washington, did.

The continued existence of slavery increasingly acted as a drag on the progress of America even after it had won its independence. Marx explained that no people can be free if it keeps another people in chains. Slavery was a heavy burden on the American people. It exercised a constant downward pressure on the wages of free labor and a permanent threat to democratic rights. Its existence tended to degrade the status of all manual labor. Any free worker was just one step above the bonded servant or slave. Even the American Revolution did not abolish this cancer. For that, a second American Revolution would be necessary.

CHAPTER EIGHT

Revolution and the U.S.A.

"[W]hat country can preserve its liberties, if its rulers are not warned from time to time that [the] people preserve the spirit of resistance? Let them take arms. The tree of liberty must be refreshed from time to time, with the blood of patriots and tyrants". (Thomas Jefferson, Letter to Col. William S. Smith, 1787.)

Nowadays, the public in the U.S.A. is taught to fear and hate revolutions. Like communism, they are regarded as un-American, something alien and a threat from without. In actual fact, from its very beginnings America has always been nourished by foreign revolutions, with waves of immigrants fleeing political repression in search of a better life. However, the above quotations show clearly that revolution is an idea that is far from foreign to the native soil of the U.S.A., which owes its very existence to a revolution. When the American colonists raised the flag of revolt against the English Crown, this was a very revolutionary act. It was this that served as the source of inspiration for the French Revolution that broke out just over a decade later. Thus, the flame of revolution in Europe was first kindled in America.

The young American bourgeoisie was rankling under the onerous rule of a foreign power based some thousands of miles away, which could introduce painful taxes, limits on trading and other burdens that hampered the free development of the American bourgeoisie. These fetters had to be broken and they were broken by revolutionary means. The imposition of the Stamp Act in 1765 was the event that set the whole process in motion. But it was only the accident through which necessity revealed itself, as Hegel would have said. In fact there were many other Acts that stoked the fires of resentment: the Navigation Acts, which regulated and restricted American commerce, the prohibition of settlement beyond the Appalachian Mountains, and the Tea Act, designed to prevent the East India Company from going bankrupt.

A revolution necessarily means the eruption of the masses onto the arena of politics and can only succeed in its objectives to the degree that it involves the mass of "ordinary people" in activity. The American Revolution was no exception to this rule. In order to succeed, the bourgeois leaders must arouse the masses and lean on them to strike blows against the enemy. Although the official histories emphasize (and over-emphasize) the role of men like George Washington, what really guaranteed the success of the revolution was the active involvement of the masses – the artisans, carpenters, apprentices, the small farmers and trappers and the elements of the lower middle class, lawyers and journalists inspired with revolutionary ideas, who spurred them on to action.

The bad conditions and absence of rights produced a ferment of discontent in the lower orders of society. So when the merchants of the colonies rebelled against the impositions of the British administrations that hampered trade and made their life impossible, the lower classes joined in with gusto. Trotsky explains that poverty alone is not enough to make a revolution. If that were the case, the masses would always be in revolt. But it is not the case. The "mob" in America already existed before 1776, but was capable of doing nothing more than to cause occasional dis-turbances. Now things were different. The poor and dispossessed now had a focal point for their discontent, a banner and a rallying cry, even if it was not exactly their own.

A decisive role was played by revolutionary agitators like Samuel Adams of Boston, the most outstanding figure of the American Revolution. His energetic agitation for the revolutionary cause struck a responsive note among the masses. He was the most able of the class of agitators but there were many unsung heroes like him whose names have not come down to us. The immediate target of the agitation was the hated Stamp Act which required all legal documents, licenses, commercial contracts, newspapers, pamphlets, and playing cards to carry a tax stamp. Stamp distributors were hanged in effigy and their houses torn down. Packages of stamps were burned in bonfires to wild cheering and the beating of drums.

The class basis of the American Revolution was well understood by the British colonialists. General Thomas Gage who was head of the British troops in America wrote in worried tones to the King's Secretary of State on December 21, 1765: "The Plan of the People of Property has been to raise the lower Classes to prevent the execution of the Law [...] with the view to terrify and frighten the people of England into a Repeal of the Act. And the Merchants, having Countermanded the Goods they had written for unless it was repealed, they make no Doubt that many Trading Towns and principal Merchants in London will assist them to accomplish their Ends.

"The Lawyers are the Source from whence the Clamors have flowed in every Province. In this Province, nothing Publick is transacted without them, and it is to be wished that even the Bench was free from blame. The whole body of Merchants in general, Assembly Men, Magistrates, etc., have been united in this Plan of Riots, and without the influence and Instigation of these the inferior People would have been very quiet. Very great Pains were taken to rouse them before they stirred. The Sailors are the only People who may be properly Stiled Mob, are entirely at the Command of the Merchants who employ them."

These lines undoubtedly contain an error. It is always a characteristic of the police (or military) mentality that it attributes strikes, disturbances and revolutions to the work of "agitators" who are so inconsiderate as to stir up the masses. The latter would otherwise, according to this view, continue meekly to submit to the yoke. Agitators there were, of course, and very talented ones, such as Sam Adams. But to imagine that they could have such a dramatic effect on the masses, unless the latter were already prepared to hear their revolutionary message, is a self-evident stupidity. The relatively small number of revolutionary agitators organized in illegal societies like The Sons of Liberty, only succeeded because the people were already preparing to move, motivated by their own experience.

CHAPTER NINE

Role of the Masses

"If ye love wealth greater than liberty, the tranquillity of servitude greater than the animat-ing contest for freedom, go home from us in peace. We seek not your counsel, nor your arms. Crouch down and lick the hand that feeds you; May your chains set lightly upon you, and may posterity forget that ye were our countrymen." – Samuel Adams

The official histories of the Revolution, as always, play down the role of the masses and concentrate on the upper strata – the wealthy Boston merchants and landowners like Washington, who were pursuing their own interests, as general Gage understood quite well. But in order to succeed in their struggle with the colonial administration, they were compelled to rely on the masses, who did all the fighting. It was the workmen in the towns who organized in the Sons of Liberty, wrecked the houses of the hated stamp agents and threw their furniture onto the streets and burned them. It was they who tarred and feathered informers. It was they who translated the speeches of the leaders into action. Later on it was the small farmers and trappers who played the decisive role in fighting against the English army of occupation.

The fact is that the American Revolution would never have succeeded unless the masses had intervened in a decisive way. It is a matter of record that the wealthy

American merchants who had set the ball rolling with their clash with the City of London on questions of trade and taxation soon recoiled from the Revolution when they saw that the poor people were getting active and taking matters into their own hands. The aims of the wealthy merchants and landowners, however, were narrow and egotistical. They aimed to destroy the rule of the British Crown in order to replace it with their own rule. This was not a very inspiring prospect, and hardly a program to set the masses on fire. More idealistic slogans were necessary. Cromwell promised the masses in England the installation of the reign of God on earth, no less, while Robespierre proclaimed the rule of Reason and Liberty, Equality, Fraternity. The American Revolution also required a banner to rally around and a program they believed in.

All this is not to say that the men who led the American Revolution did not believe what they preached. They sincerely believed that they were fighting for the sacred principles of Liberty set forth so movingly in the Declaration of Independence. A man like Thomas Jefferson, the most outstanding of the well-known leaders of the Revolution, was a product of the Age of Enlightenment, well schooled in the ideas of Locke, Hobbes, Newton and Bacon. For such a man, the fact that the American colonies were ruled by a despotic foreign power must have embittered the very depths of his being.

However, while the speeches were being made on the top, the mainspring of the revolt came from the bottom. Before the Revolution the workers – the "men of no property" – were generally deprived of political rights. Power was in the hands of wealthy merchants and magistrates who could do pretty much anything they liked. The rate of wages was decided usually by an association of owners or masters in the same trade. These were almost always on a subsistence level. The workers had no say in the matter. Associations of workers were forbidden by law. Those who owned no land had no right to vote in any of the colonies. James Truslow Adams wrote: "It was only as the Revolution approached that these unfranchised elements [...] wrested political control of the colonial government from the class of propertied freemen, and then largely by illegal, violent and terroristic methods."

The merchants were terrified that the masses would "go too far" and therefore attempted to reach a compromise with the enemy. In the moment of truth the rich American "patriots" had much more in common with their class brothers in England than with the working class and poor farmers of their own country. Many wealthy citizens deplored the actions of the "mob". Such a man was Henry Laurens, a wealthy planter and merchant of South Carolina. For this "leader of public opinion", things were getting out of hand. He asked "what would become of our estates without law, particularly ours who depend on commerce?"

While the respectable merchants fretted and dithered, the masses took decisive action from below. Hitherto the bourgeois had restricted themselves to a *voluntary* boycott of British goods. But the "Boston Tea Party", when a group of colonists thinly disguised as Mohawks, resorted to direct action, dumping British tea chests into the sea, threw down a bold challenge to the British. British public opinion was outraged. London reacted by attempting to starve Boston into submission through the imposition of a naval blockade that closed the port. But this only radicalized the whole situation. Once a revolution has aroused the masses, they are not easily intimidated even by the greatest power on earth.

Even in the moment of its birth, America was faced with the crying contradiction between rich and poor – *that is, with the class question*. From the very beginning there has been a contradiction between the theory and practice of

American democracy, an immense gulf between words and deeds. While the people were fighting for the Rights of Man, the merchants and landowners of America were really only concerned with the Rights of the Rich. Governor Morris expressed the feelings of the rich when he wrote: "...These sheep, simple as they are, cannot be gulled as heretofore. In short, there is no ruling them ... the heads of mobility [the mob] grow dangerous to the gentry and how to keep them down is the question." It has been *the question* for the American ruling class ever since. As early as 1772 – before the outbreak of hostilities with England – Sam Adams wrote in *The Boston Gazette*:

"Is it not High Time for the People of this Country, explicitly to declare whether they will be Freemen or Slaves [...] Let us [...] calmly look around us to consider what is best to be done [...] Let it be the topic of conversation in every social Club. Let every Town assemble. Let Associations and Combinations be everywhere set up to consult and recover our just Rights."

What is this but a call for the setting up of what the Russians were later to call *soviets* (which in the Russian language signifies "committee" or "council")? The American revolutionaries set up something that approximates to soviets – that is, revolutionary committees – over one hundred years before the Russian workers thought of it. They established their Liberty clubs and Committees of Correspondence, which kept the revolutionary fighting groups in contact with one another.

The town laborers detested the whole colonial system and looked forward eagerly for its destruction. They could hardly be worse off! One of the most famous of the revolutionary secret societies was The Sons of Liberty. To disguise their identity they blackened their faces and dressed up as Indians or used other disguises. They used passwords and secret signs. Their favorite weapon was tar and feathers. They also tore down houses. Unpopular customs officers and Tories (that is, supporters of British rule) would end up tarred and feathered or have their house demolished, or both.

The activities of The Sons of Liberty and other similar groups gradually became bolder, to the point where armed clashes with the redcoats became inevitable. On March 5, 1770, a clash between a mob and British soldiers led to the "Boston Massacre" when the redcoats panicked and fired into the crowd, killing four people. The murderers were let of with minor punishments. This was the spark that lit the fuse. Sam Adams worked incessantly day and night writing letters to far-flung settlements denouncing these deeds. Paul Revere – a Boston engraver and a member of The Sons of Liberty – produced an engraving of the massacre that was distributed far and wide.

The irony was that the masses who led the revolt were fighting for demands that would benefit merchants like Laurens, not themselves. These men of no property would never have to put a Stamp Act tax-stamp on a document in their lives. Not for the first or the last time, the masses were fighting and risking their lives to fight someone else's battle. As W.E. Woodward correctly points out:

"The discontent of the workingman was very real, and very bitter, though it had long been inarticulate. This dissatisfaction had nothing to do with British rule, though the illiterate mob was made to believe that Britain was the cause. The protest of the working classes was, in reality, an unconscious revolt against their position in the colonial world.

"The chief defect of colonial civilization – in respect to the common man – was not overregulation; the free white men of the time had more personal liberty than the common people in England. Its deficiency lay rather in underregulation, in a general neglect of all social problems.

The higher classes had no time to give to the consideration of such matters. Their entire attention was fixed on land and money. They never made any serious attempt to better working conditions, or to establish minimum wages or hours of labor, or to consider the poor as anything else than servile dependents on the rich." (W.E. Woodward, *A New American History*, p. 131.)

CHAPTER TEN

The Declaration of Independence

In 1774 the delegates for the Continental Congress assembled in Philadelphia. Hostilities had already broken out and the delegates, although all from the wealthier classes of society, were under pressure to adopt a more radical stand. *Originally the majority of the upper class Americans did not want independence.* But the mood of the masses made all thought of compromise impossible. The situation was explosive and this favored the most radical elements in Congress. As a result, on July 4, 1776, the Thirteen United States of America declared their independence from Great Britain.

The task of drafting the declaration was given to a committee composed of John Adams (cousin of Samuel Adams and future President), Benjamin Franklin, Thomas Jefferson, Robert R. Livingston, and Roger Sherman. Thomas Jefferson, a 33-year-old Virginian landowner and left-winger, was charged by the committee to write the declaration. He wrote one of the most inspiring revolutionary documents in history.

Here was an act of tremendous boldness and one that required great courage. The revolutionaries had thrown down the gauntlet to the most powerful imperial state in the world. Their lives were now forfeit and could only be saved by outright victory and they knew it. There could now be no turning back, as Benjamin Franklin pointed out when he uttered the famous words: "We must hang together, or assuredly we shall all hang separately". Later, when Jefferson was the American ambassador in France, he wrote:

"'If our country, when pressed with wrongs at the point of the bayonet, had been governed by its heads instead of its hearts,' he asked, 'where should we have been now? Hanging on a gallows as high as Haman's. You began to calculate and to compare wealth and numbers: we threw up a few pulsations of our warmest blood: we supplied enthusiasm against wealth and numbers: we put our existence to the hazard, when the hazard seemed against us, and we saved our country.'"

The Declaration of Independence, with its ringing endorsement of the idea of liberty and equality for all, was a clarion call to the downtrodden and oppressed everywhere. It was as revolutionary in 1776 as *The Communist Manifesto* would be in 1848.

This document seems the more remarkable because of the state of the world in which it was written. In 1776 there were kings on the throne of England, France, Austria and most of the other great powers of Europe. Russia was ruled by a tsar (or tsarina), the Ottoman Empire by the Sultan and China by its imperial dynasty. Democracy was therefore a novel and highly revolutionary doctrine.

This epoch-making document still has the power to inspire today. In it the idea of liberty is magnificently expressed. Life, liberty and the pursuit of happiness are proclaimed as *inalienable rights*. But no citizen of Russia, China or the Ottoman Empire could say the same thing. Nor could the citizens of France, Austria or Prussia, and even England was a monarchy ruled, in practice, by a corrupt and reactionary oligarchy of wealthy landowners. The Declaration shook the world. When it was announced, it caused a tremendous stir in every American city. It was read aloud to exited groups of citizens on the streets of Philadelphia. Here was something really worth fighting and dying for! "And for the support of this Declaration", Jefferson concluded, "we mutually pledge to each other our Lives, our Fortunes, and our sacred Honor."

The document would doubtless have been even more radical had it not been for the fact that it had to be subscribed by all thirteen colonies, including the slave-owning colonies from the South. In fact, the most obvious and glaring weakness of the document is that it does not deal with the issue of slavery at all. There was a considerable slave population – 539,000 or one fifth of the total population of the colonies. It seems that Jefferson wanted to include a reference to slavery and made several proposals for its abolition, but all were rejected. Finally, following the protests of the slave-owning states, all mention of the institution of slavery was omitted from the final draft. Jefferson began to temporize on the issue, postponing it to some unspecified future date. In this way, the seeds were laid for a bloody Civil War and a second American Revolution.

On the thorny question of religion, however, Jefferson was implacable. He insisted that, though the citizen had the right to hold any belief he or she chose, governments did not have the right to favour any faith. Therefore the state and religion must be radically separated. At the time when this democratic principle was proclaimed, the states had their own laws on religion, mostly of a retrograde character. Some states prohibited Roman Catholicism. In Jefferson's own state, Virginia, heresy was a capital offence. The radical separation of the state and religion is a basic democratic principle, but it is now under attack from the so-called religious right. These people wish to introduce religion into the schools and interfere with the curriculum to teach the First Book of Genesis instead of the scientific theory of evolution. These elements wish to throw America back to the Dark Ages, to the age of superstition and the Salem witch trials, and to ditch an essential feature of the Declaration of Independence.

Today the principles of the Declaration of Independence are the heritage of every American citizen. All Americans believe in these principles – at least, they would like to believe in them. Yet, if we are to be honest, there are contradictions in the very text of the Declaration and the American Constitution itself. When it is said that all men are created equal, this is clearly not in accordance with the facts. Although we may come into this world in a more or less equal state as human beings, there is inequality from the very start. The world is divided into rich and poor, and the former rule over the latter, exploit and oppress them. This was already the case when Thomas Jefferson wrote the Declaration of Independence, and it is a million times truer today.

In the 18th century, it was still possible to dream of a democratic republic comprised of small farmers (this was Jefferson's ideal), in which the differences between rich and poor would be reduced to a minimum. Over 200 years since the American Revolution, the U.S.A. is entirely dominated by a handful of giant corporations that act effectively as a law unto themselves, much as the old aristocracies of 18th century Europe did. Although theoretically the U.S. is a democracy and a republic, in fact all the important decisions are taken by small groups of unelected persons. Moreover, the power of the President, and the clique that surrounds him, is colossal and tends to constantly encroach on the rights of the citizens, the law and the Constitution itself.

For the wealthy merchants in Congress, freedom meant first and foremost freedom of trade and free enterprise. But free enterprise, as Marx explains, always begets monopoly, and today, the U.S.A. is more monopolized than any other country on earth. In place of Jefferson's democracy of small farmers we have the dictatorship of Big Business. The roots of this contradiction can already be found in the 18th century, as we shall show.

CHAPTER ELEVEN

First Shots of the Revolution

The revolutionary agitation gathered strength continually, impelled by the movement from below. There were attempts at compromise but they all broke down. It is not a question of the incompetence of lord North or the madness of George III, as some historians have tried to imply. Once the contradictions in society have reached a critical point, nothing can prevent an explosion. It is not a question then of this or that action by this or that government minister but of profound forces that, having matured over a long period, must break out onto the surface. Actually, the intention of the leaders was not to win independence from London but to reach a compromise that would lead to the abolition of the Stamp Act and other restrictive measures. When the First Continental Congress met it was overwhelmingly composed of wealthy landowners and merchants. The men of no property – the workers, artisans and dirt farmers – were conspicuous by their absence. The outlook of the majority was conservative:

"The spirit of colonial independence had not yet sunk deep into their convictions. Independence was too great a leap to take at once; they were less radical in temperament than the people who had sent them there. Why? Because all of them – or nearly all – represented some kind of vested interest and they moved with the customary caution of men of property. They regarded the Congress as a meeting of protest rather than of rebellion." (W.E. Woodward, *A New American History*, p. 145.)

We find a similar situation at the beginning of the French Revolution and the English Revolution. These were objectively bourgeois revolutions, but in practice the bourgeois elements that stood at the head of the movement in the initial stages were striving for a compromise with the old order. In every case the Revolution only succeeded to the degree that the leadership was taken out of the hands of the bourgeoisie and passed to the masses of proletarians, semi-proletarians and plebeians. If the bourgeois elements had retained control, it would have led to defeat. But that was not to be the case.

Events on the ground soon destroyed all attempts at compromise at the top. On April 18, 1775, events were brought to a head by the attempt of the British army to arrest two revolutionary leaders – John Hancock and Sam Adams. Warned in time by Paul Revere who rode out of Boston ahead of the troops, the pair escaped. Revere also warned the local militia commander at Lexington that they were in danger of losing their powder. The British, under the command of Major Pitcairn, arrived at Lexington to be confronted by some fifty armed Minutemen of the Massachusetts militia on the village green. When ordered to disperse, they stood their ground. In the ensuing fire fight, eight militiamen were killed. The first shots of the American Revolution had been fired.

The British may have won the first round but it was a pyrrhic victory. On the way back, the redcoats found themselves under fire from an invisible enemy. Farmers came straight from the fields, their clothes still caked in mud, and hid behind trees as they shot down one British soldier after another. By the end of the day, the militia had lost 93 men and the redcoats 293. Once the Revolution began it attracted all the slumbering forces of revolt that had lain dormant in the entrails of society. There were the backwoodsmen, for instance. They were not concerned with things like the Stamp Act but rather with the issue of land. For such men as these, Revolution was not just to kick out the British but also to break the power of the land companies – most of which were owned by Americans. These were the men who formed the most combative sections of the revolutionary militia – the sharpshooters whose guerrilla tactics drove the redcoats to desperation, attacking without warning and then disappearing back into the impenetrable forest.

Despite everything, the leaders continued to resist the demand for independence. Although the colonies had been advised to form temporary governments, Congress insisted that these provisional governments were to "continue only during the present unhappy and unnatural conflict." (See W.E. Woodward, *A New American History*, p. 150.)

There were many traitors who did not want the revolution to succeed. Benedict Arnold was not an isolated case. Even those in Congress who reluctantly accepted the need to fight (when the British left them with no alternative) were more afraid of the masses than of the British redcoats. In their heart of hearts many of them desired some kind of deal. In fact, most of the American aristocracy were pro-British Tories. The strength of a revolution lies in the energy, the conviction and the active participation of the masses. The period of revolutionary ascent always corresponds to the period of greatest activity of the masses. That is why a revolution is democratic by its very nature. The same is true of any strike. A strike will succeed to the degree that the rank and file workers take the running of the strike into their own hands. Bureaucratic control is the kiss of death.

The psychology of the American elite was brilliantly

conveyed by Gore Vidal in his novel about the American Revolution, *Burr*:

"'I hate the enemies of England.' There was real passion in her voice. 'I hate what your Virginia dolt is doing to our world.'

"I assured her that it would still be *our* world when the war ended; but without the inconvenience of paying taxes to England. She would not believe me."

"'It will not be ours but theirs, those wild men from the woods, from the water frontage, from the worst stews of the towns. They'll take *everything*.'" (Gore Vidal, *Burr*, p.135.)

These lines perfectly express the mentality of the wealthy Americans who were terrified by the forces unleashed by the Revolution. The men of property – even those who hated the English – were afraid that by rousing the mass of poor and dispossessed Americans to fight the English, they would put in danger the sacred rights of private property. The American ruling class in its heart has always feared democracy and done its best to curtail democratic rights because they fear that a real "government of the people, by the people and for the people" would lead to the overthrow of the dictatorship of Money. All their actions have been governed by this fear – from 1776 right up to the present day.

CHAPTER TWELVE

Expropriation of Property

The ideals expressed in the Declaration of Independence were extremely revolutionary for their day: "We hold these truths to be self-evident: *that all men are created equal.*" This proclamation of equality was like a revolutionary manifesto. In earlier documents the "inalienable rights" of Man were usually stated to be "life, liberty and *property*." The last point was of particular interest to the wealthy merchants and landlords who now stood at the head of the Republic. However, Thomas Jefferson substituted for this the phrase: "life, liberty *and the pursuit of happiness,*" leaving out any reference to property.

This was clearly a significant change the represented the pressure of the lower classes. In fact, the revolutionary government took measures that violated the sacred rights of property when it confiscated the estates of the pro-English landowners – the Tories. The estates were then broken up and sold to small farmers. In the process many of the big estates were broken up and something like an agrarian reform was carried out. This, along with independence, was one of the main gains of the Revolution. W.E. Woodward writes:

"The seizable property of the Tories, or loyalists, must have been about one-third of the total property value of the colonies. This is merely an estimate, and it is probably too low. Nearly all Tory property was confiscated, and the Tories were treated with the utmost rigor. Washington called them 'abominable pests of society,' and declared they should be treated as traitors. Their confiscated property was usually sold at auction, and it seldom brought more than a small fraction of its current value. The proceeds went into the state treasuries." (W.E. Woodward, *A New American History*, p. 166.)

The amounts of land confiscated by the revolutionaries were considerable. The Fairfax estate in Virginia covered six million acres. The Phillipse estate in New York extended for 300 square miles. Sir William Pepperell could ride for 30 miles along the coast of Maine without ever leaving his own land. Yet despite the demand from Britain that the loyalists should be given compensation, not a single cent was ever paid to them:

"Then came the question of compensation to the loyalists whose property was confiscated during the war. The American commissioners declared that the loyalists' property had been confiscated by the various states, and that Congress had no power to compel the states to make restitution. As a compromise the Americans agreed to include in the treaty a clause which would 'recommend' the states to compensate the Tories. It was also agreed that private debts owed to British creditors were still valid. The compensation clause was futile; none of the states paid any attention to it." (ibid., pp. 211-212.)

The same point is made by other authors:

"Loyalists were tarred and feathered, ridden on rails, flogged, even executed. The term 'lynch law' probably originated from the proceedings of one Charles Lynch, a justice of the peace in Virginia, who achieved a certain notoriety for his treatment of Tories.

"In addition to the brutal treatment they received, Tories had their property snatched from them by the newly formed revolutionary governments. Many Tories were forced to seek shelter behind British lines. These actions reflected not only a tradition of social antagonism but also a strong desire among revolutionaries to achieve a united front. By the war's end, nearly one hundred thousand colonial inhabitants had gone into exile in Canada and England. Their banishment brought profound psychological alienation – 'a dismal gloom', reported one unhappy exile from London." (P.N. Carroll and D.W. Noble, op. cit., pp. 117.)

CHAPTER THIRTEEN

George Washington Restores 'Order'

The main concern of Congress was to keep control of the movement and limit its scope. On June 15th, 1775, three days before the Battle of Bunker Hill, the Continental Congress assumed control of the militia that was besieging Boston as well as all the other men under arms in the colonies. Colonel George Washington, a rich landowner, was promoted to the rank of general and made commander-in-chief. This choice was no accident. The gentlemen in Congress needed an aristocrat as a guarantee against the "mob" in Boston. Discipline was to be restored. Order was to prevail. The wealthy property owners in Congress were more frightened by their own supporters than of the British army.

Washington must have been shocked at what he saw in camp. As befits a revolutionary army, there was an egalitarian spirit and a marked lack of rank. Ordinary soldiers spoke to their officers on familiar terms. They did not bother to shave and talked in the ranks. Men could come and go as they pleased. Washington soon sorted that out. He introduced courts martial. Lieutenant Whitney was convicted of "infamous conduct in degrading himself by voluntarily doing the work of an orderly sergeant."

Did these methods give better results? Actually, they did not. The men that Washington criticized so bitterly were the same American militiamen who had inflicted a terrible defeat on the British army at Bunker Hill – a defeat so resounding that after it the redcoats stayed under cover for nine months. The American troops never achieved such a result anywhere else, despite all Washington's discipline and courts martial.

George Washington was in fact a very mediocre figure. His role in the American Revolution has been greatly exaggerated, while the role of real revolutionaries like Sam Adams has been played down. "Discipline is the soul of an army" was one of Washington's favorite maxims. True – but the discipline of a revolutionary army is not the same as the discipline of any other army. Broadly speaking, every army reproduces the structures and is motivated by the spirit of the society that produced it. The army of a democracy will not be the same as the army of a fascist regime. The army of a class society needs a ferocious discipline – a reign of terror in fact – because it is maintained by force.

The discipline of a revolutionary army, on the contrary, is a voluntary discipline because it is necessarily an army of volunteers. The armies of the French Revolution, although they were composed largely of untrained volunteers, dressed in rags and barefoot, swept the best trained and equipped mercenaries in Europe before them and scattered them like the wind. The difference is that they knew what they were fighting for. They believed in it and were willing to die for it. This made them virtually invulnerable.

A revolutionary army must be run on democratic lines. This does not at all contradict the requirements of discipline in the battlefield. The Russian Red Army under Trotsky was very democratic. The Bolsheviks abolished the saluting of officers and all the outward trappings of command: the medals and gaudy uniforms. The officers and men ate in the same canteens and the soldiers were no longer required to use the polite form (*vy* in Russian, like *vous* in French or *usted* in Spanish) when addressing an officer. But when in battle strict discipline was expected and all orders had to be obeyed. The Red Army became a formidable fighting force while maintaining the norms of proletarian democracy. By the way, a similar regime existed in Oliver Cromwell's Model Army during the English Revolution in the 17th century.

The aristocratic Washington, who was very much in favour of pomp and circumstance, medals and smart uniforms, and who tried to impose strict (bourgeois) discipline in an army of revolutionary volunteers, did not make them a more effective fighting force but rather the opposite. In the same way the Stalinists in Spain in the Civil War of the 1930s, using the same arguments as Washington, actually destroyed the basis of the revolutionary army and undermined its fighting spirit, leading to its defeat at the hands of Franco's fascist army.

Far from improving the military efficiency of the revolutionary forces, Washington committed a major blunder. The strength of the revolutionary army lay in its guerrilla tactics, combining flexibility with great mobility. They could inflict considerable casualties on the British and then vanish into thin air. The farmers' boys and backwoodsmen were fine sharpshooters, but could not stand a bayonet charge by regular troops. Washington attempted to turn them into regular soldiers and made a mess of it. Charles Francis Adams, who was a soldier in the revolutionary army as well as a historian, wrote:

"Washington measured himself and his army up against his adversary at the point where they were strongest and he was least so. He offered infantry to infantry; oblivious of the fact that the British infantry were of the most perfectly organized kind, while his own was at best an extemporized force."

The main problem was not military but political. Both Washington and the bourgeois and landlords in Congress lacked the will to pursue the fight against the British to the finish. They admitted there was a war but denied it was a war against the king! As a result the war dragged on inconclusively for years. Washington was a careerist, more suited for political intrigues and manoeuvres at the top than fighting the enemy. As Gore Vidal wittily (and correctly) says: "[...] though Washington could not defeat the enemy in battle, he had a fine talent for defeating rival generals in the Congress." (Gore Vidal, *Burr*, p. 73.)

There can be no doubt that the British were actually winning the war before the French came in on the American side. The French were motivated not by the love of liberty (they lived under an absolutist monarchy a hundred times more oppressive than the British equivalent), but by hatred of England, their old rival. This tipped the balance in favour of the American colonists. Britain was already worn down by the costs of a prolonged war that was draining them financially and disrupting trade, especially when Spain and Holland also joined in.

In 1781 the British general Cornwallis found himself trapped in Yorktown, with the American forces in front of him, and the French fleet in his rear. There was no escape. He was forced to surrender. At this time the ruling administration in London was led by men who were unenthusiastic about continuing the war. They added up their sums and concluded that it was costing them more to hold down the American colonies than what they could ever hope to get back. They decided to pull the British army out. The war was over.

Washington's alleged military skills therefore had little or nothing to do with the victory. The war itself was really mainly a series of inconclusive skirmishes. As a military chief his record was very poor. In the first three years he lost every single engagement, except for a small victory at Trenton, and that was achieved more by luck than judgement. In a Christmas Eve skirmish in the middle of a snowstorm, he managed to defeat a whole brigade of Hessians. It helped a little that the Hessians, who had been celebrating the Festive season, were blind drunk at the time and did not know what they were doing.

Other revolutionary generals were more capable and more successful than Washington. And the most successful actions of the revolutionary forces were carried out by the guerrillas, whom he despised. The reason that Washington's image has been boosted by the official historians of the Revolution is that he represented the most Conservative wing of the leadership – a "moderate", a respectable man of property – a man in the image of the present-day rulers of the U.S.A., with whom the modern bankers, capitalists and Republican leaders can feel comfortable.

The attempts of Washington to control the revolutionary army from the top and impose a ferocious military discipline were not dictated by military necessity but rather by the wish of the bourgeois and landowners in Congress to police the revolutionary masses and prevent the revolutionary movement from getting "out of hand". Even in the course of hostilities, the men of property were preparing for the moment of victory, when it would be necessary to reassert their "sacred right to rule" and crush the very people who had won the victory.

CHAPTER FOURTEEN

The New Oligarchy

> *"Democracy has never been and never can be so desirable as aristocracy or monarchy, but while it lasts, is more bloody than either. Remember, democracy never lasts long. It soon wastes, exhausts and murders itself. There never was a democracy that did not commit suicide."* (John Adams)

The fears of the "Moneyocracy" were fully confirmed by what happened after the British were driven out. With the removal of the common enemy, the class divisions emerged with renewed force. The wealthy upper class was itself divided between the Whigs, who supported the Revolution, and the Tories, the most con-servative wing of the bourgeois and landowning aristocracy, who had supported the British Crown. But after the defeat of the English and the departure of the Redcoats, the Tories had no alternative but to throw in their lot with the winning side.

Although the right to vote was extended to include new layers of property owners, it was still highly restrictive. A new oligarchy was being created, in which the rich and powerful joined forces in a reactionary bloc against democracy and the demands of the lower orders. They attempted to give the most restrictive interpretation to the Constitution, stressing property rights above all else. Their model was the principles of the British government – that is, an aristocratic constitution that excluded the bulk of the people from government. The common people had shed their blood to drive the British out, while the American ruling class conspired in Congress to reintroduce the corrupt and undemocratic British system of government. For them, all the rights and privileges were the monopoly of the rich, while all the obligations and duties were for the poor. As long as the rich were all right, everybody was assumed to be all right. (The same idea is basically behind what is today called the "trickle-down" theory.)

A section of the bourgeoisie favoured a strong central state, while others wanted a weaker centre. From this arose the Federalist and anti-Federalists. Some of the Whigs became anti-Federalists, while others like Hamilton (who was really a monarchist in disguise) became strong Federalists. Tory Federalists became Republicans, while anti-Federalist Republicans became Jeffersonian Democrats. The Tories were in favour of strong central government in order to protect property, although previously they had been opposed to any government since they supported the British Crown.

The fact is that Alexander Hamilton and John Adams were conspiring to reintroduce an English-style monarchical system. The differences between Jefferson and Hamilton were between the right wing of the bourgeoisie, who wanted a deal with the counter-revolutionaries, and the more radical wing that was prepared to lean on the masses for support, but without surrendering an atom of real power. Of the 13,000 men who lived in New York City, only 1,300 owned enough property to qualify as voters. In the election of 1789 there were over 200,000 residents in New York State, of whom only 12,000 were eligible to vote for governor. In Massachusetts the property qualifications for voters were twice as high as under British rule. The Federalists were firm supporters of oligarchic rule and in essence opposed to democracy:

"Supporters of the new Constitution – people who styled themselves Federalists – argued that state governments were too susceptible to popular control, that the masses did not respect the interests of property, that liberty threatened the stability of the republics. The Federalists appealed to people with interstate interests – merchants, commercial farmers, public creditors, and urban workers whose livelihoods depended upon the prosperity of their employers. They also attracted politicians who lacked power within the existing state governments, men who hoped to supplant the entrenched political groups. As defenders of property, the Federalists saw a strong national government as a bulwark against the caprice of popular politics."

"In framing a government which is to be administered by men over men," Madison declared, "the great difficulty lies in this: you must first enable the government to control the governed; and in the next place oblige it to control itself." These lines strikingly express the attitude of the oligarchy to the people. The first task of government is not to represent the people, but to *control* them. The real attitude of the ruling elite was shown by the words of John Adams, who together with Hamilton had founded the Federalist Party (though he later described Hamilton as "the bastard son of a Scotch peddler").

Party lines constantly shifted and the arguments between the rival factions were acrimonious at times, but in the last analysis, the entire ruling class was united against the demands of the workers and the poor. Having aroused the masses to fight against Britain, it was not easy to get them to accept the rule of a privileged oligarchy after the redcoats had left. In fact, for all the talk of "Liberty", the victory of the Revolution had only transferred power from a corrupt and reactionary colonial government to an equally corrupt and reactionary American oligarchy.

The Revolution proclaimed the inalienable Rights of Man, but these did not include women, slaves, Native Americans or the great majority of the population who owned little or no property. When the revolutionary armies were disbanded, there was no money to pay the arrears of wages. Some of the men were paid off in land warrants, which were later sold to speculators for paltry amounts. Half the members of Congress had their pockets full of these warrants. George Washington was one of the big buyers. As President, Washington tried to give the impression of standing above classes and party strife. But in practice he represented the oligarchy, whose interests and psychology he shared:

"He was a practical man, not troubled much by unrealizable ideals. His intellectual outlook was that of an industrialist or a banker. It was what we call today the 'banker-mind.' The banker stands for stability, and Washington was for that. The banker is for law and order, for land and mortgages, for substantial assets – and Washington believed in them too. The banker wants the nation to be prosperous; by that he means that he wants the common people to have plenty of work and wealthy people to have plenty of profits. That was Washington's ideal." (W.E. Woodward, op.cit., pp. 255-6.)

CHAPTER FIFTEEN

Shays' Rebellion

In every great revolution we see more or less clearly defined stages, which recur with a strange regularity and with uncanny similarity. The initial stage, which corresponds with the first awakening of the masses and the growth of their self-awareness, is characterized by a mood of euphoria and a spirit of unity. But gradually this illusory unity dissipates and there is a growing division between the more revolutionary elements and the more moderate party. The period of revolutionary ascent is marked by a movement to the left, in which the more revolutionary wing and the most audacious leaders gain the upper hand and sweep all before them.

However, as Trotsky explains, revolution is a powerful devourer of human energies. As the masses become exhausted by their exertions and sink into passivity, the conservative wing tends to regain control and elbow the revolutionaries to one side. This happened in every bourgeois revolution in history, and corresponds to the inevitable dialectic of such a revolution. The Declaration of Independence stated that all men were born free, and proclaimed the equality of all men as "self-evident." These were ideals worth fighting and dying for. But once the British had been defeated, the American bourgeoisie soon made it clear that all men were not equal, and that they intended to rule and exploit the people, just as the British had done before them.

There is a stage in every great revolution when the masses – or at least the most militant section of the masses – begin to feel that they have been cheated of the fruits of victory, that power is slipping through their fingers and they have to act to prevent this from happening. A desperate minority moves to take power and is crushed. This marks a decisive turning point in the revolution, where the conservative wing crushes its former allies and proceeds to consolidate its power as a new ruling class. This stage in the American Revolution was Shays Rebellion.

When the cannons had fallen silent and the smoke had finally cleared from the battlefields, the small farmers, workers and artisans who had done all the fighting looked around them and saw that they had gained nothing from the Revolution. They were crushed by debts and taxes. Interest rates were charged at up to forty percent. Poor settlers, crossing the mountains in search of land, found the best farming country in the hands of land companies. All the power was in the hands of the rich –the merchants, the landowners, the moneylenders. Runaway inflation made money worthless. To make matters worse, the war was followed by a deep trade depression that lasted from 1783 to 1788. Prices and taxes soared. As a result, thousands languished in debtors' prisons. In Massachusetts alone, 90 percent of those in prison were debtors. The discontent of the masses reached boiling point.

There were serious uprisings in Massachusetts. In New Hampshire a mob of several hundred men marched to the legislature with clubs, stones and guns to demand relief. The rebels assumed (erroneously) that the problem was a shortage of currency. "Print money and lower the taxes" was their slogan. But there is no doubt that the high taxes fell disproportionately on the poor. They particularly targeted the courts where moneylenders would secure eviction orders against poor farmers who had fallen into debt. In the *New York Picket* of September 11, 1786 we read:

"On Tuesday the 29th [of August] ... the day appointed by law for the sitting of the Court of Common Pleas [...] there assembled in the town from different parts of the county four or five hundred people some of whom were armed with muskets, the others with bludgeons, with the professed intention to prevent the courts from proceeding to business [...]."

This movement culminated in what was known as Shays' Uprising – an armed insurrection led by Captain Daniel Shays, a former officer in the revolutionary army, and now, like so many others, a ruined small farmer. About 1,000 men armed with muskets, swords and clubs, succeeded in closing the courts for several months. Leo Huberman writes:

"The upper classes throughout the country were thoroughly frightened at this armed uprising of the poor people. There was no money in the treasury to pay the state troops, so a number of rich people contributed enough to do so. Shays and his followers headed for Springfield, where there was a public storehouse containing 7,000 muskets and 13,000 barrels of gunpowder, stoves, camp kettles and saddles. They were stopped by the state troops, a few shots were fired, and the mob dispersed." (Leo Huberman, *We the People*, p. 94.)

It was at this time that Thomas Jefferson made his famous remark that the Tree of Liberty must be watered from time to time by the blood of patriots. He also wrote that "a little rebellion now and then is a good thing, and as necessary in the political world as storms in the physical." However, this view was anathema to the majority of the American ruling class. Again, Gore Vidal accurately expresses the views of the oligarchy in the following imaginary dialogue between George Washington and Aaron Burr, a controversial figure in the American Revolution and the central figure in his novel of that name:

"Washington spoke through me, but not to cut me off: he was going deaf and did not hear half what was said to him. 'When word came to me of the treasonous acts of a certain Captain Daniel Shays – a dirty fellow once known to me – it was apparent that we must have a strong government to protect our property. Mr. Hamilton concurred with me and we summoned a constitutional convention at which I, at great personal sacrifice, let me say, presided. I regard, Sir, that convention as the most important event of my own career. Because had we not invented this federal govern-ment, *they* would have taken away *everything*.'

"The face was dark with sudden color. The hands that were stretched to the fire trembled. 'By now that Massachusetts rabble would have divided all property amongst the worthless classes. Not even your French have dared go so far. This is not natural, I said at the time. This must be stopped. We did not fight and win a war with a despot across the sea to be in turn tyrannized by a bloody mob whose contribution to our victory, if I may say so, was considerably less than that of those gentlemen who sacrificed all that they had in order that we be a separate nation. So what we won in that war we mean to keep, Colonel Burr. And I am sure that you agree with that sentiment.'" (Gore Vidal, *Burr*, p.192.)

The true significance of Shays' rebellion can only be understood in class terms. Later general Knox wrote to George Washington to explain the dangerous character of the ideas of the insurgents. In particular, Knox said that the rebels believed that "the property of the United States has been protected from […] Britain by the joint efforts of all *and therefore ought to be the common property of all.*" He added: "Our government must be braced, changed, or altered to secure our lives and property." (Quoted in W.E. Woodward, op. cit., p. 228, my emphasis, AW.)

The rebellion was crushed and fourteen of its leaders, including Shays, were sentenced to death, though later pardoned. In Shays' rebellion, the masses, feeling that the power that they have fought and died for is slipping from their hands, tried desperately to seize the initiative again. But the movement was doomed to defeat. The class nature of the American Revolution of the 18th century was objectively bourgeois. It could not go beyond the limits prescribed by the capitalist mode of production. Consequently, the attempt of Shays to do so was condemned in advance to failure, as the similar attempt of the English Levellers and the Left Wing of the Puritans was condemned to defeat over a century earlier in England.

The challenge thrown down by Shays terrified the oligarchy that was quietly concentrating political and economic power into its own hands. They understood the need to create a strong state power immediately as a bulwark against the masses. At the same time they were under the pressure of the masses.

CHAPTER SIXTEEN

The Constitution

When the 55 delegates met in 1787 to revise the Articles of Confederation, not one of them was from the working class or the class of small farmers. The class that had done all the fighting and dying in the Revolution was rigorously excluded from the decision-making process. So were a number of the most prominent revolutionary leaders. Patrick Henry was not there. They asked him to serve, but he would have nothing to do with it. Nor was Samuel Adams, the most outspoken of the revolutionaries. Nor was Christopher Gadsden, of South Carolina, organizer of mechanics and laboring men. Their day had passed; the moving spirits of the convention did not want any organizers of rebellion, or leaders of the populace. Thomas Jefferson, idealist and democrat, was in France serving as the American ambassador.

The men who drafted the American constitution were all moneylenders, merchants, manufacturers, bondholders or slaveholders. They met behind closed doors, and all the delegates were pledged to secrecy. When the Constitution was finally announced most people were surprised. They knew nothing about it. The secrecy with which the Constitution was drawn up is no accident. It is possible to draw a parallel between this phase of the American Revolution and the Thermidorean counterrevolution in

France, that is to say, the beginnings of a conservative reaction against the egalitarian spirit of the Revolution in its flood tide. In the sense that it marked the inevitable stage of stabilization when the men of money, the big landowners and wealthy merchants grabbed power out of the hands of the plebeian radical wing, this is a fair comparison. That is precisely why the proceedings had to take place behind the backs of the people.

Gradually, the voice of the radical elements was drowned out by the men of property. Hamilton was openly contemptuous about democracy. He was not the only one. Listen to what Madison had to say: "In future times a great majority of the people will not only be without landed, but any other sort of property. These will either combine under the influence of their common situation; in which case, the rights of property and the public liberty will not be secure in their hands, or, which is more probable, they will become the tools of opulence and ambition; in which case there will be equal danger on another side."

These lines are perfectly clear. The fierce debates that raged over the Constitution were the parting shots of class conflict. The central contradiction may be simply stated: *most of the authors of the Constitution did not believe in the equality of man, but the common people certainly did*. It required a second revolution (the Civil War) to get the question of the suffrage included in the Constitution in the Fifteenth Amendment of 1870. But at that time the question was left up to the individual states. This meant that three quarters of the free white men in all states except two or three were excluded from voting because they did not posses enough property. However, at the proposal of Jefferson and other Left-wingers, a Bill of Rights was approved.

The discussions on the Constitution dragged on for months. The disputed questions were numerous: should large states have more say in the national government than small states? Should black slaves be counted as white people? And so on. But there was one question upon which they all agreed: that *those with little or no property should not have too much power*. In the end, the Constitution of the United States was only approved after bitter argument and even then was only passed by a narrow margin by those few who were eligible to vote, as these figures show:

	For	*Against*
New York	30	27
New Hampshire	57	47
Massachusetts	187	168
Virginia	89	79

The American Republic at its birth was a revolutionary power that owed its existence to the workers and small farmers and was, at least in the beginning, under their pressure. Later, as the lava of Revolution cooled, the big landowning and merchant interests prevailed. But in the beginning, the American Revolution was a beacon of hope to the entire world.

CHAPTER SEVENTEEN

America and the French Revolution

The international significance of the American Revolution was far greater than what most people realize today. The connection between the American and French Revolutions was very close. That great English-American revolutionary Thomas Paine lived in France and developed the most radical ideas. The proclamation of *The Rights of Man* was a most revolutionary idea for its time. People like Thomas Paine were the most advanced revolutionary democrats of their day. The ideas of liberty, equality and fraternity that they advocated shook the ruling classes of all Europe.

What is even less understood is the impact these revolutionary ideas from America had on the infant workers' movement in Britain. Tom Paine's writings were passed from hand to hand in underground workers' groups known as corresponding societies. Nowadays, the British establishment likes to parade its democratic credentials. But this is a blatant lie. The British ruling class fought tooth and nail against democracy. They opposed every attempt to establish the right to vote. This was conquered in struggle by the British working class, which paid a heavy price in martyrs, with imprisonment, deportation and even death as its reward. In those dark days when the working class of Britain was struggling to win the most elementary rights, when the trade unions were illegalized by Pitt's notorious

Combination Acts, the flame of freedom was kept alight, not only by the example of revolutionary France, but by the revolutionary democratic ideas of Thomas Paine, who for generations was the hero of British workers.

The American Revolution provided a stimulus for the French Revolution of 1789-93. But in its turn the French Revolution had a considerable impact on America. The news from Paris exacerbated the split between Right and Left inside Washington's cabinet, especially after the execution of Louis XVI and Marie Antoinette in April 1793. Jefferson, who stood on the Left, welcomed it, but the Conservative wing recoiled in horror, probably picturing themselves on the steps of the guillotine. Although the French Revolution appalled the American Conservatives, much as the Russian Revolution did later, it inspired the Left Wing and reaffirmed their revolutionary identity and aspirations. Even before 1789, Thomas Jefferson was strongly anti-monarchical in his views. He was sent as ambassador of America to Paris – probably to get him out of the way.

While in Paris he had occasion to note that France was divided between sheep and wolves, with an abyss separating rich and poor. Among all that aristocratic gang he felt like "a savage from the woods of America". It was not therefore surprising that Jefferson greeted the Revolution enthusiastically. "Was ever a prize won with so little human blood?" he asked, answering the attacks of the enemies of the Revolution who (as they always do) tried to portray it as an orgy of bloodletting.

The French Revolution opened up a deep rift that expressed itself on party lines. The Jeffersonian Republicans were pro-French in foreign policy and advocated a loose confederation of states in America with less power for the centre. It based itself on the support of the small farmers and proletarian and semi-proletarian elements in the cities.

The Federalists, on the other hand, were pro-British (their opponents called them "the English Party"), stood for a strong central government and represented the interests of the big merchants and manufacturers.

In October 1789 Jefferson returned to America. Revolutionary France was attacked by the reactionary powers of Europe: England, Austria, Sardinia and the Netherlands. The Republicans wanted war against England, whereas the Federalists wanted war against France. The Republican Party at that time stood on the left and were a very different Republican Party than that which was later founded in the mid-1850s and which still exists today. They were pro-French, anti-British, and argued for greater egalitarianism. The leaders included Thomas Jefferson, James Madison, George Clinton and Aaron Burr.

The Federalists were the right wing and included many former Tories. This was the party of the oligarchy par excellence, and was backed by Alexander Hamilton, John Adams, John Jay, and (surreptitiously) by Washington himself. However, realizing that for America to unite with Britain against France was politically impossible, Washington insisted on strict neutrality.

The impact of the French Revolution in America was tremendous. It gave fresh heart to the revolutionaries and the Left Wing and threw the Conservatives into a panic. They feared that the example of the Jacobins would lead to a second Revolution in America that would lead to the overthrow of the oligarchy. This did not happen because the vast open spaces to the West provided a safety valve. The energies of the downtrodden that in France were the mainspring of the Revolution, in America could be channelled into the movement to the West. Nevertheless, the contradictions remained and would burst to the surface in the Civil War.

The French Revolution, with its slogan Liberty, Equality, Fraternity also inspired an uprising of black slaves in Santo Domingo. This terrified the big landowners of the Southern States even more. Gabriel Prosser led an uprising of slaves in America, which was put down with great ferocity. Thousands of black slaves were slaughtered in Virginia.

The war in Europe had serious repercussions in America. Both the British and French seized American vessels. This was used as an excuse to bring in the Alien and Sedition Act that gave the executive the power to arrest and deport any foreigners and arrest citizens for criticizing the government. Here we see the beginnings of an attempt to limit and even undermine the democratic rights established by the Constitution and the Bill of Rights. The Act was used to harass, arrest and imprison anti-Federalist elements. We see exactly the same thing now with the anti-democratic Patriot Act legislation introduced after September 11. Jefferson and others attempted to resist the attacks on democracy by insisting on states' rights. Although the same demand was later filled by a reactionary content – to defend the right of the southern states to keep slaves – at this time it had a progressive character.

CHAPTER EIGHTEEN

Federalists and Anti-Federalists

The struggle between Federalists and anti-Federalists was in essence the struggle between the American Thermidorean counter-revolutionaries and those who sought to uphold the original aims of the American Revolution. Thomas Jefferson even spoke openly of the need for a second Revolution. This was actually took place in the Civil War. The third – and greatest – American Revolution is currently in the process of being prepared. The victory of the conservative faction led to a state of affairs which had very little to do with the revolutionary-democratic ideals of 1776.

P.N. Carroll and D.W. Noble point out:

"The importance of the legislatures made questions of political representation more pressing than ever before. In organizing republican governments, American politicians assumed that the legislatures represented specific constituencies and spoke for that amorphous group they called 'the people'. They agreed, nevertheless, that the power of the people could easily degenerate into anarchy and destroy the governmental balance. To reduce the likelihood of mob rule, the state constitutions restricted political participation to male property owners and often established still higher property qualifications for officeholding. Despite occasional demands for wider democracy, the older habits of elitist politics prevailed.

Consequently political representation remained with the more affluent citizens even though there is some evidence that members of state senates were slightly less wealthy than the councillors of the colonial period.

"The conservative nature of these changes tells much about the American Revolution. Despite the revolutionary implications of the Declaration of Independence – the demands for government by consent of the governed and the assumptions about political equality – power generally remained in the hands of moderate leaders who were concerned as much with the interests of property as with the cause of liberty." (P.N. Carroll and D.W. Noble, op. cit., pp. 120-21.)

Needless to say, the Federalists attacked Jefferson viciously, using exactly the same kind of language the U.S. reactionaries later used against socialists. When he stood against Adams in the election of 1800, it was said that a Jefferson victory would destroy religion and undo the bounds of society, and that a vote for Jefferson was a vote against God, etc. However, the people showed that they would not be bullied and voted for Jefferson, risking the wrath of the Almighty in the hopes of achieving justice in this life.

Even the geography of the new capital was a reflection of the class struggle. By moving the capital of the Republic to Washington, the Federalist faction clearly intended to remove the government and Presidency from the pressure of the masses of New York. The new capital, conveniently situated near to the conservative agrarian states of the South, was a place where hardly anybody lived. The scale and style of the White House and Capitol suggested grand imperial ambitions. Jefferson, who was allergic to monarchy, commented ironically that the White House was big enough to house "two Emperors, one Pope and the Chief Lama."

To his credit, Jefferson immediately took measures to counteract the Federalists' attempt to move in the direction of monarchy. He banned the use of his image on coins, forbade the celebration of his birthday and opened up the White House to anyone who wanted to visit him. He dressed so modestly that a visiting diplomat took him for one of the servants. This is quite in the spirit of the Bolshevik leaders who after the October Revolution would take no more wages than those of a skilled worker, walked the streets without armies of bodyguards and were easily accessible to anyone who wanted to meet them.

When the famous English writer Arthur Ransome visited Moscow in 1919 he met Bukharin, who at that time was a key figure in the revolutionary government. He gave Bukharin a packet of sugar, and the Bolshevik leader was delighted because he did not have any sugar. This was absolutely typical of all the Bolshevik leaders at that time. The situation only changed after the Stalinist political counterrevolution, itself the result of the isolation of the Revolution in conditions of frightful poverty and backwardness.

This democratic, egalitarian spirit of the founders of the American Republic stands in stark contrast to the conduct of America's present-day political leaders. Thomas Jefferson was a true son of the Enlightenment with a classical education and a healthily sceptical attitude to religion. He dressed like a servant and when he died he did not have enough money to pay his debts. George W. Bush is an illiterate billionaire who cannot utter a single coherent sentence and has a brain that is chock-full of the crudest religious superstition. He also has pretensions to imperial grandeur to rival those of Nero or Caligula. We leave it to the reader to decide whether this represents progress or regression.

CHAPTER NINETEEN

Rich and Poor

"I think our governments will remain virtuous for many centuries, as long as they are chiefly agricultural; and this will be as long as there shall be vacant lands in any part of America. When they get piled upon one another in large cities, as in Europe, they will become corrupt as Europe." (Thomas Jefferson)

The conquest of independence for the American colonies, although it was a great step forward, did not mark the final victory of democracy in America. Power was in the hands of a wealthy oligarchy: "The most serious problem inherited from the Revolution was its failure to carry out its declaration of the equality of all men. We have pointed out that half-consciously the leaders of the Revolutionary period confined the application of equality to those men whom they recognized as parties to the social contract and members of the political community. Even among them equality was never rigorously asserted. Property qualifications for voting and unequal representation of sections in the state legislature gave distinct advantages to the wealthier men and the wealthier areas. Literacy tests as the years passed were substituted for property tests as a more defensible means for disfranchising the poor, but with almost the same effect. Those inequalities have persisted to the present day, operating now primarily to give white men an advantage over Negroes, and rural areas an advantage over urban areas at the ballot." (Dan Lacy, *The Meaning of the American Revolution*, pp. 282-3.)

The ideal of many of the founding fathers, especially Thomas Jefferson, was that of a democratic republic of small farmers. "Those who labor in the earth", he wrote, "are the chosen people of God." To further this aim, in 1804 Jefferson purchased the vast territory of Louisiana from France for the immense sum (for those days) of 15 million dollars (double the total Federal budget) – the biggest land deal in history. By the stroke of a pen, Jefferson removed Britain, France, Russia and Spain from a massive swath of North America, and provided a huge area of land for the expansion of the population.

As usual, the losers were the Native Americans who were deprived of their ancestral lands and pushed to the West. Although he was an advanced democrat in many ways, Thomas Jefferson was incapable of thinking of them as human beings with the same rights as the European settlers. There was no place in his agrarian scheme for the First Americans whose lands were expropriated. "The backward [tribes] will yield," he wrote in 1812, "and we shall be obliged to drive them, with the beasts of the forests, into the Stony [Rocky] Mountains." (Quoted in P.N. Carroll and D.W. Noble, op. cit., p. 137.)

However, Jefferson's dream of a free agrarian republic was already obsolete before he died. The development of capitalism in America, made possible by the Revolution, signified the rapid growth of industry in the North and East that brought in its wake a growing gap between rich and poor, workers and capitalists. The dream of an agrarian paradise became the nightmare of industrial capitalism. As far as democracy was concerned, it was fine in theory but in practice was little more than a fig-leaf to disguise the rule of a wealthy elite:

"The government in Washington had grown, through successive administrations, into a pleasant little oligarchy. A handful of men ran everything, and when they departed from the scene they chose their successors in the manner of one who writes a last will and testament. Jefferson chose Madison and Madison chose Monroe."

(W.E. Woodward, *A New American History*, p. 361.) The rich and powerful vied with each other to get their hands on the pork barrel of political power, just as they do today. The only important business in Washington was office-holding and related matters, just as it is today. No wonder Jefferson remarked shortly before his death: "I like the dreams of the future better than the history of the past."

CHAPTER TWENTY

In a Few Hands

A Whig journalist in the early years of the 19th century wrote: "Ours is a country, where men start from an humble origin, and from small beginnings rise gradually in the world, as the reward of merit and industry, and where they can attain to the most elevated positions, or acquire a large amount of wealth, according to the pursuits they elect for themselves." (Quoted in P.N. Carroll and D.W. Noble, op. cit., p. 155.) So much for the self-satisfied rhetoric of the American dream. The reality, however, was very different. Not only were the Native Americans, black slaves and women excluded from this dream, but also the growing number of property-less industrial workers laboring in the sweat-shops of the cities of the northeast.

The conquest of formal democracy and the proclamation of the Rights of Man did not prevent the concentration of economic and political power into a few hands. The position of the working class did not improve but worsened, as shown by the following Appeal to the Working People of Manayuk to the Public, published in *Pennsylvanian*, August 28, 1833:

"We are obliged by our employers to labor at this season of the year, from 5 o'clock in the morning until sunset, being fourteen hours and a half, with an intermission of half an hour for breakfast, and an hour for dinner, leaving thirteen hours of hard labor, at an unhealthy employment, where we never feel a refreshing breeze to cool us, overheated and suffocated as we are, and where we never behold the sun but through a window, and an atmosphere thick with the dust and small particles of cotton, which we are constantly inhaling to the destruction of our health, our appetite and strength.

"Often we feel ourselves so weak as to be scarcely able to perform our work, on account of the over-strained time we are obliged to labor through the long and sultry days of summer, in the impure and unwholesome air of the factories, and the little rest we receive during the night not being sufficient to recruit our exhausted physical energies, we return to our labor in the morning, as weary as when we left it; but nevertheless work we must, worn down and debilitated as we are, or our families would soon be in a starving condition, for our wages are barely sufficient to supply us with the necessaries of life. We cannot provide against sickness or difficulties of any kind, by laying by a single dollar, for our present wants consume the little we receive and when we are confined to a bed of sickness any length of time, we are plunged into the deepest distress, which often terminates in total ruin, poverty, and pauperism.

"Our expenses are perhaps greater than most other working people, because it requires the wages of all the family who are able to work (save only one small girl to take care of the house and provide meals) to furnish absolute wants, consequently the females have no time either to make their own dresses or those of the children, but have of course to apply to trades for every article that is wanted." (J. Kuczynski, *A Short History of Labour Conditions under Industrial Capitalism*, vol.2, p. 25.)

The condition of women workers was underlined in a report by the National Trades' Union Convention in

September, 1834: "Mr. Douglass observed that in the single village of Lowell, there were about 4,000 females of various ages, now dragging out a life of slavery and wretchedness. It is enough to make one's heart ache, said he, to behold these degraded females, as they pass out of the factory – to mark their wan countenances – their woe-stricken appearance. These establishments are the present abode of wretchedness, disease and misery; and are inevitably calculated to perpetuate them – if not to destroy liberty itself."

Another report states: "It has been shown that the number of females employed in opposition to male labor, throughout the United States, exceeds 140,000 who labor on an average from 14 to 15 hours per day, without that pure air and wholesome exercise which are necessary to health, and confinement with the consequent excess of toil, which checks the growth of the body, destroying in effect the natural powers of mind, and not infrequently distorting the limbs."

Even more ghastly was the position of children: "If children must be doomed to those deadly prisons," said the New Haven delegates to the above mentioned convention, "let the law at least protect them against excessive toil and shed a few rays of light upon their darkened intellect. Workingmen! Bitter must be that bread which your little children earn in pain and tears, toiling by day, sleeping by night, sinking under oppression, consumption and decrepitude, into an early grave, knowing no life but this, and knowing of this only misery."

The class struggle has accompanied the American Republic ever since it was born. In 1778, when the ink was scarcely dry on the Declaration of Independence, journeymen printers of New York City combined to demand an increase in wages. The first strike of wage earners took place in Philadelphia as early as 1786 when the printers fought for a weekly minimum wage. The first general strike, that is, the first strike of a considerable number of workers in a large number of trades in one big strike movement, took place in 1827, again in Philadelphia. In this period, many trade unions were formed and there were numerous strikes.

The bosses ferociously resisted the right of workers to organize in unions and go out on strike. In 1806 members of the Philadelphia Journeymen Cordwainers were tried for criminal conspiracy after a strike for higher wages. The charges were (1) combination to raise wages and (2) combination to injure others. Bankrupted as a result, the union disbanded. This was not an isolated case. Wherever possible the employers brought in scab labor to break strikes and appealed to the courts to declare trade unions illegal. Far from trade union organization being recognized as a democratic right, the unions were dragged through the courts and prosecuted for "conspiracy in restraint of trade" – a phrase copied from English common law. For decades, strikes, boycotts and other forms of working class struggle were subject to legal action on the grounds of "conspiracy".

CHAPTER TWENTY-ONE

Andrew Jackson

Andrew Jackson was a self-made frontiersman from Tennessee. The son of a poor family from the West, he took on the rich W.A.S.P. (White Anglo Saxon Protestant) clique that held power in Washington in the name of the small man. One of his biographers says of him: "He became imbued with the doctrine that [...] the banker is vastly overpaid for his services in expediting commerce, and that for bankers in Philadelphia and New York to have the power of life and death over business enterprises in Tennessee is criminal injustice."

There was growing discontent among the property-less masses, small farmers, frontier settlers and religious minorities. Although Jackson was an outsider to politics, he got a surprisingly large popular vote when he ran for President in 1824. The W.A.S.P. elite was alarmed. The ruling class in the U.S.A. has, contrary to the well-known mythology, never been fond of democracy. One of them, James Kent of New York voiced the real feelings of the rich and powerful concerning democracy: "It is not to be disguised that our governments are becoming downright democracies. The principle of universal suffrage, which is now running a triumphant career from Maine to Louisiana, is an awful power, which, like gunpowder, or the steam engine, or the press itself, may be rendered mighty in mischief as well as in blessings."

The fears of the wealthy elite were well founded. In the election of 1828 Jackson swept the board. Overnight the flood tide of democratic protest had swept away the old Massachusetts and Virginia dynasties. Jackson ("Old Hickory") became the first west-of-the-mountains President. On his inauguration day he allowed the people of Washington – "from the highest and most polished," reported a disgusted Justice Story, "to the most vulgar and gross in the nation" – to enter the White House and consume ice cream and cake, lemon and punch. This turned into a riot and was dubbed "the reign of King Mob" by Judge Story. For the conservatives the American people have always been "King Mob" – people to be feared, not trusted.

Honest and blunt-spoken, Andrew Jackson tried to represent the interests of the small man, the farmer and the West. The Jackson Democrats were mainly the party of the agrarian masses, the rural areas and the West. However, as with all agrarian parties in history, it was characterized by the lack of a clear program, aims and perspectives. The only common denominator of Jackson's party was Jackson himself. And he was always better at saying what he was against than what he was in favor of. Nevertheless, the masses looked upon Jackson as their man in the White House – the People's Champion.

That is, of course, unless you were Native American. An energetic advocate of westward expansion (later termed "manifest destiny"), Jackson, like his predecessors, looked down on the peoples who originally lived in those lands. He was an active proponent of their removal – more often than not by brute force. His signing into law of the "Indian Removal Act" legalized the wholesale killing, enslavement, and land theft that had begun with the arrival of the first Europeans. The infamous episode of the "Trail of Tears", during which the Cherokee were herded from Georgia to Oklahoma was a direct result.

Jackson had no clearly defined political program, but he spoke for millions when he denounced the most obvious symptoms of capitalist robbery and exploitation: paper money, chartered corporations and banks. The Jacksonian Democrats condemned the moneyed aristocracy that had robbed the people of their birthright. This was the period of intense struggles over issues like tariffs and the United States Bank. The masses hated the Bank, which had received a charter for twenty years in 1816. Jackson himself shared the common view of all bankers as a bunch of parasites and slick swindlers. During the panic and ensuing depression of 1819 and 1820, the Bank had deflated the currency, denied credit to merchants and local banks and rapaciously levied on assets in cases where loans were in default. In other words, it acted as banks always act. As W.E. Woodward put it:

"It was an inveterate foe of everybody who owed it money unless the debtor was a member of Congress or the editor of a newspaper. [...] Its funds were intelligently mobilized; its drafts were readily honoured in all commercial centres, and in Europe; its notes never fell below their par value; it provided a stable currency. But it was in the hands of men who carried it on as a private enterprise, a magnified pawnbroker's shop endowed with extraordinary privileges. In spirit it was antisocial and greedy." (W.E. Woodward, *A New American History*, p. 398.)

The fact that an outsider from the West could overthrow the old political dynasties, the cliques of landowners who had been in power ever since the Revolution was in itself of tremendous symptomatic importance. The Jacksonian period was a period of tremendous ferment and unrest that came from the unresolved contradictions that lay within the foundations of American society:

"It was like a chemical mixture which has never composed itself, but wherein its biting acids continually fume and struggle. The social chemistry of America was in a state of extreme tension." (Ibid., p. 393.)

Jackson's confrontation with the United States Bank led to what is known as the Bank War. It expressed the conflict between rich and poor, the oligarchy and democracy. Following his re-election in 1832, Jackson abolished the Bank. This was an utopian attempt to fight against tendencies that were irresistible. Capitalism, market forces and banks were firmly entrenched. But the Bank War showed that The Revolution had left many unpaid bills. These now demanded to be paid.

Among the unresolved contradictions was the conflict between the northern free states and the slave-holding states of the South. This expressed itself as a struggle over tariffs. This in turn led to an attempt at secession by the state of South Carolina after the adoption of the Tariff Act of 1828. Jackson had to back down on the tariff question but denounced the secessionist leaders and appealed to the people of South Carolina to repudiate them. "Their object is disunion," he thundered. "Disunion by armed force is *treason*." Here already were the first rumblings of the Civil War.

CHAPTER TWENTY-TWO

The Second American Revolution

> *"I believe that to have interfered as I have done, as I have always freely admitted I have done, in behalf of his [God's] despised poor, I did not wrong but right. Now, if it is deemed necessary that I should forfeit my life for the furtherance of the ends of justice, and mingle my blood further with the blood of my children and with the blood of millions in this slave country whose rights are disregarded by wicked, cruel, and unjust enactments, I say let it be done."* (John Brown)

The growth of capitalism was expressed in the rapid development of the textile factories in England and the northeastern United States, beginning in the last decades of the 18th century. This in turn led to an insatiable demand for raw cotton. The perfection of the cotton gin in 1793 guaranteed rich profits for the Southern planters. Thus, slave labor entered as an important component part of the accumulation of capital. It made fabulous fortunes, not only for the Southern slave owners but for the most Christian industrialists of the North and Britain. America, which proclaimed the sacred principle of liberty, was stained by the evil of slavery. Men and women, torn from their homes and lands in black Africa by the monstrous trade in human beings, were bought and sold like chattel by Christian gentlemen who worshipped the Lord in church every Sunday, and tortured, beat, raped and killed their slaves every other day of the week.

Although the African slave trade was already illegal, the Southern planters continued to import slaves after 1808. It is estimated that as many as 150,000 slaves were sent to the New World every year, compared to 45,000 towards the end of the 18th century. And although many of them were not shipped directly to the U.S.A., most of them must have ended up there. In the *Charleston Courier* of April 12, 1828 we read: "As valuable a family [...] as ever was offered for sale, consisting of a cook about 35 years of age, and her daughter about 14 and son about 8. The whole will be sold together or a part of them, as may suit a purchaser."

The slaves were regarded as chattel or animals, as the following description of a slave sale shows: "About a dozen gentlemen crowded on the spot while the poor fellow was stripping himself, and as soon as he stood on the floor, bare from top to toe, a most rigorous scrutiny of his person was instituted. The clear black skin, back and front, was viewed all over for sores from disease; and there was no part of his body left unexamined. The man was told to open and shut his hands, asked if he could pick cotton, and every tooth in his head was scrupulously looked at."

The class outlook of the slave owners was well expressed in the comments of Senator Hammond of South Carolina: "In all social systems there must be a class to do the mean duties, to perform the drudgeries of life [...] we call them slaves. We are old-fashioned at the South yet; it is a word discarded now by ears polite; I will not characterize that class in the North by that term; but there you have it; it is there; it is everywhere; it is eternal [...] The difference between us is that our slaves are hired for life and well compensated; there is no starvation, no begging, no want of employment among our people, and not too much employment, either. Yours are hired for the day, not cared for, and scantily compensated, which may be proved in the most deplorable manner, at any hour in any street of your large towns. Why, sir, you meet more beggars in one day, in any single street of the city of New York than you would ever meet in a lifetime in the whole South. Our slaves are black, of another inferior race [...] your slaves are white, of your own race; you are brothers of one blood."

These lines are interesting because they let slip the smiling mask of the ruling class to reveal the brutal hypocrite that hides beneath it. In order to defend the indefensible – chattel slavery – the Southern slave owner points an accusing finger at the Northern capitalist. The attempt to prettify chattel slavery is, of course, absurd. Yet there is just a grain of truth in this attack against the hypocrisy of the Northern capitalists. The pro-slaver says to them: "Why do you condemn us, when in reality you are just as bad as us? Our slavery is open and self-evident. We do not hide it. But your slavery is just as bad, if not worse, except it is hidden and hypocritical." We need not accept the logic of the slaver to understand that the attitude of every exploiting class in history –slave owners, feudal lords and capitalists – to the exploited class is very similar. The Northern manufacturers were lukewarm about abolition because they feared – not without reason – that any attempt to challenge the "sacred rights of property" in the South would set an unwelcome precedent for the working class in the North.

There were a number of slave revolts that were put down with the utmost savagery. The whites were always concerned with intimidating the blacks, inculcating in them a sense of inferiority and fear of their masters. By all manner of cruelty, the blacks, both free and slaves (and many were free in some states) had to be *put in their place*. A few thousand wealthy slave owning families ruled the South, while four million black slaves did all the work, the gap being filled by a population of poor whites who could always be depended upon to support their masters against the slaves.

In order to end this abomination and finish the job begun in 1776, a new revolution was necessary: a long and bloody Civil War. This took great courage and determination. The name of Abraham Lincoln will forever have a place of honour in the annals of the long struggle for democracy. In the course of this struggle, he grew in stature as a man and a leader. The initiative for this epic struggle, however, came from below, from the militant abolitionists and the slaves themselves. A movement that began as a small minority, despised as "extremists" and "subversives", shunned by the "moderate mainstream" succeeded, by heroic efforts, in turning America upside down.

The expansion of the United States created conditions for a struggle between the North and South as they advanced westward in parallel lines. In 1818 the state of Missouri applied for admission to the Union. Slavery existed in Missouri and New England and the North were opposed to the extension of the slave system. They therefore opposed the acceptance of Mississippi or any other state that accepted the institution of slavery. The reason for this opposition was not wholly humanitarian. On the one hand, slavery had no place in the capitalist industrial economy of the North. On the other hand, the Northerners and New Englanders feared that they would come under the political domination of the southern slave states.

When Missouri applied for admission there were eleven free states and eleven slave states, so that its admission could tilt the delicate balance one way or the other. On the other hand, Maine, which was free, had also applied to join the Union, and this was blocked by the South for the same reason. The deadlock was broken by the so-called Missouri compromise. The southern border of Missouri is the 36 degree 30 minutes parallel of latitude. According to the compromise, the northern limit of slavery (from the

Mississippi westwards) was to be that parallel, with the sole exception of Missouri, which, although north of the line, was admitted as a slave state. In return, Maine was also admitted.

Such a geographical compromise obviously had an extremely tenuous and fragile nature and could be upset by the slightest disturbance. Like all such agreements, it merely expressed the balance of forces at a given moment. As soon as the balance of forces changed, it would be torn to shreds. The whole logic of the situation was tending to war. The main result of the Missouri Compromise was to create a powerful Southern self-consciousness, born out of suspicion and hatred of the North. On the other hand, the acceptance of Missouri as a slave state outraged public opinion in the North and gave rise to increasingly militant anti-slavery groups, opposed to compromise and inclined to direct action. In the words of W.E. Woodward: "The Civil War was built up as a house is built, brick upon brick. One of its cornerstones was the Missouri Compromise." (W.E. Woodward, *A New American History*, p. 354.)

There was a militant anti-slavery tendency that used revolutionary methods to free the slaves. The struggle between slaveholders and abolitionists erupted into open civil war in 1856, when John Brown led his militant abolitionist forces into Kansas to do battle with the slavers. In October, 1859, John Brown led a band of 18 armed men, of which four were black, to capture the Federal arsenal at Harper's Ferry, Virginia. The raid failed and Colonel Robert E. Lee, the future commander of the Confederate forces, led a detachment of U.S. Marines which captured John Brown. Amidst a lynch-mob atmosphere, Brown was sentenced to death by hanging, the sentence being carried out in December 1859. His execution had far-reaching consequence and only exacerbated the accumulated social contradictions. During the war, the song "John Brown's

Body", which includes the line "John Brown died that the slaves might be free," would become a rallying cry for the Union troops.

The defeat of the South – that bastion of landowning reaction – and the emancipation of the slaves was undoubtedly a progressive task, and one that merged imperceptibly with a war of emancipation of the black slaves. But the bourgeoisie dragged its feet, looking for a compromise up to the very last moment when the first cannon balls were fired at Fort Sumter on April 12, 1861. It was the pressure from the anti-slavery militants and the working class and lower middle class that forced the North into action. The workers of the Union were prepared to sacrifice their lives in this cause. And the workers of Europe instinctively understood this and took a truly internationalist position in relation to the Civil War – *the Second American Revolution*.

CHAPTER TWENTY-THREE

The Civil War

Historical legend presents the picture of the "anti-slave" North conducting a campaign for freedom against the slave-holding South. Like all historical legends, however, this is a gross oversimplification. The fact of the matter was that a significant section of the capitalist class in the North and also of the political Establishment – including in Lincoln's own party – did not want to fight against slavery and were in favour of reaching a compromise with the Southern slave owners. Lincoln himself was originally a compromise candidate between the openly abolitionist wing and the compromisers on the right wing.

Like every other serious conflict, at bottom the American Civil War was a class struggle. The Northern manufacturers necessarily had to come into conflict with the Southern landowning classes. The conflict of interest between the two lasted for sixty years and finally ended in civil war. However, the mutual hatred between the northern capitalists and the slave owners of the South, grounded in economics, was only half the story. There was a genuine sense of moral outrage among sections of the northern working class and middle class against the evils of slavery. The abolitionists waged an energetic campaign of agitation and propaganda aimed at arousing public opinion in the North.

Pamphlets and books like Harriet Beecher Stowe's *Uncle Tom's Cabin* caused widespread indignation against the institution of slavery and prepared the ground for more active revolutionary measures. A section of the abolitionist movement was inclined to direct action. The execution of John Brown brought matters to a head. Historian Lloyd Lewis explains that the incident at Harper's Ferry "was to the South a gathering thunderhead on the Northern sky, promise of the hurricane to come." Fearful of slave uprisings and interference from Northern abolitionists, the South began to organize militias that would form the basis of the Confederate Army. Mass anti-slavery rallies and demonstrations took place in the North.

It was this mass agitation that led, the following year, to the election of Abraham Lincoln. This was taken as a signal for the secession of the slave states. Lincoln was immediately faced with a serious crisis provoked by the secession of South Carolina, followed by the five states of Georgia, Alabama, Mississippi, Louisiana and Florida on February 4th 1861. Virginia, Arkansas, Tennessee and North Carolina followed, making a total of eleven states. The immediate cause was the old argument over tariffs. The South produced nothing that needed tariff protection, whereas the northern capitalists needed a tariff barrier to protect their infant industries against competition from Europe.

The ruling class in the South had no interest in developing industry. The southern slave owning aristocracy based itself on backwardness. The big landowners were quite happy to remain as England's cotton field and in return they would import English manufactured goods without the imposition of a tariff that would only benefit the manufacturers of the North. The secession was a direct challenge to American nationhood. If accepted it would undermine everything the American people had fought for since Independence. But from the standpoint of the South it was a defensive war "for Southern rights".

When South Carolina and ten other slave states declared themselves to be no longer part of the union, Lincoln's main priority was to prevent the break-up of the Union. As a minority President, Lincoln was compelled to do deals with other parties and groups. He could not even rely on the support of all members of his own party. On the contrary, the upper circles of the party were constantly conspiring to remove him and replace him with some political baron. Therefore he was obliged to tack and compromise. But compromise was in vain.

In vain did Lincoln attempt to reassure the slave-owners that his government would "not interfere with the institution of slavery in the states where it exists". He was merely echoing the position of an important section of the Northern bourgeoisie that wanted to avoid a conflict with the South. This fact explains why Lincoln was so cautious at the beginning. His own views were quite clear from the beginning when he said: "*A house divided against itself cannot stand; this government divided into free states and slave states cannot endure, they must all be free or all be slave; they must be one thing or the other*." But he did not have a firm base of support. This only came in the course of the War itself, which galvanized and hardened public opinion. By the end of this terrible conflict, however, Lincoln was not the same man as at the beginning. From a political tussle to preserve the Union, the Civil War evolved inexorably into a revolutionary war against slavery.

The industrial bourgeoisie of the North wished to consolidate its power by destroying the outmoded slave system in the South. It suited their interests. But they did not pursue the task with any enthusiasm. On the contrary, a significant section of the Northern capitalists would have been willing to reach a compromise with the Southern reactionaries. They feared a war that would disrupt trade and preferred to confine themselves to a series of parliamentary maneuvers, like the "Missouri Compromise". But the logic of the situation ruled out any compromise, and these parliamentary intrigues and political struggles culminated in the civil war that the bourgeoisie had hoped to avoid.

While the South was eager for war and immediately began its preparations, the North dragged its feet and was unprepared for the conflict when it finally erupted in the attack on Fort Sumter. But as soon as it became clear that war was unavoidable, Lincoln acted with tremendous determination. He ordered the removal of two million dollars of Southern funds from the Treasury and the confiscation of Western Union's files. He also suspended the right of *habeus corpus*, by executive order, although according to the Constitution only Congress has the right to do this. Thousands of men were arrested and held indefinitely without even charging them with any offence. These measures were strictly anti-constitutional. They were *dictatorial* measures. But they were absolutely necessary in the given situation.

Under the Constitution the power to raise armies and to declare war is invested in Congress. Lincoln paid no attention to this. He immediately assumed the authority to create armies and to wage war on the secessionist states. A drastic measure, certainly. But what else could he have done? Nor did the freedom of speech fare any better. Lincoln's subordinates raided the offices of newspapers and stopped their publication, in spite of the First Amendment of the Constitution. This states that the federal authority shall not abridge the freedom of speech or of the press.

The Maryland Legislature was due to convene on September 17, 1861. The military commander of the district was instructed by the secretary of war to arrest all the members who were *suspected* of disloyalty. Many were arrested and thrown into prison, although none of them was actually charged with having committed acts of treason or disloyalty. There were many such actions. In his inspired historical novel *Lincoln*, Gore Vidal writes:

"Currently, by Seward's order, the mayor of Baltimore and the mayor of Washington were both in prison, where they would remain without trial until such time as he or the President was inspired to let them go. As a Lawyer and as an office-holder, sworn to uphold the Constitution and its Bill of Rights, not to mention those inviolable protections of both persons and property so firmly spelled out in Magn*a* Cart*a* and in the whole subsequent accretion of the common law, Seward found that he quite enjoyed tearing up, one by one, those ancient liberties in the Union's name. Never before had anyone ever exercised such power in the United States as he did now, with Lincoln's tacit blessing. Although, officially, the secret service was under the military, regular reports were made to Seward, in whose name letters were opened, copies of telegrams seized, arrests made." (Gore Vidal Lincoln, p. 273.)

Nowadays it is assumed that everyone was behind Lincoln (in the North at least). But this is very far from the truth. Most of the rich hated him. There were constant conspiracies to get rid of him, and a constant avalanche of calumnies and insults in the press. *Harpers Weekly* described the President as a *"Filthy story-teller, Despot, Liar, Thief, Braggart, Buffoon, Usurper, Monster, Ignoramus, Abe, Old scoundrel, Perjurer, Robber, Swindler, tyrant, Field-Butcher, Land Pirate."* This was typical. It was also in the Civil War that the (then) revolutionary measure was introduced to tax the incomes of the rich to finance the war. No wonder the rich denounced Lincoln as a dictator and called for his removal! Nowadays he would have been called a communist as well.

However, unless Lincoln had been prepared to override the private interests of the capitalists, the Union would never have won the War. In every war situation, certain liberties are suspended or curtailed. The same is true in a revolution, although the degree to which such "exceptional" measures is necessary depends on many things. If the Southern slave-owners had been prepared to accept the will of the majority and obey the democratically elected government, Lincoln would never have had to take the measures he did to curtail democratic rights. But the slave-owners' rebellion forced him to do so.

To those who argue that a socialist revolution necessarily means the abolition of democracy, we answer: not so! Marxists stand for democracy and are its most fervent defenders. We will make use of all the democratic openings to present our ideas and fight to win the majority. We stand for a democratically elected socialist government. We do not advocate violence. But we are also realists and know that the ruling class will never surrender its power, wealth and privileges without a fight with no-holds-barred. What happened in the American Civil War proves this.

If a democratically elected socialist government is faced by another slave-owners' rebellion, we reserve the right to act in the same way that Abe Lincoln acted. To do anything else would be to accept the right of Capital to continue its dictatorship forever and deny the right of the People to determine its own destiny. Of course, it goes without saying that any suspension or curtailment of democratic rights must be only temporary, for the duration of the emergency, not a moment longer. That was the case in Britain and the U.S.A. during the Second World War, which most people thought was a war for democracy (in fact, it was not, but that is another matter). The workers in the U.S.A. and Britain had democratic traditions but were prepared *voluntarily* to accept certain limitations for the duration of the war and *for that only*.

Nobody nowadays condemns Abraham Lincoln for his actions during the Second American Revolution, when he took measures against big business, confiscated wealth and arrested counter-revolutionaries without trial. Few people even remember such things. Yet they throw their hands up in horror at the actions of Lenin and Trotsky in 1917 in Russia. Why such a hypocritical difference should be made between the two is not clear.

CHAPTER TWENTY-FOUR

The Problem of Leadership

At the start of the war, in fact, things went very badly for the Union. The South had better generals, who were not afraid to go on the offensive, making up with courage and energy for their numerical disadvantage compared to the more populous and wealthy industrial North. The white population of the South believed they were fighting a defensive war –a war for self-determination and independence, in fact– and they fought with conviction. As a result the Confederate forces won victory after victory.

By contrast, at the beginning of the war the Union forces did not display the necessary determination and energy. They were continually forced onto the defensive by the Confederates who fought better and had far more capable generals. Even the cel-ebrated defence of Fort Sumter, which Union propaganda made a great deal of at the time, was little more than a charade. Major Anderson, the Fort's defender, declined to haul down the flag after the first volleys but stated complacently that even if he were not attacked he would have to hand over the Fort in a few days, as there would be nothing to eat. The resistance was merely formal. The surrender of Fort Sumter seems to have been quite an amicable affair. Major Anderson had dinner with General Beauregard, the Confederate commander, and then the Union Flag was hauled down to the accompaniment of a salute and full military honors.

This was typical of the attitude of most Union commanders at the beginning of the Civil War. It is strikingly similar to the position at the start of the English Civil War in the 17 century, when Royalist and Parliamentarian commanders often exchanged letters on the eve of battle professing their friendship for each other and their abhorrence of the conflict that pitted one against the other. In a civil war above all, political questions predominate over military ones. At bottom, the problem was not military but political. The Northern general staff simply reflected the opinions of most of the ruling class, which did not believe in the war and was looking for a compromise.

The Confederates, quite naturally, had a poor opinion of the North's military potential. When Lincoln announced his appeal for 75,000 volunteers, the Confederate cabinet met the news with roars of laughter. Actually, the Union army increased rapidly to the point where it was already the strongest army in the world, with close to 200,000 well-trained troops in the area of Washington alone. But this advantage was initially thrown away by a succession of incompetent Union generals. General McClellan was one of the most notorious cases. His supine inactivity exasperated Lincoln, who wrote him a stream of letters like the following:

"Major-General McClellan,

I have just read your despatch about sore-tongued and fatigued horses. Will you pardon me for asking what the horses of your army have done since the battle of Antietam that fatigues anything?"

This angry correspondence culminated in a laconic outburst of despair:

"My dear McClellan; if you don't want to use the army I should like to borrow it or a while.

Yours respectfully, A. Lincoln."

At one point McClellan came within six miles of the rebel capital Richmond, but failed to take the city although his army outnumbered the Confederate forces by at least five to one and their commander had been seriously wounded. The real reason for this situation was not just that McClellan was a bad general (which he was). The real reason was that he was intriguing against Lincoln. McClellan, who secretly aspired to become a dictator, an American Bonaparte, was, like a significant section of the Northern ruling class, in favour of doing a deal with the South to end the War. Most of the other generals in the Union army were not much better. General Hooker, ironically nicknamed "Fighting Joe" is another example of a useless Northern general. He was a champion at the art of whisky drinking, though not at the art of war. At the battle of Chancellorsville he led 130,000 Union troops against Lee's Confederate army of only 60,000. Yet Lee managed to inflict the greatest defeat on the Northern army in the history of the war. General Hooker is today remembered for something not directly connected with the military profession but with a rather older one. His camp, according to a contemporary witness, resembled something in between a brothel and a casino. So addicted were the general and his staff to the sins of the flesh that the female visitors to his camp were known as "Hooker's girls", or simply *hookers*.

General Sherman was a more effective, if extremely brutal, commander. He had been removed from command early in the war because his superiors thought he had gone mad. His "crime" was to predict that hundreds of thousands would die in the coming conflict – a prediction that tragically came true. Politically he was a reactionary who believed in slavery. In December 1859, when the abolition uproar was at its height, he wrote: "'I would not if I could abolish or modify slavery.'And in July, 1860, he wrote: 'All the Congresses on earth can't make the negro anything else than what he is; he must be subject to the white man, or he must amalgamate or be destroyed. Two such races cannot live in harmony save as master and slave'." He is quoted as saying (correctly) that the war did not begin professionally until after Vicksburg and Gettysburg (that is, not until July 1863). Paradoxically, General Robert E. Lee the Southern Commander, was opposed to slavery. Before the War he wrote that it was a "moral and political evil" and hoped it would be abolished. But his loyalty lay with his state of Virginia, and he fought with great valor and ability to establish a nation that would have been based on that same "moral and political evil", while Sherman's army emancipated the slaves as it marched through Georgia. The personal and moral values of the individuals were subordinate to the class content of the struggle. This was basically a war between two incompatible socio-economic systems – capitalism and slavery. Capitalism won and that changed everything.

The war dragged on and the cost in lives was without precedent. In a single campaign, the Union army under Grant lost 50,000 dead and wounded. And these figures do not include the Confederate casualties. This further strengthened the capitulationist trend of the Northern bourgeoisie. The mood of the capitalists was to sell out and get peace at all costs. The so-called Peace Democrats were on the rise, reflecting the bourgeois' lack of enthusiasm for the War. War was bad for business (although not in all cases).

But the Northern employers should not have worried. In the long run the South could not prevail. The industrial might of the North, its far greater wealth and bigger population proved decisive. Industrial output in the state of New York alone was four times that of the entire Confederacy. The population of the United States at the beginning of the War was about 31.5 million. Of these about 8.7 million were in the Confederacy, from which we must deduct 3.6 million slaves. The Confederate army had to be drawn from the white population of just over five million, plus some reinforcements from three Southern states that did not secede: Maryland, Kentucky and Missouri. By contrast, the Union had a population of about 23 million.

That means the North could put four times as many men on the field and take many more losses without affecting their fighting capacity. In addition the North had command of the sea and was able to blockade the southern ports more or less effectively from the beginning. The blockade caused shortages that led to food riots even in Richmond, the Confederate capital. This shows the falsity of the propaganda of the pro-Confederate historians, according to whom the entire population of the South were united in their enthusiasm for the Confederate cause. The initial enthusiasm wore off and by 1864 the Confederacy was held together by arbitrary and despotic measures backed up by state repression.

As the war dragged on there were also problems in the North. After years of hardship there was discontent among a layer of the masses. The Conscription Act, which allowed the sons of the rich to buy their way out of military service, provoked riots in New York, where the measure was seen as "a rich man's war and a poor man's fight." In what turned out to be a prolonged war of attrition, the North was able to tolerate the terrible casualty rate far better than the South. However, to win the war it was necessary to adopt a revolutionary policy that would rouse the masses in the North to fight with the spirit of conviction.

CHAPTER TWENTY-FIVE

Role of the Working Class

War is undoubtedly terrible, and civil wars are more terrible than any other. Yet war is also a source of profit to some, and great fortunes can be coined by the few from the blood, sweat and tears of the many. The American Civil War was no exception. In the spring of 1864 it was possible for a speculator to take $600 in gold, exchange it for $1,000 in dollars, buy a $1,000 bond with the dollars and get $60 a year interest on the bond or a 15 percent profit on his initial investment. All measures to limit this profiteering proved futile. Despite its fundamentally revolutionary character, the Civil War led inexorably to increased centralization of power and wealth in a few hands. This explains the resentment of the masses, as expressed in outbursts like the New York riots.

Bondholders plundered the treasury, crooked manufacturers plundered the army, speculators plundered the whole population and made their fortunes out of blood, death and misery. In his *Life of Thaddeus Stevens*, James A. Woodburn writes:

"One may well doubt whether there was ever a more outrageous fleecing and robbery of a patriotic people than that perpetrated through the influence of capitalists and money lenders by the manipulation of government finance during and immediately following the American Civil War."

Lincoln realized that the masses would not be prepared to give their lives willingly just to prevent the South from seceding. He therefore proposed a most revolutionary measure. On September 22 1862, President Lincoln summoned the cabinet and took them by surprise. He told them he had an important paper to read. But when they came into the room it appeared the President was reading a humorous story – which he often did. Then he closed his book and informed them that he had been thinking a lot about the relation between the war and slavery. "I think the time for action has now come and I have got you together to hear what I have written down." This was the Emancipation Proclamation. It read as follows:

"I, Abraham Lincoln, President of the United States of America, do proclaim that on the first day of January, 1863, all persons held as slaves within any State, or designated part of a State, the people whereof shall then be in rebellion against the United States, shall then be, thenceforward and forever, free; and the executive Government of the United States, including the military and naval authorities thereof, will recognize and maintain the freedom of such persons, and will do no act, or acts, to repress such persons, or any of them, in any efforts they may make for their actual freedom."

It must be realized that this proclamation, like so many of Lincoln's acts during the war, was an executive order, issued under the war powers conferred on the president by Congress. In effect, he went over the heads of Congress and the cabinet to speak directly to the American people. He understood that in order to win the war it was necessary to inspire and motivate the masses by adopting a revolutionary program. The Civil War would not be won by guns and bayonets alone, but by the moral force behind the guns and bayonets. As long as people in the North suspected that this was a rich man's war in which the poor were called on to fight and die for the interests of the wealthy merchants and industrialists of the North, the war could not be won. He therefore decided to appeal directly to the masses.

In order to wage war against the slave-holding South, Abraham Lincoln relied upon the support of the mass of American workers and small farmers. After some initial hesitation (he was afraid of losing the support of the four border states of Delaware, Kentucky, Maryland and Missouri, where slavery still existed), he accepted the recruitment of black soldiers into the Union armies. He also openly espoused the cause of labor, making comments that nowadays would automatically make him suspect of subversion and communism. He said, among other things: *"All that harms labor is treason to America. No line can be drawn between these two. If any man tells you he loves America, yet hates labor, he is a liar. If a man tells you he trusts America, yet fears labor, he is a fool."* He also defended the right to strike as a democratic right of working people: *"I am glad to see that a system of labor prevails under which laborers can strike whenever they want to... I like the system which lets a man quit when he wants to and wish it might prevail everywhere."*

After two years of bloody fighting, the Emancipation Proclamation freed the slaves in those states fighting against the Union. Later the slaves were also freed in the neutral border-states. No longer were four million human beings to be held in bondage. Inspired by the message of freedom, the workers of the North threw themselves enthusiastically into the struggle. Many trade union locals were dissolved for the duration of the conflict, as the entire workforce was often away at war. In the conflict between Northern industrial capitalism and Southern landlordism and slavery, it was clear which side the workers supported. American trade unionists also played a decisive role in the fight against slavery, as Northern workers signed up in droves for the Union Army.

The victory of the North was due only to a small extent to the military capabilities of general Ulysses S. Grant. Although undoubtedly a better general than his predecessors (he could hardly be worse!) Grant was no military genius. As W.E. Woodward expresses it: "Grant just happened to be swimming with the tide and he was a man who swam extremely well in that particular kind of tide." (W.E. Woodward, op. cit., p. 563.) Later he proved to be a spectacularly incompetent President at the head of a voraciously corrupt administration. As a general, he combined a mule-headed stub-bornness with an indifference to the horrific scale of casualties on his own side. These qualities, however, were sufficient to wear down the South and bring it to its knees.

The Battle of Gettysburg was the decisive turning point. The battle was fought over three days of bloody slaughter from July 1st to the 3rd, 1863. The Confederates lost 20,000 men, killed, wounded or captured. The Union army had 23,000 casualties. But these losses were far more serious to the South than to the North. In the end, the wealth, population and industrial muscle of the Union was decisive and the Confederates' early victories proved unsustainable. But it was above all the courageous decision of Abraham Lincoln to fight a revolutionary war against the slave-owning South that tipped the balance. Lincoln's Gettysburg address is one of the great revolutionary democratic documents of all time. With its clarion call of government of the people, by the people, for the people stands alongside the Declaration of Independence as a landmark in the struggle for democracy.

By the spring of 1864 the Confederacy was on its knees. One hard blow would be enough to topple it. Congress created the grade of lieutenant general and Lincoln immediately conferred this rank on Grant. The victory of the Union was not in doubt. But the losses in the Union army were horrendous, in large measure because of the way Grant conducted himself. We see the character of the man in the short but bloody battle of Cold Harbour, where the Union forces lost 7,000 men in an hour, compared to 600 of Lee's men. The army was on the brink of mutiny. Some regiments refused to participate in what was obviously a suicidal assault on the rebel capital.

More successful was Sherman's advance through Georgia and the Carolinas, which was accompanied by a merciless scorched earth policy. Sherman's army burnt everything in its path. The actions of a section of the soldiery were a disgrace to the Northern cause. But this burning and plundering was enthusiastically greeted by sections of Northern public opinion. Especially bloodthirsty (as it often the case in times of war) were the preachers. Phillip Brooks, a devout Massachusetts pastor and author of *The Influence of Jesus,* when he heard about the torching of Columbia, exclaimed: "Hurrah for Columbia! Isn't Sherman a gem?" Despite its savagery, Sherman's campaign severely weakened the already enfeebled South. Grant's forces overwhelmed Lee's defences. Finally, Lee faced Grant at Appomattox, about 80 miles from Richmond, with a force of only 28,000 starving and exhausted men against Grant's army of 72,000. Lee was compelled to surrender.

Lee presented himself to Grant dressed in a splendid uniform of Confederate grey made from English cloth and handed grant a handsome sword with a jewel-studded hilt. Grant was dressed in the travel-stained uniform of a private to which the shoulder straps of a lieutenant general had been attached. The contrast had a deep symbolic value. The aristocratic slave-owning gentry of the South was overthrown by the capitalist North. The past was defeated by the future.

The victory of the North was a revolutionary victory. It transformed the face of the United States. At a stroke the rule of the slave owners was overthrown. The reactionary class of Southern planters was deprived of two billion dollars worth of property, with not a single cent in compensation. *Thus, there is nothing "un-American" about the expropriation of tyrants and oligarchs, which was carried out both in 1776 and in 1865. The United States was established at birth with an act of revolutionary expropriation. In the same way a socialist U.S.A. in the future will be established by the expropriation of the property of the big banks and corporations that exercise their dictatorship over the people and have turned democracy into an empty word.*

By the end of the War, Abraham Lincoln was a changed man. He was drawing ever more radical conclusions. Lincoln's revolutionary measures earned him the love and admiration of the working class in the U.S.A. and internationally. But it aroused the bitter hatred of the ruling class – and not only in the South. Even at the height of the war, Lincoln did not have a firm base of support in his own party. A section put forward the cowardly and reactionary scoundrel McClellan as the Presidential candidate. Lincoln's popular majority was tiny – only half a million votes. In spite of everything, Lincoln was re-elected and the Thirteenth Amendment for the unconditional abolition of slavery was passed. It was a new dawn for the American people. But Lincoln also took measures in the interests of the poor farmers in the North. The Homestead Act was the first in American history to give public land free of charge to citizens who agreed to settle on it. What new measures he would have passed had he lived we shall never know. The slave-owners took their revenge for their defeat. On April 14 1865, Abraham Lincoln was shot down in cold blood by a Confederate assassin.

CHAPTER TWENTY-SIX

International Repercussions of the Civil War

At the outbreak of the Civil War there was a considerable amount of British capital invested in American enterprises, including the railroads, banking, coal, timber and land. The sympathies of the British ruling class were with the South. A reactionary coalition of textile manufacturers, landowners and imperialists put heavy pressure on the British government to recognize the Confederate States. *The Times* of London could hardly conceal its glee when commenting on how short-lived the Union of American states had been.

The Confederates were confident in their belief in the power of King Cotton. And since Britain took five-sixth of all the exports of American cotton and there were about 400,000 workers in English cotton mills who depended on cotton for their livelihood (making a total of about two millions with their families and dependents), they were convinced that within three months Britain would recognize the South, smash the blockade and if necessary fight the Union to guarantee supplies of cotton to British mills. During the Civil War several Confederate warships were built in English shipyards or purchased from British subjects. Their crews were mostly made up of English sailors. Three of these vessels – the *Alabama*, *Florida* and *Shenandoah*

– did a lot of damage to Northern commerce. Yet none of these vessels ever entered a Confederate port. This open connivance of the British government with the rebels constituted a flagrant provocation and a blatant breach of neutrality.

In fact, Britain came close to declaring war on the Union in November 1861 when an American ship, *the San Jacinto*, stopped *the Trent*, a British mail packet boat, off the coast of Cuba and seized two Confederate Commissioners on their way to London. A military intervention by Britain would have drastically changed the balance of forces to the disadvantage of the Union. If the British government finally backed down it was mainly for fear of the reaction of British public opinion and especially the working class.

While the British ruling class openly sympathized with the slave owners of the Confederacy, the working people of Britain wholeheartedly backed the Union. This was quite remarkable if we bear in mind that the Civil War in America badly disrupted the trade in cotton and caused a depression in the cotton mills of Lancashire and terrible unemployment and suffering for the workers. The English radical John Bright toured Lancashire explaining the plight of the American slaves:

"The jobless mill hands resolved to stick by their black brothers in the Southern states of America, although their allegiance compelled them to feed at soup kitchens and live on charitable relief." (W.E. Woodward, op. cit., pp. 527-8.)

In this war against the forces of reaction, the International Workingmen's Association (the First International) sided unequivocally with the North against the South. It is not generally known that Karl Marx wrote two letters to Abraham Lincoln on behalf of the IWA, expressing his admiration and support for the latter in his fight against slavery. Thus, in this decisive moment in American history, Marxism stood shoulder to shoulder with the American people, and not just in words. Members of the IWA fought in the ranks of the Union army, and thus fulfilled their internationalist duty. Working class revolutionaries like Anneke and Weydemeer – the latter a close friend of Marx – served with distinction in the ranks of the Union army.

CHAPTER TWENTY-SEVEN

An Interesting Comparison

Recently the author of these lines was invited to participate in a television documentary about the French Revolution. The filmmakers were charming and intelligent young Americans, who apparently wanted to know what the Marxist perspective on the French Revolution was. During our preliminary conversations, they asked me whether I considered the French Revolution to be justified, in view of all the violence and bloodshed it involved. I think they were a bit surprised at my answer. I drew their attention to the fact that America won its independence through a revolution, and that in that revolution they did not treat the British very gently. Moreover, the second American Revolution was a very violent and bloody affair. Yet nobody has ever asked me whether the American War of Independence was justified, or whether Abraham Lincoln was right to use violence against the Southern slave-owners.

In the French Revolution of 1789-93, almost two millions died out of a population of only 26 millions – that is, about 7.7 per cent. Yet few French people (excepting a handful of eccentric people nostalgic for the good old days of Louis XVI) would argue that they would have been better off under the *ancien régime*. Even fewer Americans would argue that, in order to avoid bloodshed, they should have remained under the blessed rule of George III!

The critics of Bolshevism also frequently raise the question of revolutionary violence. Actually, the October revolution was a relatively peaceful affair, particularly in Petrograd, since the Bolsheviks had the support of the overwhelming majority, and practically nobody was prepared to fight for the old regime. The real bloodbath began in the Civil War, which was the exact equivalent of the slaveholders' rising in the U.S.A. Soviet Russia was invaded by 21 foreign armies of intervention: British, French, German, Poles, Czechs, Japanese – and Americans. Many people were killed unnecessarily because of this, and the Russian people suffered terrible hardship. Incidentally, this was when the parties that opposed the Bolsheviks were banned -since every one of them took arms against the Soviet government.

Lenin and Trotsky originally had no plans to prohibit other parties. After the October Revolution the only party that was outlawed was the fascist and anti-Semitic Black Hundreds. But in the same way that Abraham Lincoln was obliged to take drastic measures against the rebels during the Civil War, so Lenin and Trotsky were compelled to act against parties that not only agitated against the Revolution but took up arms against it. It is not generally realized that, relative to population size, many more people were killed in the American civil war than in the civil war in Soviet Russia. Yet very little is said on this subject, and certainly nobody ever accuses Abe Lincoln of being a bloodthirsty monster as they accuse Lenin and Trotsky with tedious regularity. Let us make a brief comparison of the two.

Because of the chaotic character of the period, there are no exact figures for casualties in the Russian Civil War. But the total deaths incurred in both the First World War and the subsequent Civil War adds up to about three million. If we assume that one third of these died during the Civil War (which is certainly an exaggeration), the result would be one million. Since the population of Russia was 150 million at that time, that is 0.7 per cent. In the American Civil War, according to the most accurate figures I could find, the total killed (not including wounded) on both sides was 558,052 out of total population of 34,300,000. That would mean 1.63 percent of the population was killed. That is already more than in the Russian Revolution. However, if we include the wounded – many of whom were horribly crippled and deformed -then the percentage of the total killed *and* wounded would actually be 2.83 percent of the population. In other words, a lot more blood was shed in the American Civil War.

	Population (millions)	*Enrolled (thousands)*	*Ratio*
Union	26.2	2,803.3	10.7%
Confederate	8.1	1,064.2	13.1%
Combined	34.3	3,867.5	11.1%

		<——— Casualties ———>			
			[—Deaths—]		
	Enrolled	*Combat*	*Other*	*Wounded*	*Total*
Union	2,803.3	110,070	249,458	275,175	634,703
Confederate	1,064.2	74,524	124,000	137,000+	335,524
Combined	3,867.5	184,594	373,458	412,175+	970,227

The Civil War in the U.S.A. was a revolution, just as much as the French Revolution of 1789-93 or the October Revolution in Russia. Many people lost their lives in it, yet nobody considers it a "crime". In fact, while naturally regretting the loss of life, the historians are unanimous in agreeing that it was worth it, that is to say, *the end justi-fied the means*. Yet this is supposed to be the original sin of Bolshevism!

We might add that there is no reason to suppose that the Socialist Revolution in America will be a bloody affair. The U.S.A. is not tsarist Russia! The American working class is an overwhelming majority of the population. It could easily take power, brushing aside the resistance of the big corporations, on one condition: that it is organized, disciplined and determined to overcome all obstacles. There is one other condition that would guarantee a peaceful transformation: a courageous and far-sighted leadership that would not be afraid to adopt the most audacious measures to disarm the ruling class and render it impotent. The American workers need a revolutionary party and a leadership like that of Abraham Lincoln and Sam Adams: men and women who are not hypnotized by the power of the oppressors, their rules and regulations, but prepared to rely only on the revolutionary initiative and power of the masses.

CHAPTER TWENTY-EIGHT

How Capitalism Failed African Americans

The Second American Revolution was a tremendous step forward, but it never realized its promise to Black Americans. The real winners in the Civil War were the Northern capitalists who opened up new markets and obtained a huge new supply of dirt-cheap labor. Nearly a century and a half after the abolition of slavery in the U.S.A., we are very far from achieving genuine equality for all, regardless of race, color or sex. Despite a number of advances achieved through the struggles of black people in the 1960s, the position of blacks remains one of clear disadvantage. Michael Moore points out that in the U.S.A. today:

- About 20 percent of young black men between the ages of sixteen and twenty-four are neither in school nor working – compared with only 9 percent of young white men. Despite the "economic boom" of the nineties, this percentage has not fallen substantially over the last ten years.
- In 1993, white households had invested nearly three times as much in stocks and mutual funds and/or IRA and Keogh accounts as black households. Since then, the stock market has more than doubled its value.

- Black heart attack patients are far less likely than whites to undergo cardiac catheter-ization, a common and potentially lifesaving procedure, regardless of the race of their doctors. Black and white doctors together referred white patients for catheterization about 40 percent more often than black patients.
- Whites are five times more likely than blacks to receive emergency clot-busting treatment for stroke.
- Black women are four times more likely than white women to die while giving birth.
- Black levels of unemployment have been roughly twice those of whites since 1954.
- In the first nine months of 2002, the U.S. unemployment rate averaged 5.7 percent, compared with the first nine months of 2000, when it averaged 4 percent. About 2.5 million more workers are unemployed now than in 2000. But the unemployment rate for African-Americans has risen about 60 percent faster than for all workers. Some 400,000 more are now out of work than were out of work in 2000, a two-year rise of 30 percent.

Capitalism has failed all Americans, with the exception of the tiny minority that own and control the means of production and treat the country and its government as their private property. But the biggest losers are the twenty percent at the bottom of the pile, and of these the biggest majority are blacks and Latinos. Despite the attempts to disguise this situation by the kind of tokenism that allows a handful of privileged blacks like Colin Powell or Condoleeza Rice to figure prominently on the stage, the position of the great majority of working class and poor black people has not been substantially improved.

The conclusion is clear. The only way to eliminate racism is by pulling it up by the roots. The black slaves were first brought into the U.S.A. as a form of cheap labor serving the wealthy Southern planters. As a result of the Second American Revolution, they are formally free. But they remain as before cheap labor at the disposal of Big Business. The link between racism and capitalism was eventually clearly understood by Malcolm X and the Black Panthers, who attempted to organize on class lines and link the struggle of blacks for advancement to the general struggles of the American working class. This represented a deadly menace to the establishment that has thrived for so long on the policy of divide and rule. That is why the Black Panthers and Malcolm X were targeted and ruthlessly hunted down and killed.

Marxists consider the basic principles of the American Revolution to represent a great historic advance, but also consider that the only way to breathe life into these great principles is by overthrowing the rule of the big banks and monopolies that exercise a dictatorship over the people and have turned the idea of democracy into an empty shell. The overthrow of the dictatorship of Big Business demands the utmost unity in struggle of all working people – black and white, Native American and Irish, Hispanic and Asian, Arab and Jewish, white and blue collar, men and women, old and young. We make no distinction on grounds of color, sex or creed. It is necessary to unite all the oppressed, underprivileged and exploited people under the banner of the labor movement and socialism.

On the basis of a genuine socialist society –which has nothing to do with dictatorship or totalitarianism – the idea of the Rights of Man and Woman will cease to be an empty phrase and become a reality. Not only life, liberty and the pursuit of happiness, but a genuine freedom to develop the potential of human beings to the full – this is the meaning of socialism.

CHAPTER TWENTY-NINE

"Give Me Your Huddled Masses"

The emigration of the Pilgrims was the first influx into America of people fleeing from a defeated revolution, but by no means the last. Over the last two centuries we observe the following phenomenon: after every defeat of a revolution in Europe, there was a big influx of refugees into America. That rich mosaic of peoples that fused together to form the modern American nation was formed in the first place out of Poles, Hungarians, Germans, Italians, Russians, Scandinavians, Jews, Irish, and Asians, with the admixture of the descendants of African slaves and more recently, people from Latin America.

Where did these people come from? If we leave aside the native Americans and the millions of black slaves forcibly torn from their native lands and shipped to the plantations of the South and consider the European immigrants who formed the central core of the population of the U.S.A. in the 19th century, the great majority were, like the Pilgrims, political refugees fleeing from either victorious counterrevolution or national oppression. The defeat of the Polish uprisings of 1830 and 1863, the crushing of the German revolution of 1848, the persecution of Jews and revolutionaries by Russian Tsarism, the defeat of numerous uprisings of the Irish people against their British tormentors – all these things provided America with a steady flood of human material that made it what it is today.

The opening up of the West was undoubtedly an historically progressive development (although it was a terrible tragedy for the native peoples who were regarded as an obstacle to be removed). Americans refer proudly to the "pioneer spirit" that made this development possible. But where did this spirit come from? In order to conquer the vast open spaces of North America, to clear the dense forests, to brave the innumerable dangers of an untamed and hostile environment – all this required a special kind of people, motivated by a special kind of spirit. If we examine this question more closely, it will immediately become evident that those heroic pioneers who threw themselves with such energy into the opening up of America were to a very large extent revolutionaries who, having lost all faith in the possibility of changing the Old World, looked for and found a new life in the New World. The very same energy and courage with which they fought against the ruling regimes in Europe was now turned to other purposes. *Thus, the celebrated American "pioneer spirit" was to a very large extent the product of a revolutionary psychology and spirit that simply found a different outlet.*

This fact was already understood by the great German philosopher Hegel, who pointed out that if France had possessed the prairies of North America, the French Revolution would never have taken place. Here we also find the historical explanation for the celebrated "American Dream", the idea that it is possible for anyone to succeed on the basis of individual initiative and work. In a period when America possessed vast expanses of uncultivated land, this vision was not altogether without foundation. The apparently unlimited possibilities meant that the idea of revolution was subsumed and absorbed. In place of the struggle between the classes, there was the struggle of individual men and women against nature, the unceasing fight to tame the wilderness and carve a living out of mother earth. This is the true origin of that element of rugged individualism that has for so long been regarded as the basic ingredient of the "American character".

W.E. Woodward writes: "Like those who were better off, the average laboring man or farmer was an individualist too. He detested authority and was inclined to be rowdy and pugnacious. His class consciousness was dissipated by his individual self-asser-tiveness. The working class had no leaders, and it is doubtful if any set of leaders, however gifted, could have organized the laboring men of that time into a permanent association or a working class political party. Laborers' revolts took the form of spontaneous and senseless riots which usually began and ended in a few hours.

"The spirit of our early civilization was the spirit of the pioneer. It pervaded all classes of society. Four out of five men were pioneers in something or other, or the sons of pioneers. A feeling for adventure, a pride in single-handed accomplishment, was a necessity of social life.

"Through the generations the pioneering spirit has persisted in its various sublimated forms, long after the need for it has passed away. It has become so thoroughly infused in the American character that it has acquired the dignity of an honored tradition, and in that role it adds enormously to our present-day vexations and befuddlements. You may observe it in the ardent worship of individualism; in the widespread opposition to collective efforts for human betterment; in the stubborn attempts to preserve, in individualistic patterns, activities which are inherently social. There is a time and a place for the pioneer, the individualist, but in a modern, compact, highly organized society, he is not helpful but destructive." (W.E. Woodward, op. cit., p. 252.)

In the 19th century, the famous French sociologist and historian Alexis de Tocqueville wrote a well-known book called *Democracy in America*, which ever since has enjoyed the status of a classic. His basic thesis is that democracy in the United States had such profound roots because the difference between rich and poor was relatively small, and certainly much less than in Europe. He also observed that many rich Americans had started out poor and worked their way up the social ladder. When de Tocqueville wrote his book, this was largely true. With the exception of the South, where slavery still ruled supreme and a wealthy white aristocracy existed, in most of the States of the Union, there existed a remarkable degree of equality between citizens. Of course, there were still rich and poor. But even the poorer citizens felt that it was still possible to "get on" with a little effort. Class divisions existed – there were the so-called range wars between the big ranchers and smallholders that sometimes assumed a violent character. But in general, until the last decades of the 19th century, the class struggle, although clearly present, remained relatively undeveloped.

This had certain consequences. For example, for a long time the state was relatively weak, and America was not cursed with the heavy burden of bureaucracy and militarism that weighed so heavily on most nations in Europe. However, all that began to change with the rapid development of industrial capitalism towards the end of the 19th century. The growth of the big trusts, the search for markets and the commencement of America's involvement in foreign adventures, beginning with Spanish-Cuban-American War of 1892-1898, marked the inexorable transformation of the U.S.A. into a country dominated by giant monopolies and the most powerful imperialist state the world has ever seen.

CHAPTER THIRTY

The Golden Calf

"'To think', he said to Gallatin, 'what has happened to our country since your father's day! Since the time of Jefferson!'

"Gallatin was astonished. 'But surely everything is so much better now, Mr. Tilden. The country is so big, so very rich...' This was some weeks before the panic. 'Railroads everywhere. Great manufactories. Floods of cheap labor from poor old Europe. America is El Dorado now, whilst in my father's time it was just a nation of farmers –and not very good farmers at that.'

"'You misunderstood me, Mr. Gallatin.' Tilden's sallow cheeks now each contained a smudge of brick-colored red. 'I speak of corruption. Of judges for sale. Of public men dividing amongst themselves the people's money. Of newspapers bought, bought by political bosses. Even the Post.' Tilden nodded gravely to me, knowing that I often wrote for that paper. 'The Post took a retainer from Tweed. That's what I mean by change in our country, this worship of the Golden Calf, of the almighty dollar, this terrible corruption.'" (Gore Vidal, *1876*, p. 15.)

American capitalism in the nineteenth century was an historically progressive force, and the victory of the North laid the basis for the economic expansion and domination of the U.S. on a world scale. It freed up a massive labor pool for capitalist enterprise, and allowed for the domination of a handful of industrialists, paving the way for the giant trusts and monopolies of the 1890s. While the working class was fighting and dying in the war against slavery, the monopolists-to-be were busily enriching themselves in the lucrative war industry. The early fortunes of Carnegie, Mellon, Armour, Gould, Rockefeller, Fisk, Morgan, Cooke, Stanford, Hill, and Huntington were made during this period.

The triumph of capitalism in the U.S.A. signified an unprecedented development of the productive forces. This is nest shown by the explosive growth of the railroads:

In 1860 there were 30,000 miles of railroad track in the U.S.A. In 1880 there were three times as much – 90,000 miles. By 1930 the figure was 260,000 miles.

The supporters of the market economy cite this as a shining example of the achievements of free enterprise. In reality the railway bosses received huge state subsidies. Twelve million acres of government land along the railway's right of way were given outright to the Union Pacific Railway, which, in addition, received a government loan of $27 million in U.S. bonds. Union Pacific, which set out with no funds at all, then entered into an agreement with a small financial entity in Pennsylvania called Crédit Mobilier, to build the railway. One of the directors of Crédit Mobilier was a member of Congress, Oake Ames, who sold stock in the company to his fellow congressmen. The Congressional investigation later discovered that the bank, its stockholders and friends had obtained a profit of $23 million on an initial investment of less than a million.

It is also worth noting that the U.S.A., which today (theoretically at least) stands for "free trade" was originally firmly committed to protectionism and tariffs. Indeed, this was an important element in the conflict between the capitalists of the North and the slaveholding South. The Tariff Act of 1870, which pretended to be a step in the direction of tariff reduction, in fact raised tariffs steeply on things like steel rails that were of fundamental importance to the northern industrialists. The manufacturers of the North and East, sheltering behind high tariff barriers, were making vast fortunes in easy, unearned profits at the expense of the South and West.

Up to 1860 the government of the United States was largely in the hands of the landowners of the South. From 1865 the Northern capitalist oligarchs pushed them aside and took over the power. Cornelius "Commodore" Vanderbilt, whose rapacious greed was equalled only by his crudeness and ignorance, was the richest man in America. The attitude of these men was shown by his words: "Law! What do I care about law? Hain't I got the power?" Yes, the Vanderbilts and their like had the power, and they still have it. W.E. Woodward provides us with a good account of this capitalist adventurer:

"He was considered a great constructive genius and a pattern for poor boys. But there was in him no constructiveness of any kind. He waited for the other fellow to do all the preliminary work, and when the industry – steamships, railroads, or whatever it was – had turned the corner and was about to be a big thing, then Cornelius Vanderbilt proceeded to crowd out the originators and inventors and get control of the property by methods which would fill an ordinary cardsharp with envy. He was a financial gangster with many lesser gangsters working for him. When he died the reverend gentleman who officiated at his funeral said that 'riches and honors had been heaped on Vanderbilt, that he might devote all his ability to the cause of humanity and seek to lay up treasures in heaven.'

"The net worth of the treasures he laid up in heaven is unknown, but the value of his worldly assets was large. He left about one hundred million dollars." (W.E. Woodward, *A New American History*, pp. 607-8.)

The American ruling class has always surrounded itself in the "rags to riches" myth, made popular in Horatio

Alger's penny novels. In fact, it has its origins in crime, swindling and downright robbery. The present rulers of America are descended from a real rogue's gallery of speculators and crooks, such as the pious Daniel Drew, who was a deacon of the church on Sundays and a common stock market swindler the rest of the week. He began his career as a cattle drover who sold cows to the butcher by weight and just before they got to market fed them salt and gave them large quantities of water to drink to increase their weight.

Drew saw no contradiction between this kind of activity and religion. Religion has its place in the church and the home, he said, but not in business. He took this principle to its logical conclusion when he unloaded a pile of worthless stock on the unsuspecting members of his congregation. But that was done on a weekday, so it was presumably OK. When he died he left a fortune to Drew Theological Seminary, an institution that trains preachers – presumably in the same moral principles.

Under the Grant Presidency, gangsters like these were allowed to rule unchecked by any controls. The administration was in their pocket, and Grant himself was corrupted by big business, although not as much as other members of his entourage:

"Since the War Grant had played the part of little Jack Horner with much gusto. In his particular corner the plums were numerous. He accepted valuable presents from anybody and everybody. The gifts ran from horses to houses. A group of 'fifty solid men' of Boston gave him a library which had cost seventy-five thousand-dollars. Alexander Stewart, a wealthy department store proprietor of New York, sent Mrs. Grant a thousand-dollar shawl, which was gratefully accepted. Whisky distillers contributed cases of their product, and there were donations of furniture, paintings, choice hams, boxes of sausages, and a vast collection of elaborate toys for the general's youngest son." (ibid., p. 605.)

The Grant administration was the first to reveal the real content of bourgeois democracy in the U.S.A. The government was firmly wedded to big business and served it faithfully, while the new class of capitalist robber barons showed their gratitude by generously filling the pockets of the politicians. And all of them regarded the state and its treasury as a gigantic pork barrel from which it was legitimate to help oneself.

The salary of the President was raised from $25,000 to $50,000 a year – a fortune in those days. Senators and representatives also did quite well, their stipends being boosted from $5,000 to $7,500 a year. But unfortunately Congress got too greedy. It proposed to make the measure retroactive for two years. This outstanding piece of legislation became known as the *Back Pay Grab*. It caused a public uproar almost as furious as the Union Pacific bribery case. In the end the Grant Presidency sank under a heap of financial scandals. The President's private secretary adviser and friend, Babcock, had received valuable presents and money from the leaders of the Whisky ring, which he had used to finance Grant's election campaign. There were many other such cases. Grant wrote: "Let no guilty men escape." But they nearly all did and have been escaping ever since. The clique of super wealthy oil barons who control the Bush administration today behave no differently to the crooks and swindlers of the Grant administration. Only the quantities involved are infinitely larger.

CHAPTER THIRTY-ONE

Inequality

> *"It matters not one iota what political party is in power or what President holds the reins of office. We are not politicians or public thinkers; we are the rich; we own America; we got it, God knows how, but we intend to keep it if we can by throwing all the tremendous weight of our support, our influence, our money, our political connections, our purchased senators, our hungry Congressmen, our public-speak-ing demagogues into the scale against any legislature, any political platform, any presidential campaign that threatens the integrity of our estate."* (Frederick Townsend Martin, *The Passing of the Idle Rich.*)

Progress in the last decades of the 19th century was tremendous, but the fruits of progress were not equally enjoyed by all. The growth of the economic might of the U.S.A. signified a simultaneous growth in the power of Big Business. By 1904 the Standard Oil Company controlled over 86 per cent of the refined illuminating oil of the country. By 1890, gigantic corporations were in control of each great industry. The Aluminium Company produced 100 per cent of the output of virgin aluminium in the United States. The Ford Motor Company and the General Motors Corporation together produced three out of every four cars. The Bell Telephone Company owned four out of every five telephones in the United States. The Singer Sewing Machine

Company made at least three out of every four sewing machines sold in the United States. And so on.

The huge polarization between Labor and Capital, between rich and poor, was the real basis on which the class struggle developed on the soil of the United States. In the old days the difference between rich and poor were so small that a man like de Tocqueville could regard them as insignificant. But for the last hundred years or more the gulf between rich and poor, between haves and haves not, has widened into an abyss. The bosses were utterly indifferent to the conditions of their workers. These so-called Christians were all ardent believers in *laissez-faire* and "Social Darwinism".

John D. Rockefeller is reported to have said: "the growth of a large business is merely a survival of the fittest." For millions of Americans living and working conditions were very bad, and the hope of escaping from a lifetime of poverty virtually non-existent. As late as the year 1900, the United States had the highest job-related fatality rate of any industrialized nation in the world. Most industrial workers worked a 10-hour day (12 hours in the steel industry), yet earned from 20 to 40 percent less than the minimum deemed necessary for a decent life. The situation was only worse for children, whose numbers in the work force doubled between 1870 and 1900.

Under these conditions socialist ideas were beginning to get an echo in the U.S.A. In 1892 the People's Party noted in its platform:

"The fruits of the toil of millions are boldly stolen to build up colossal wealth for a few [...]

"Wealth belongs to him who creates it, and every dollar taken from industry without an equivalent is robbery. If any will not work, neither shall he eat [...]

"We believe that the time has come when the railroad corporations will either own the people or the people must own the railroads [...] Transportation being a means of exchange and a public necessity, the government should own and operate the railroads in the interests of the people [...]

"The telegraph and telephone, like the post office system, being a necessity for the transmission of news, should be owned and operated by the government in the interest of the people..."

Karl Marx pointed out that without organization the working class is only raw material for exploitation. The American workers began to organize quite early on. The roots of the labor movement were already well established in the nineteenth century. William Sylvis, an early trade union activist, founded the Iron Moulders' Union, and helped found the National Labor Union, which he wanted to affiliate to the International Workingmen's Association – the body in which Marx played the leading role. He was far ahead of his day on issues of black workers and women – he wanted them in the unions – against considerable opposition. This great advocate of working class unity, cutting across all artificial lines, died in great poverty at age 41.

The attempts of working people to defend themselves against rapacious employers were met with extreme brutality. As one contemporary labor leader wrote: "a great deal of bitterness was evinced against trade union organizations, and men were blacklisted to an extent hardly ever equalled." In response the workers formed a clandestine union – The Noble Order of the Knights of Labor – founded in 1869. Originally a secret society organized by Philadelphia garment workers, it was open to all workers, including African Americans, women and farmers. The Knights grew slowly until they succeeded in defeating the great railroad baron, Jay Gould in the strike of 1885. Within a year they added 500,000 workers to their membership.

The Knights of Labor had a very advanced program that called for the eight hour day, equal pay for equal work for women, the abolition of convict and child labor, the public ownership of utilities and the establishment of co-operatives. The terrible conditions and brutality of the bosses sometimes provoked a violent response. The "Molly Maguires" were a secret society of Irish immigrant coal miners who fought for better working conditions in the coalfields of northeastern Pennsylvania. Called murderers and framed, 14 of their leaders were imprisoned and ten of them were hanged in 1876.

In reply to the labor movement the bosses sent in their shock troops, the Pinkerton Detective Agency – those hated private cops of the monopolists, scabs, strike breakers, hired guns and murderers – to fight the workers. The bosses also had at their disposal the forces of the state. Workers were imprisoned, beaten up and killed for the "crime" of fighting for their rights. This state repression was carried out on behalf of private interests, in particular Lehigh Valley Railroad founder, Asa Packer, as well as Franklin Gowen of Philadelphia and Reading Railroad, and the coal company bosses who wanted to crush the fledgling labor organizations.

CHAPTER THIRTY-TWO

The Workers' Uprising of 1877

> *"The power of money has become supreme over everything. It has secured for the class who control it all the special privileges and special legislation which it needs to secure its complete and absolute domination. ... This Power must be kept in check. It must be broken or it will utterly crush the people."* (*The New York Sun*, quoted in Philip S. Foner, *The Great Labor Uprising of 1877*, p. 7.)

In 1876, as the nation prepared to celebrate a hundred years of American In Independence, an economic depression (or panic, as it was then known) gripped the country. Millions had been thrown out of work. In New York one quarter of the workforce was unemployed. The already meagre wages of the workers were cut. The police attacked meetings of the unemployed, mercilessly beating up men, women and children.

This was the period of the most violent labor conflicts in the history of the United States. The first of these occurred with the Great Rail Strike of 1877, when rail workers across the nation went out on strike in response to a 10-percent pay cut. A contemporary labor paper called the Great Strike the beginning of a Second American Revolution. The Journal of the Brotherhood of Locomotive Engineers asked in April 1873:

"Are not railway employees in this year of grace, 1873,

enduring a tyranny compared with which British taxation in colonial days was as nothing, and of which the crack of the slave whip is only a fair type?"

Attempts to break the strike led to a full scale working class uprising in several cities: Baltimore, Maryland; Chicago, Illinois; Pittsburgh, Pennsylvania; Buffalo, New York; and San Francisco, California. At several locations the military was called in to crush the uprising workers. Many workers were killed and wounded. The first victim of this repression was shot on July 17 by the militia in Martinsburg, West Virginia, and died a few days later of his wounds. But the workers were not intimidated and the strike continued to like wildfire along the main railroad lines. On July 20, a clash between strikers and militia at the Camden depot in Baltimore left eleven unarmed people dead and many more wounded. President Hayes called in three companies of regular soldiers to deal with the subsequent protests.

In Pittsburgh the militia fraternized with the workers, obliging the authorities to call in the First Division of the National Guard from Philadelphia. These "heroes" shot into an unarmed crowd of men, women and children, killing ten people and wounding another eleven. A report in the Pittsburg*h* Pos*t* described the scene of carnage: "Women and children rushed frantically about, some seeking safety, others calling for friends and relatives. Strong men halted with fear, and trembling with excitement, rushed madly to and fro, tramping upon the killed and wounded as well as upon those who had dropped to mother earth to escape injury and death." (Quoted in Philip S. Foner, op. cit., p. 63.)

The workers responded by burning the property of the railroad. Everywhere there was the same insurrectionary spirit. The situation in Baltimore was so serious that the marines were called in to guard the railroad company's buildings and equipment with artillery. Six companies of the Fourth National Guard arrived in Reading, Pennsylvania, where they shot into a crowd, killing eleven more. Everywhere the authorities responded to the strike with great brutality, beating up strikers and demonstrators. But still the strike spread.

On July 25th there was a monster demonstration in St. Louis, including many black workers, closing down businesses and carrying out a general strike. The women of the working class played a prominent role, fighting shoulder to shoulder with their men, as the following account from the *Chicago Inter-Ocean* shows:

"Women with babes in arms joined the enraged female rioters. The streets were fluttering with calico of all shades and shapes. Hundreds were bareheaded, their dishevelled locks streaming in the wind. Many were shoeless. Some were young, scarcely women in age, and not at all in appearances. Dresses were tucked up around the waist, revealing large underthings. Open busts were common as a barber's chair. Brawny, sunburnt arms brandished clubs. Knotty hands held rocks and sticks and wooden blocks. Female yells, shrill as a curfew's cry, filled the air. The swarthy features of the Bohemian women were more horrible to look at in that scene than their men in the Halsted Street riots. The unsexed mob of female incendiaries rushed to the fence and yards of Goss Phillips' Manufacturing company. The consternation which this attack created extended to Twenty-second Street, at that hour very quiet. A crowd of men gathered on Fisk Street to witness this curious repetition of the scenes of the Paris commune. The fence surrounding the yard gave way, and was carried off by the petticoated plunderers in their unbridled rage. There was fear for a while that the Amazonian army would continue their depredations. Word was dispatched to the Himmon Street Station, and a force of officers under

Lieutenant Vesey pushed down to the corner of the contest. The women hissed as they saw the blue coats march along. Some of the less valorous took to their heels... Others stood their ground.

"A shower of missiles greeted the boys as they came smiling along left front into line. One woman pitched a couple of blocks at the heads of the officers, and then moved on to attend to her family duties. The men were weak in the strength and forcefulness of their language compared to these female wretches. Profanity the most foul rolled easily off their tongues with horrid glibness. Expressions were made use of that brought the blood mantling to the cheek of the worst-hardened men in the crowds of spectators. It was awful." (Quoted in Philip S. Foner, op. cit., pp. 154-5.)

The police showed no sign of sex discrimination. They beat up the women with the same enthusiasm as they beat up the men.

One significant element in this great strike that was close to an insurrection was the active participation of the Workers' Party of the United States, an anticipation of the great Party of American Labor, which one day must emerge and lead the working class to victory. The Workers' Party played a most active role in the strike, issuing leaflets and proclamations and providing practical guidance to the strikers. At a rally organized by the WPUS., one of the speakers, an Englishman named John E. Cope, a former member of the International Workingmen's Association, spoke in favour of the nationalization of the railroads:

"In his speech, Cope insisted that the workingmen were not going to destroy the railroads. Rather, the railroads were going to become national property for the benefit of the people, and the working class would not destroy its own property. If the railroad corporations starved their workers, he went on, it was as if they murdered them, and whoever murdered a man should be hung. Yet under the existing system, these 'murderers' were honoured: 'A man who stole a single rail is called a thief, while he who stole a railway is a gentleman.' Cope concluded by warning the workers to be prepared to meet the military once the authorities called them in to crush their strike." (Philip S. Foner, op. cit., p. 167.)

The strikers were accused in the press of being communists (the Paris Commune just six years earlier had terrified the ruling class of America). Someone signing himself "a red-hot striker" replied: "You challenge me to compare 'the Communist and the Railway.' The way to do it is, first to see what is the idea of both, what each of them demands. Now, I say, – and I challenge you, or any other fellow like you, to show I'm not right, – I say the 'Commune' *represents the cause of the poor in this: that its object is to give every human born into this world a chance to live; live long, and die well.* And I say of the 'Railway,' it *represents the few rich who don't want everybody to have a chance for a decent living, but intend to grind out of the rest of the world all the wealth possible for their own special benefit.* I say this, and don't fear you can show the contrary. The difference is, the one is struggling to make it possible for all the world to get on; the other is doing its damnedest to make it impossible for anybody to get on, save the few rich it represents. Let the public judge which side is most worthy, – as it will judge in good time, and don't you forget it." (Quoted in Philip S. Foner, op. cit., p. 211.)

Marx followed the unfolding of the Great Strike with tremendous interest. Writing to his friend and comrade Frederick Engels, he called it "the first uprising against the oligarchy of capital which had developed since the Civil War." He predicted that, although it would inevitably be suppressed, it "could very well be the point of origin for the creation of a serious workers' party in the United States." (Letter to Engels, July 24, 1877.)

Marx's prediction proved to be premature. The spectacular upswing of the productive forces in the United States was sufficient to give capitalism a new lease of life and blunt the political consciousness of the masses for far longer than Marx or anyone else could have anticipated. But the need to create a class-independent mass party of labor in the U.S.A. remains as correct and necessary today as then. Sooner or later the American working class, through the experience of struggle, will come to the same conclusion.

CHAPTER THIRTY-THREE

The Chicago Martyrs and May Day

The bosses met the workers' movement with extreme violence. The list of the martyrs of American Labor is endless, the most celebrated being the Chicago martyrs of 1886 – as a result of which the American working class gave May Day to the rest of the world. It is ironic that in the U.S.A., "Labor Day" is now held at the beginning of September, far from the more significant date of May 1. It is generally seen as a last 3-day weekend of summer with lots of grilling and beer drinking. The union marches in major cities have been emasculated in order to reduce the importance of May Day by moving it to September and making it a "fun" weekend. In this way the ruling class in the U.S.A. does everything possible to make the working class forget its own history and traditions.

On May 1, 1886, Albert Parsons (his wife Lucy was a tireless activist who campaigned to have him pardoned), the head of the Chicago Knights of Labor, led a demonstration of 80,000 people through the city's streets in support of the eight-hour day. In the next few days they were joined nationwide by 350,000 workers who went on strike at 1,200 factories, including 70,000 in Chicago. On May 4, Spies, Parsons, and Samuel Fielden were speaking at a rally of 2,500 people held to protest the police massacre when 180 police officers arrived, led by the Chicago police chief. While he was calling for the meeting to disperse, a bomb exploded, killing one policeman. The police retaliated, killing seven of their own men in the crossfire, plus four oth-ers; almost two hundred were wounded. The identity of the bomb thrower remains unknown.

Of course another Red Scare was invoked ("Communism in Chicago!") when all the workers were fighting for was the eight-hour day. On June 21, 1886, eight labor leaders, including Spies, Fielden, and Parsons went on trial, charged with responsibility for the bombing. The trial was rife with lies and contradictions, and the state prosecutor appealed to the jury: "Convict these men, make an example of them, hang them, and you save our institutions."

Even though only two were present at the time of the bombing (Parsons had gone to a nearby tavern), seven were sentenced to die, one to fifteen years imprisonment. The Chicago bar condemned the trial, and several years later Governor John P. Altgeld pardoned all eight, releasing the three survivors (two of them had had their sentences reduced from hanging to life imprisonment). Unfortunately, the events surrounding the execution of the Haymarket martyrs fueled the stereotype of radical activists as alien and violent, thereby contributing to ongoing repression. On November 11, 1886, four anarchist leaders were hanged; Louis Lingg had committed suicide hours before. Two hundred thousand people took part in the funeral procession, either lining the streets or marching behind the hearses.

As the crisis of capitalism deepens, workers need to arm themselves with a program that can answer their needs and aspirations. In doing so they need to reclaim May Day's tradition of struggle. May Day itself was born out of struggle. The fight for the 8-hour working day in the United States in the 1880s was the issue that gave birth to May Day as International Labor Day. In 1884 the Convention of the Federation of Organized Trades raised a resolution that was to act as a beacon to the whole working class: "that eight hours shall constitute a legal day's labor from and after 1st May 1886". This call was taken up by the Labor movement with the creation of Eight Hour Leagues, which wrung significant concessions out of the bosses, and led to the doubling of trade union membership.

Shortly after the Chicago tragedy of May 1886, which became known thereafter as International Workers Day, workers representatives set up the Second (Socialist) International in 1889, under the banner of workers' internationalism. A key resolution of the Congress was that on every May Day workers in every country would strike and demonstrate for the 8-hour day. On May 1, 1890 workers struck all over Europe, with 100,000 demonstrating in Barcelona, 120,000 in Stockholm, 8,000 in Warsaw, while thousands stayed at home in Austria and Hungary where demonstrations were banned. Strikes spread throughout Italy and France. Ten workers were shot dead in Northern France. In the words of the Austrian Social Democratic leader, Adler, "Entire layers of the working class with which we would otherwise have made no contact, have been shaken out of their lethargy."

In Britain and Germany, huge demonstrations were held on the Sunday following May Day. The importance of these developments was not lost on Frederick Engels, the lifelong comrade of Karl Marx, who had lived through the long period of quiescence in the British Labor movement after the great Chartists days of the 1840s. He wrote enthusiastically about May Day: "more than 100,000 in a column, on 4th May 1890, the English working class joined up in the great international army, its long winter sleep broken at last. The grandchildren of the old Chartists are entering the line of battle." *Yet again, a great tradition of international labor was "made in the U.S.A.".*

CHAPTER THIRTY-FOUR

Craft Unionism

The rise of American capitalism as a world power in the last decades of the 19th century was marked by a sharp upturn of the productive forces, booming industry and high profits that permitted certain concessions to the upper layer of the working class in the skilled trades. This "labor aristocracy" formed the basis of the kind of "craft unionism" typified by the AFL.

In 1881, six prominent unions, the printers, iron and steel workers, moulders, cigar-makers, carpenters and glass workers met together with other groups to launch the Federation of Organized Trades and Labor Unions (FOTLU), led by Samuel Gompers and Adolph Strasser. With only 45,000 members, it was initially weak and overshadowed by the Knights of Labor. But on the basis of the booming economy, the tendency towards class collaborationism gathered ground. In the 1880s the tendency of "practical trade unionism" or "pure and simple unionism" gained ground at the expense of the Knights of Labor who, by 1890, had only 100,000 members.

The strength of the AFL – as it later became – was primarily in the crafts already named. It began with a membership of around 138,000 in 1886 and slowly doubled that number in the next twelve years. Gompers and his ilk represented what one might call the aristocracy of labor.

By appealing to craft prejudices with their narrower outlook, they succeeded in turning the labor movement away from the socialist views of earlier labor leaders. In this sense it represented a big step back as compared to the Knights of Labor.

Lenin explained that apolitical trade unionism is bourgeois trade unionism. The idea that the unions must be non-political inevitably leads to them falling under the domination of one or other of the bosses' parties. This assertion has been proved by the history of the American trade union movement from this time onwards. Samuel Gompers, a real bosses' man, was elected first president and held onto the position until his death in 1924.

The rise of this so-called trade unionism "pure and simple" was no accident, but flowed from the material conditions at that time. In the exceptionally privileged position of U.S. capitalism, which was already beginning to challenge Britain's position as the main industrial power by the beginning of the 20th century, concessions could be given to buy off the labor aristocracy. A similar situation led to the national-reformist degeneration of the labor and Social Democratic organizations in Britain, France and Germany in the years before 1914. From 1900 to 1904, the membership of the AFL went from half a million to a million and a half, and then to two million on the eve of the First World War. During and immediately following the War, membership again increased rapidly to more than four million in 1920. During this period, an estimated 70 to 80 percent of all unionized workers in the U.S.A. were in the AFL.

However, the organizational and numerical strengthening of the unions was accompanied by a process of bureaucratic degeneration at the top. In this period the basis was laid for the policies of class collaboration and non-political, that is for "yellow" trade unionism that has characterized the leadership of the AFL ever since. Leaders like Gompers and Meany accommodated themselves to capitalism, preaching the unity of interest between Capital and Labor – which is like preaching the unity of interest between horse and rider. Meanwhile, the vast majority of American workers remained unorganized, unrepresented and oppressed.

Moreover, the class collaborationist views of the AFL leaders were not at all shared by the bosses, who viewed the growth of trade unionism with alarm. Caroll Dougherty writes in his book *Labor Problems in American Industry*: "Most of the powerful ones [employers], believing that unionism was growing too strong and fearing further encroachments on their control of industry, decided to break off relations, and the years from 1912 to World War I, were characterized by a definitely increasing anti-unionism. […]

"Scientific management and 'efficiency' systems were introduced in many plants, much to the discomfiture of many skilled craft unions. A variety of union-smashing tactics were adopted by employers. Vigilante groups and citizens' committees were fostered to resist unionization activities. Court decisions upheld as a rule most of the employers' anti-union practices. In the face of these new difficulties, the membership of the AFL at first fell off a little and then resumed growth at a much slower rate than before 1902."

This is the eternal contradiction of reformist politics in general – that it produces results that are the exact opposite to those intended. The compromising attitude of the labor leaders always leads to a hardening of attitudes on the part of the employers: *weakness invites aggression.* This is shown by the record of that period – and the same applies today.

In spite of the class collaboration of Gompers and Co., the class struggle reached a fever pitch. In 1892 the bitter Homestead strike by the Amalgamated Association of Iron,

Steel and Tin Workers at the Carnegie steel mills in Homestead Pa., resulted in the death of several strikers and Pinkerton guards. A group of 300 Pinkerton detectives the company had hired to break the strike by the Amalgamated Association of Iron, Steel and Tin Workers were fired upon and 10 were killed. Unions were not let back into the plant until 1937. The workers were sacked from most of the mills in the Pennsylvania area.

Two years later a strike of the American railway Union led by Eugene V. Debs against the Pullman Co., was defeated by the use of injunctions and federal troops sent into the Chicago area. The National Guard was called in as a result to crush the striking workers; non-union workers were hired and the strike broken. Debs and others were imprisoned for violating the injunctions, and the union was defeated.

Then, as now, workers could not rely on the law to come to their aid. The bosses could buy expensive lawyers and bend the law to their will. The following example is quite typical. Wage cuts at the Pullman Palace Car Company just outside Chicago led to a strike, which, with the support of the American Railway Union, soon brought the nation's railway industry to a halt. As usual, as soon as labor began to fight for its rights, the federal government stepped in on the side of capital. U.S. Attorney General Richard Olney, himself a former lawyer for the railroad industry, deputized over 3,000 men in an attempt to keep the rails open. This was followed by a federal court injunction against "union interference" with the trains.

CHAPTER THIRTY-FIVE

The IWW

In the stormy years before and after the First World War, the labor movement in the U.S.A. was alive and vibrant. This was a period of giants – people like Eugene Debs, the "grand old man" of U.S. labor. Born in Terre Haute, Indiana, Debs left home at 14 to work in the railroad shops. As a locomotive fireman, he became an early advocate of industrial unionism, and was elected president of the American Railway Union in 1893. His involvement in the Pullman Strike led to a six-month prison term in 1895. In 1898 he helped found the U.S. Socialist Party; he would run as its presidential candidate five times in the period from 1900 to 1920. In 1905 he helped found the Industrial Workers of the World. Debs was charged with sedition in 1918 after denouncing the 1917 Espionage Act; he conducted his last presidential campaign from prison, winning 915,000 votes, before being released by presidential order in 1921.

During the early 1900s, mass production industries had expanded rapidly. Most of the workers in these industries lacked union representation. The AFL opposed unionizing these largely unskilled or semi-skilled workers, arguing that such attempts would fail. This view was challenged – successfully – by one of the most extraordinary militant union movements ever seen in any country. The Industrial

Workers of the World (the IWW.), also known by their nickname of Wobblies - would prove to be the most radical and militant movement in the nation's labor history.

Formed from an amalgam of unions fighting for better conditions in the West's mining industry, the IWW, or "Wobblies" as they were commonly known, gained particular prominence from the Colorado mine clashes of 1903 and the singularly brutal fashion in which they were put down. In 1905 a handful of the nation's most radical political and labor figures met in Chicago. Featuring Big Bill Haywood of the Western Federation of Miners and Eugene V. Debs of the Socialist Party, the group aimed to ignite a grassroots fire that would sweep the nation and pull down an evil and unjust system, brick by brick.

The IWW, engaged in militant action in the years before the war. Led by larger-than-life figures like Joe Hill and Big Bill Haywood, the "Wobblies" succeeded in organizing layers of the working class that had never been organized. They were free from all routinism, reformist prejudices and craft narrowness, and approached the class struggle with enthusiasm and verve. Fresh from his acquittal on murder charges in Idaho, Bill Haywood soon became a driving force for the IWW. Convinced that the Western Federation of Miners was not the answer, Haywood wanted the IWW to represent all workers in one big union – and to bring that union into a head-on clash with the centers of power in America.

The ideas of the IWW were a peculiar and colorful mixture of anarcho-syndicalism and Marxism. At its founding convention in 1905, it adopted a preamble that was a stirring statement of the class struggle: "The working class and the employing class have nothing in common. There can be no peace so long as hunger and want are found among millions of working people and the few, who make up the employing class, have all the good things.

"Between these two classes a struggle must go on until all the toilers come together on the political, as well as the industrial, field, and take and hold that which they produce by their labor, through an economic organization of the working class without affiliation with any political party."

The IWW declared war on the kind of narrow craft unionism represented by the AFL: "The rapid gathering of wealth and the centering of the management of industries into fewer and fewer hands make the trade unions unable to cope with the ever-growing power of the employing class, because the trade unions foster a state of things which allows one set of workers to be pitted against another set of workers in the same industry, thereby helping defeat one another in the wage wars."

The answer of the IWW was to fight for the principle of industrial unionism under their famous slogan "One Big Union". In combating craft narrowness and fighting to organize all workers in one union, they were undoubtedly on the right lines, and although their policies were distorted by some anarcho-syndicalist prejudices, they led the way with militant class politics. In 1908 they approved another preamble, which ended with a call for the abolition of capitalism: "Instead of the conservative motto 'A fair day's pay for a fair day's work', we must inscribe on our banner the revolutionary watchword, 'Abolition of the wage system'.

"It is the historic mission of the working class to do away with capitalism. The army of production must be organized, not only for the everyday struggle with capitalists, but also to carry on production when capitalism shall have been overthrown. By organizing industrially we are forming the structure of the new society within the old."

In reality, the organizations of the labor movement in the U.S.A. and every other country are just that: *the embryo of the new society that has taken shape and is slowly maturing in the womb of the old*. That is why the capitalists have historically shown such bitter hostility to the unions and try to destroy, by one means or another, any attempt of the workers to organize in defence of their class interests. The IWW, uniting in its ranks the most advanced, resolute and revolutionary elements of the American working class, led a series of militant strikes before the First World War, in the teeth of the most ferocious repression by the employers and their state.

By openly calling for class warfare, the Wobblies gained many adherents. Among other mass actions, they organized a brilliantly successful strike by textile workers in Lawrence, Massachusetts, in 1912. Their militant actions in the midst of World War I, however, provided the excuse for a government crackdown in 1917, which virtually destroyed the IWW. Some of the leaders later joined the young American Communist Party. The IWW degenerated into a small sect.

The reason for this was only partly state repression. It had a sectarian attitude to the AFL, which represented the big majority of the American workers. This conduct tended to separate the most militant and revolutionary workers from the mass, doom-ing them to impotence. In the end, the Left Wing of the union movement emerged through a big split in the AFL with the founding of the CIO.

CHAPTER THIRTY-SIX

Joe Hill

> *"Tomorrow I expect to take a trip to the planet Mars and, if so, will immediately commence to organize the Mars canal workers into the IWW and we will learn to sing the good old songs so loud that the learned star-gazers on earth will once and for all get positive proof that the planet Mars is really inhabited [...]. I have nothing to say for myself only that I have always tried to make this earth a little better for the great producing class, and I can pass off into the great unknown with the pleasure of knowing that I have never in my life double-crossed a man, woman or child."* (Joe Hill to editor Ben Williams, *Solidarity*, October 9, 1915.)

On November 19, 1915, a 33 year-old Wobbly songwriter was executed by a firing squad in the prison yard of the Utah State Penitentiary, framed on a murder charge. Thus ended the life of one of the most extraordinary figures of the history of American labor – Joe Hill.

Joe was born in Gavle, Sweden, on 7 October 1879, and, like so many of his compatriots, immigrated to the lower east side Bowery section of New York City via Ellis Island in 1902. Joe Hill, also known as Joseph Hillstrom and Joel Hagglund, was an American labor songwriter and martyr of the working class. His naive idealism about American society was soon shattered by the harsh conditions and exploitation of immigrant workers that he witnessed. He became an itinerant laborer, working in mines, the lumber industry, and as a longshoreman. He also developed skills as a hobo, traveling on freight trains and living off the land.

Joe joined the IWW around the year 1910 and became the "Wobbly bard", showing tremendous ability as a poet and songwriter. He was the author of dozens of Wobbly songs, which were printed on song cards and published in the *Industrial Worker, Solidarity* and in the IWW's little red songbook. These songs were based on his personal experience of the lives of the ordinary working people of his day. His most famous songs, including *Rebel Girl, The Preacher and the Slave*, and *Casey Jones*, became world - famous and were used in labor organizing drives and in rallies supporting strikes.

The Wobblies used many varied weapons in their fight against Capital, including art, poetry and music. These songs, with their air of cheerful proletarian defiance, were not written only for amusement. *They were weapons of struggle.* One of the participants in the Lawrence strike recalled:

"It is the first strike I ever saw which sang. I shall never forget the curious lift, the strange sudden fire of the mingled nationalities at the strike meetings when they broke into the universal language of song. And not only at the meetings did they sing, but in the soup houses and in the streets. I saw one group of women strikers who were peeling potatoes at a relief station suddenly break into the swing of the *Internationale*. They have a whole book of sings fitted to familiar tunes – *The Eight Hour Song, The Banners of Labor, Workers, Shall the Masters Rule Us?* But the favorite was the *Internationale*." (Ray Stannard Baker, *The Revolutionary Strike*, in *The American Magazine*, May, 1912.)

The IWW also used that most devastating proletarian weapon, particularly important in the United States: humour. This is a good example:

"On one occasion a non-union man entered a butcher's

shop to purchase a calf's head. As the butcher was about to wrap it up for him the customer noticed the union shop card.

"'Say, is that a union calf's head?' he asked.

"'Yes, sir,' answered the butcher.

"'Well, I'm not a union man and I don't want union meat,' said the customer.

"'I can make it non-union,' said the meat man, picking it up and retiring to the back room. He returned in a few minutes and laid the head on the counter with the remark, 'It's all right now.'

"'What did you do to make it non-union?' asked the prospective buyer.

"'I just took the brains out of it.'"

Joe Hill arrived in Utah in 1913 and found employment in the Park City mines while becoming acquainted with the Swedish community in Murray, Utah. In 1914 he was accused of the murder of a Salt Lake City storeowner, John A. Morrison, and convicted on circumstantial evidence. There ensued an international battle to prevent his execution by the State of Utah. What exactly happened can never be ascertained. But it is certain that the business interests of the West, especially the Copper Bosses of Utah, had conspired to eliminate him.

The bosses used all manner of dirty methods against the labor movement but were always careful to cover their tracks. The climate of opinion in the West and in Utah was decidedly hostile to the IWW and to Joe Hill and he could never get a fair trial. Under today's laws, Joe Hill would not have been executed on the evidence presented at his trial. President Woodrow Wilson intervened twice in an attempt to prevent the execution, but Hill was executed at the Utah State Prison in Sugar House, Utah, on November 19, 1915.

Joe Hill has become a folk hero and labor martyr, a

symbol of the American revolutionary tradition and the fight to defend the working class and the poor and downtrodden sections of society. One of his final statements, "Don't mourn, orga-nize!" has become a labor-rallying cry. There can be few more moving human documents in world literature than Joe Hill's Last Will, written while he was awaiting execution in the condemned cell:

"My will is easy to decide,
For there is nothing to decide.
My kin don't need to fuss and moan -
'Moss does not cling to a rolling stone.
"My body? – Oh! – If I could choose,
I would to ashes it reduce,
And let the merry breezes blow
My dust to where some flowers grow.
"Perhaps some fading flower then
Would come to life and bloom again.
This is my last and final will.
Good luck to all of you.
Joe Hill.

There have been many attempts to portray Joe Hill's life in different media over the years: biographies, novels, songs, plays, and movies have been written about him. *I Dreamed I Saw Joe Hill Last Night* by Alfred Hayes and Earl Robinson has become an American folk song of enduring quality. Today the songs of Joe Hill, the Wobbly bard, class fighter and martyr of the American labor movement, are known, loved, and sung around the world.

CHAPTER THIRTY-SEVEN

Literature and Revolution

Joe Hill showed how music and poetry could be powerful weapons in the class struggle. His example was followed by others, including the great Woody Guthrie. The beloved "dust bowl" and "hobo" folksinger, established a new genre of radical folk song that marries the best traditions of the songs of the American West with revolutionary class politics. Spokesperson of the working class, one of greatest American songwriters of any genre, and a continued influence on musicians today, especially singers and songwriters like Bob Dylan and Pete Seeger. Although most Americans know the song *"This Land is Your Land"*, few know that it is a socialist song. As the song says – *"this land was made for you and me"*!

It is a shame that many young Americans today are unaware that there was a great American tradition of left wing writers, starting with Jack London who was a committed and active socialist. Jack London, at his peak, was the highest paid and the most popular of all living writers. He is best known as author of wildlife novels *Call of the Wild* and *White Fang*, which remain popular with young readers. But how many have ever read his inspiring essays such as *War of the Classes*, *Revolution*, and *How I became a Socialist*? One of the most interesting is the autobiographical sketch called *What Life Means to Me*:

"So I went back to the working-class, in which I had been born and where I belonged. I care no longer to climb. The imposing edifice of society above my head holds no delights for me. It is the foundation of the edifice that interests me. There I am content to labor, crowbar in hand, shoulder to shoulder with intellectuals, idealists, and class-conscious workingmen, getting a solid pry now and again and setting the whole edifice rocking. Some day, when we get a few more hands and crowbars to work, we'll topple it over, along with all its rotten life and unburied dead. Its monstrous selfishness and sodden materialism. Then we'll cleanse the cellar and build a new habitation for mankind, in which there will be no parlour floor, in which all the rooms will be bright and airy, and where the air that is breathed will be clean, noble, and alive.

"Such is my outlook. I look forward to a time when man shall progress upon something worthier and higher than his stomach, when there will be an incentive to impel men to action than the incentive of today, which is the incentive of stomach. I retain my belief in the nobility and excellence of the human. I believe that spiritual sweetness and unselfishness will conquer the gross gluttony of today. And last of all, my faith is in the working-class. As some Frenchman as said, 'The stairway of time is ever echoing with the wooden shoe going up, the polished boot descending'."

One of Jack London's most remarkable works is his novel the *Iron Heel*, which both Lenin and Trotsky admired. In it he predicts the rise of fascism and depicts the heroic struggle of the American workers for socialism – long before the Russian Revolution and the rise of Hitler proved how eerily accurate he was.

"In reading it," states Trotsky in his introduction, "one does not believe his own eyes: it is precisely the picture of fascism, of its economy, of its government technique, its political psychology! The fact is incontestable: in 1907 Jack London already foresaw and described the fascist regime as the inevitable result of the defeat of the proletarian revolution. Whatever may be the single 'errors' of the novel – and they exist – we cannot help inclining before the powerful intuition of the revolutionary artist."

There were many other great American socialist novels. Upton Sinclair's novel *The Jungle* is a vivid exposure of conditions in the stockyards and slaughterhouses of America, ending with an uncompromisingly socialist message, its root-and-branch condemnation of capitalism that still reads well today, and its depiction of the appalling conditions of the workers in the slaughterhouses.

Sinclair's novel appeared as early as 1906, when it caused a major scandal in America. Ever since the Cuban War, when thousands of American soldiers died as a result of the rotten meat supplied to the army by the Chicago meat packers, the industry had been the target of public suspicion. Sinclair himself had got a job in a large Chicago meat packing firm and obtained first-hand information about the appalling conditions of the workers. As a result his novel comes close to the best work of Emile Zola. The characters in it are mostly workers in packing plants like the one Sinclair worked in:

"There was no heat upon the killing beds; the men might exactly as well have worked out of doors all winter. For that matter, there was very little heat anywhere in the building, except in the cooking rooms and such places – and it was the men who worked in these who ran the most risk of all because whenever they had to pass to another room they had to go through ice-cold corridors, and sometimes with nothing on above the waist except a sleeveless undershirt. On the killing beds you were apt to be covered with blood, and it would freeze solid; if you leaned against a pillar, you would freeze to that, and if you put your hand upon the blade of your knife, you would run a chance of leaving your skin on it. The men would tie up their feet in newspapers and old sacks, and these would be soaked in blood and frozen, and the soaked again, and so on, until by night-time a man would be walking on great lumps the size of the feet of an elephant. Now and then, when the bosses were not looking, you would see them plunging their feet and ankles into the steaming hot carcass of the steer, or darting across the room to the hot-water jets. The cruelest thing of all was that nearly all of them – all of those who used knives – were unable to wear gloves, and their arms would be white with frost and the hands would grow numb, and then, of course, there would be accidents. Also the air would be full of steam, from the hot water and the hot blood, so that you could not see five feet before you; and then, with men rushing about at the speed they kept up on the killing beds and with butcher's knives, like razors, in their hands – well, it was to be counted as a wonder that there were not more men slaughtered than cattle."

The Jungle became a best seller in a week. It sold hundreds of thousands of copies. The sales of canned meat plummeted. A board of investigation was set up that substantiated all of Sinclair's assertions. Legislation was put before Congress to control the industry. The owners tried to kill it but it was passed. Even the stupidest congressman must have realized that failure to act would have led to a collapse of the sales of American canned meat abroad. Almost a hundred years later, however, they are up to the same tricks, putting profits before people.

The powerful U.S. food and agriculture lobby, which, despite its hostility to socialism and state control, gets huge subsidies from the U.S. government. It is currently trying to force reluctant European consumers to eat genetically modified food. This is just the tip of a very large and ugly iceberg that potentially menaces the health of the entire planet. We look forward to the appearance of a new Upton Sinclair who will be capable of exposing the scandals of adulteration perpetrated by the modern food monopolies that will undoubtedly make the activities of the Chicago meat packers in 1906 look like child's play.

CHAPTER THIRTY-EIGHT

Imperialism

The end of the 19th century saw the birth of imperialism. Germany, France, Britain and Belgium struggled to gain possession of markets, territory, raw materials and spheres of influence. This policy led to the establishment of colonies and empires in Africa, Asia and the Middle East. On the Pacific, Japan's development followed a similar pattern, following the Western lead in industrialization and militarism, enabling it to gain a foothold or "sphere of influence" in China. As Germany emerged as a great power after victory in the Franco-Prussian War, which completed the process of German unification, so the U.S. would emerge as a great power after the victory of the North in the Civil War.

The United States, as the youngest member of the capitalist club, entered late into the scramble for markets and colonies. As a result it found itself at a disadvantage with respect to the older imperialist nations of Europe. The Panic of 1893 exacerbated the already fierce competition over markets in the growing "spheres of influence" of the United States, which tended to overlap with Britain's, especially in the Pacific and South America. Like all newly industrializing great powers, the U.S. adopted protectionism, seized a colonial empire of its own (the Spanish-American War of 1898), and built up a powerful navy (the "Great White Fleet"). Following the example of Germany, the United States tried to solve the depression by the adoption of protective tariff protection with the passage of the McKinley Tariff of 1890.

The nascent trend of American imperialism found its voice in a new generation of U.S. politicians, such as Henry Cabot Lodge, William McKinley, and Theodore Roosevelt, all of whom advocated a more aggressive foreign policy as a means of pulling the United States out of the depression of the second Grover Cleveland administration.

In addition to the strictly economic content of imperialism, it also fulfilled an important social and political role. Europe in this period witnessed the re-emergence of far more militant working-class organization and mass strikes. The existing social order felt threatened by the growth of the trade unions and Social Democratic Parties. A period of increasing unemployment and deflated prices for manufactured goods gave an additional impulse to imperial expansion.

Very soon after it had thrown off the yoke of British and European imperialism and established itself as a young and vigorous capitalist power, the U.S.A. began to flex its muscles and assert its power, developing territorial designs on its neighbors, especially Mexico. This was expressed in the Monroe Doctrine, which, as early as 1823, proclaimed that the American Continent was closed to European colonization, that America was for the Americans and that any attempt on the part of Spain or any other European state to reconquer the South American republics would be considered "a manifestation of unfriendly disposition towards the United States."

On this subject W.E. Woodward writes: "[…]the South American republics were not grateful then and are not grateful now. On the contrary, they hate us heartily on account of the Monroe Doctrine, as they assume that the doctrine is our indirect way of asserting an overlordship over the countries to the south of us." (W.E. Woodward, *A New American History*, p. 358.) Whatever may have been the original intention, there can be no doubt that that has been precisely the result.

Under the pretext of reaffirming the Monroe Doctrine, U.S. imperialism in reality extended it beyond all recognition through the Roosevelt Corollary of 1904. In practice, this was taken to mean that the U.S.A. claimed the exclusive right to "lead" the entire American continent – North and South. Under McKinley's Republican administration, the U.S.A. aimed to restore prosperity and obtain new markets through the "Open Door" policy. The meaning of this was already demonstrated in the U.S.-Cuban War.

Spain was the weakest of all the European imperialist states, and its last remaining possession in the New World, Cuba, was an obvious target. In 1895 the people of Cuba rose in revolution against their Spanish colonial masters. The Madrid government sent 200,000 soldiers but were unable to put down the uprising. The Cubans made use of guerrilla war, avoiding pitched battles and resorting to hit and run tactics – just like the Iraqis at the present time. The Spanish imperialists resorted to brutal repression. All suspected rebels were rounded up and placed in concentration camps, where many died of disease and starvation. These events were followed with great interest in the United States, and not only from humanitarian motives. American citizens had about $50 million worth of Cuban property, including sugar and tobacco plantations and iron mines. American property was being destroyed.

A vociferous campaign began in the U.S.A. in favour of "going to Cuba and sorting out the whole damn mess." This was an early expression of the pent-up chauvinism that was pushing America to assert its power on the world stage. President McKinley was not sympathetic to the imperialists and attempted to keep the U.S.A. out of war. But he was under increasing pressure from the imperialists who made sure that every Spanish atrocity, real or imaginary, was splashed all over the front pages of American newspapers in what was called "yellow journalism".

We know from more recent experience how easy it is to whip up pro-war feelings by using the mass media to create hate figures and manipulate public opinion – as George W. Bush and his administration did very effectively after the 11th September. It was even easier at that time because the American public had no experience of foreign wars. In such a situation, some incident is always needed to spark off war hysteria. In this case it was provided by the notorious *Maine* incident. The U.S. war party had a very vocal leader in the person of Theodore ("Teddy") Roosevelt, who imagined that the U.S.A. should act on the world stage in the same way as General Custer leading the Seventh Cavalry into battle against the "injuns". He declared that President McKinley had "no more backbone than a chocolate éclair". All the war party needed was that useful little incident. They got it on February 15, 1898 when the *Maine* was blown up in Havana harbour.

Late in January 1898, the U.S. government sent the battleship *Maine* to Havana on what was supposed to be a "good will" mission. In fact, "good will" had nothing to do with it. The *Maine* had been sent to protect U.S. property and citizens in Cuba. Despite this act of blatant interference, the Madrid government swallowed hard, maintained a diplomatic silence and publicly accepted the "good will" fairy story. It could hardly do anything else!

To this day nobody knows what happened. It may be that the Maine was blown up by Spanish loyalists, indignant at the affront to their government. But it is also possible that it was the work of Cuban rebels, intending to provoke a U.S. military intervention against Spain. It is even possible that the ship's magazine may have blown up through some kind of accident or spontaneous combustion. Certainly the official report on the incident was inconclusive. But it really made no difference. All this has quite a modern ring about it. After the 11th September, the right wing clique in the White House found the perfect excuse for carrying into practice the plans for the invasion of Iraq that they had already prepared long before. The destruction of the Twin Towers was the perfect excuse for this, although it is well known that Iraq had nothing whatever to do with it. Once the war machine starts to roll, like the Juggernauts of ancient India, it crushes everything in its path.

Is it not remarkable how every war is always humanitarian and pacific in intent, no matter how many lives are lost? Chauvinistic and anti-foreigner feeling is whipped up and all kinds of false moralizing arguments are put forward to dress up an act of aggression under the banner of the noblest and most humanitarian sentiments. But behind the scenes the most sordid self-interest is at work. Listen to Senator Thurston of Nebraska: "War with Spain," he said, "would increase the business and earnings of every American railroad, it would increase the output of every American factory, it would stimulate every branch of industry and domestic commerce." In other words, war was just another department of big business, or, as old Clausewitz might have said *"the continuation of business by other means"*.

Faced with pressure of such intensity, McKinley took the honourable way out and joined the war party. In his speech to Congress, the President was economical with the truth. He did not inform Congress that Spain had agreed to accept all the terms imposed by Washington for reform in Cuba. He doubtless understood that a "splendid little war" would not do his prospects for re-election any harm.

He would have been right, except that his Presidential aspirations were cut short by an assassin's bullet.

On April 19th, Congress declared war on Spain. The U.S. Navy moved in with gusto, although it was based on the other side of the world in Asia. Admiral Dewey entered Manila where the Spanish fleet was anchored and reduced it to scrap iron in the space of five hours. U.S. land forces backed by Filipino insurgents defeated the Spanish. But later the same insurgents were fighting the U.S. forces. Not for the last time, one imperialist power had simply replaced another.

From the American point of view the Spanish War was a brilliant success. Casualties on the U.S. side were few. The U.S. Navy lost fewer than 20 men, having destroyed the entire Spanish fleet. The total fatalities of the U.S. army in Cuba were 5,462. Of these, 379 were killed in action. The rest died from disease and bad food sold to the army by unscrupulous Chicago meat companies and accepted without question by stupid or corrupt military managers.

CHAPTER THIRTY-NINE

The Seizure of Panama

It was the "splendid little war" in Cuba that brought fame to Teddy Roosevelt, the man who discovered the art of public relations, photo opportunities and political marketing. He commanded a division known as the "Rough Riders" made up, supposedly, of cowboys from "out West", whose barnstorming tactics were excellent material for the front pages back home. War correspondence has never been the same since. The face of TR is the face of the American bourgeoisie in its expansionist phase: crude, vigorous, self-confident, greedy and uncultured. He enriched the English-American language with picturesque words like *"muckraker"*, *"mollycoddle"*, *"big stick"*, *"undesirable citizen"* and other gems.

Here was a plain, ordinary American millionaire, proud of his lack of culture, a man who hated the kind of educated, highfalutin' language of politicians, or *"weasel words"*, as he called them. His main interest in life was shooting lions and tigers, and especially being photographed in the performance of this manly activity. His moral views were slightly more progressive than those of Atilla the Hun. He opposed birth control as "wilful sterility" and "more abasing, more destructive than ordinary vice." He also condemned divorce. His taste in literature was as refined as those of the class he represented. He denounced Tolstoy's *Kreutzer Sonata* as "filthy and obscene".

George W. Bush may trace his political line of descent back to Teddy Roosevelt. But there is an important difference. When the U.S.A. invaded Cuba and occupied Philippines, capitalism was still on its ascending curve. It easily dominated countries that lagged behind historically and economically. But now we are in an entirely different historical period. Capitalism on a world scale has long since outlived its historical usefulness. Its progressive role is played out. That is why it is faced with crises, wars, instability and terrorism everywhere.

The decline of capitalism can be seen by comparing the invasion of Cuba with the invasion of Iraq. Even the comparison between the persons of Bush and Roosevelt reveals all the symptoms of decline. They have many things in common: reactionary politics, provincial narrowness and cultural philistinism. But Theodore Roosevelt possessed the élan, the drive and the raw pioneer energy of the American capitalist class in the period of its expansion. In his rhetoric there was a certain defiant style, and he showed personal courage in spite of the theatricalities. Yes, the man was a gangster, but he was a gangster with style. This was a reflection of the boundless self-confidence of rising American capitalism thrusting its way to world domination.

George Bush has all the negative features of his illustrious predecessor without any of his virtues. A mean-spirited provincial, this cowardly and hypocritical second-rater from the Bible Belt perfectly personifies the nature and intellect of the class he represents: the monopoly capitalists in the age of capitalism's senility. Here is no great idea, no broad horizon, no audacious rhetoric, only vicious intrigues combined with shameless bullying covered with a thin veneer of religious hypocrisy. Insofar as Roosevelt gave any thought to the Almighty, it was to thank Him for the invention of the machine-gun. And despite his aversion for

Tolstoy, at least he was capable of putting together a coherent sentence when he wanted to.

The truth is that for the U.S.A. the Cuban war was a small war, though not for Spain, for which it began a period of national humiliation and soul-searching that eventually had revolutionary consequences. For America, on the contrary, it marked the beginning of a long career of imperialist expansion and a fatal involvement in world affairs. The war was supposed to have been fought for Cuban independence from Spanish tyranny. But at the Paris Peace Conference the U.S.A. demanded the control over Puerto Rico and the Philippines. The Spanish were in no position to argue. As a cover for their actions the U.S.A. paid Spain $20 million for the Philippines, and as we know, fair exchange is no robbery. The opinion of the people living on the islands was not asked.

There is a Russian proverb: appetite comes with eating, and the appetite of the new member of the imperialist club was insatiable. Theodore Roosevelt was determined that the United States should control the passage from the Atlantic to Pacific oceans. This was a vital objective both militarily and economically, a major step in the U.S.A.'s march towards world domination. Admittedly there was a small snag: *Panama was part of Colombia, a sovereign nation.* However, such trifles have never been known to deter imperialists from Teddy Roosevelt to George W. Bush.

Roosevelt proceeded to negotiate with the Colombians to obtain the necessary permission to control the all-important canal. In early 1903 the Hay-Herran Treaty was signed by both nations, but the Colombian Senate failed to ratify the treaty. Not deterred, Roosevelt got into contact with Panamanian rebels (as George Bush got in touch with the Northern Alliance in Afghanistan and later the Iraqi Kurds and Shiites) and gave them to understand that if they revolted the U.S. Navy would assist their cause for independence. Panama proceeded to proclaim its independence on November 3, 1903, and the *U.S.S. Nashville* in local waters impeded any interference from Colombia – a classic case of gunboat diplomacy.

When the fighting began Roosevelt ordered U.S. battleships stationed off of Panama's coast for "training exercises". Fearing war with the United States, the Colombians avoided any serious opposition to the uprising. As we know, one good turn deserves another. The "independent" Panamanians returned the favour to Roosevelt by generously handing over to the United States control of the Panama Canal Zone on February 23, 1904 for the quite modest amount of $10 million. All in all, a very nice little business deal!

CHAPTER FORTY

The Philippine-American War

The ambitions of U.S. imperialism went far beyond the New World. The successful outcome of the war with Spain led to bigger things. Although U.S. capital investments within the Philippines and Puerto Rico were relatively small, nevertheless these colonies were strategic outposts for expanding trade with Asia, particularly China and Latin America. The United States suppressed an armed independence movement in the Philippines in the first decade of its occupation. During the ensuing (and largely forgotten) Philippine-American War, 4,234 U.S. soldiers were killed, and thousands more were wounded. Philippine military deaths were estimated at roughly 20,000. Filipino civilian deaths are unknown, but some estimates place them as high as one million.

U.S. attacks into the countryside often included "scorched earth" campaigns where entire villages were burned and destroyed, torture (the "water cure") and the concentration of civilians into "protected zones." As a result many Philippine civilians perished of disease and famine. All these methods were later repeated and developed in Vietnam, where civilians were forced into so-called fortified villages. The depersonalization of colonial peoples as a justification for treating them as animals, to be tortured and killed without a second thought – all were put into practice in the Philippine-American War, and even earlier in the genocidal wars against the Native American peoples.

As in Vietnam and Iraq, reports of the execution of U.S. soldiers taken prisoner by the Filipinos was used to justify disproportionate reprisals by American forces. Many U.S. officers and soldiers called the war a *"nigger killing business."* In the same way, the Vietnamese were described as *"gooks"* and the people of Iraq are depicted as *bloodthirsty terrorists.* Racism is always the inevitable concomitant of imperialism.

The forcible interference of one nation in the internal affairs of another is conveniently justified on the grounds of alleged racial and cultural superiority. This is supposed to give "our" people the right to decide what another people is supposed to believe and how they should organize their internal government and laws. During the U.S. occupation of the Philippines, English was declared the official language, although the languages of the Philippine people were Spanish, Visayan, Tagalog, Ilokano and other native languages. Six hundred American teachers were imported aboard the U.S.S. *Thomas*. The people of the Philippines were compelled to accept the language, culture and religion of the conquerors, whether they wanted it or not. In 1914, Dean C. Worcester, U.S. Secretary of the Interior for the Philippines (1901-1913) described "the regime of civilization and improvement which started with American occupation and resulted in developing naked savages into cultivated and educated men." In 2004, the Iraqi people are being treated in exactly the same way; only the politicians do not speak so honestly.

CHAPTER FORTY-ONE

The United States and World War One

The U.S.A.'s entry into World War One (the "War to End All Wars") in 1917 marked a qualitative new stage in American history. The whole logic of America's position in the two decades prior to 1914 rendered American intervention inevitable. The enormous and growing economic strength of the U.S.A. and its resulting military power made a clash with the older imperialist powers of Europe a certainty. That is why during the 20th century the U.S. was involved in two World Wars. However, when World War I began in 1914, the United States at first firmly protested neutrality – and none more loudly than the President, Woodrow Wilson. He was a strange figure in history. Wilson was neither a socialist nor a radical but a man of rigid views who tried to reconcile imperialism with democracy and pacifism. This was approximately like trying to reconcile a man-eating tiger with the principles of vegetarianism. No wonder Wilson died a bitter and disappointed man.

To imagine that the U.S.A. could keep out of the war in Europe, given America's important and growing role in world affairs, was utopian. The logic of events was pushing her into the war. All that was required was the usual incident to justify intervention. This was provided when early in 1917 Germany resumed its policy of unrestricted submarine warfare. The *RMS Lusitania*, a British ship carrying many American passengers, was sunk by German submarines. The *Lusitania*, like the *Maine*, Pearl Harbor, and the Gulf of Tonkin incident later, served as a convenient excuse to justify intervention in a European War, in a way that was to turn the U.S.A. into the de facto arbiter of the destiny of Europe – and hence the world. This created the necessary public indignation and led to a final break of relations with the Central Powers. President Wilson requested that the United States Congress declare war, which it did on April 6, 1917.

All sides in this War claimed that they had entered it with the purest and most Christian and civilized reasons. But, as in all other imperialist wars, this was only for the gallery. That goes just as much for the "idealist" Wilson as for Lloyd George and Clemenceau. The British and French insisted that the United States emphasize sending infantry to reinforce the line. They needed more cannon fodder to replace the millions who had been already led like sheep to the slaughter since the summer of 1914. The United States Army and the National Guard had already been mobilized in 1916 to pursue the Mexican "bandit" Pancho Villa, which helped speed up the mobilization. However, it would be some time before the United States forces would be able to contribute significant manpower to the Western and Italian fronts.

With American help, Britain, France and Italy won the war. The latter naturally (from an imperialist point of view) took their revenge on the defeated and imposed savage economic penalties on Germany in the Treaty of Versailles. Wilson gained a short-lived popularity by proposing his famous Fourteen Points, which proposed a democratic peace without annexations or crippling indemnities, as well as self-determination for all peoples etc., etc. As a list of good intentions it was admirable. But as a program for the post-war world it was useless. The British and French leaders, Lloyd George and Clemenceau, thought Wilson was mad. But they needed America's money and soldiers, and so they bit their tongues. Lloyd George was the wilier and more cunning of the two. He loudly demanded small concessions on matters of no importance, in order later to abandon them in exchange for getting his way on all the important questions later.

The style of the French President George Clemenceau was of a different type, although the substance was the same. As W.E. .Woodward correctly states:

"Clemenceau spoke English well. He was annoyed by Wilson's abstractions and ideals, and by his dissertations on the inalienable rights of mankind. His only com-ment on Wilson's essays was frequently an expressive, obscene and unprintable English word, which has been expunged from the record.

"Clemenceau did not want to be considered a gentleman; he looked upon all that as a lot of flummery and a waste of time. He made it perfectly plain that he was not in sympathy with the Fourteen Points, except those which gave something substantial to France." (W.E. Woodward, *A New American History*, p. 794.)

The conduct of Lloyd George and Clemenceau has rightly earned them the reputation of callous brigands. But there was a definite logic behind their conduct. It was largely determined by the relations between Europe and America. The Allies owed a large amount of money to the U.S.A. and they intended to squeeze it out of Germany. Despite all President Woodrow Wilson's calls for reasonable terms, *the Versailles Treaty amounted to a decision to plunder Germany.*

CHAPTER FORTY-TWO

A New World Power

> *"I spent 33 years in the Marines. Most of my time being a high-classed muscle man for Big business, for Wall Street and the bankers. In short, I was a racketeer for capitalism. I helped purify Nicaragua for the international banking house of Brown Brothers in 1909-1912. I helped make Mexico and especially Tampico safe for American oil interests in 1914. I brought light to the Dominican Republic for American sugar interests in 1916. I helped make Haiti and Cuba a decent place for the National City Bank boys to collect revenue in. I helped in the rape of half a dozen Central American republics for the benefit of Wall Street...."*
>
> -Smedley D. Butler (1881-1940) Major General (U.S. Marine Corps)

Somebody once said to Lenin "war is terrible", to which he replied: "Yes, terribly profitable." In 1922, the U.S. government created the Nye Committee to investigate the reasons the United States got involved in the war. The committee reported that between 1915 and April 1917, the U.S. loaned Germany 27 million dollars ($27,000,000). In the same period, the U.S. loaned Britain and its allies 2.3 billion dollars ($2,300,000,000), or about 85 times as much. They concluded that the U.S. entered the war because it was in its commercial interest for Britain not to lose. In other words, the decision to enter the War was *the result of a simple business calculation.*

The human balance of the First World War was as follows: Allied soldiers killed: 5,497,600; Central powers soldiers killed: 3,382,500; Civilians killed: 6,493,000. However, the economic balance of the War was quite satisfactory. The American firm J.P. Morgan and Co. bought approximately three billion dollars' worth of goods during the War on behalf of the Allies, and made a profit of thirty million dollars from this source. In addition they made a great deal more from the sale of Allied War Bonds in the U.S.A.

The World War turned the U.S.A. into the most powerful nation on earth. As the world's creditor, it was in a position to put Europe on hunger rations. The Allies were in debt to America to the tune of $10,350,000,000. Italy owed $2,000,000,000 and was given 62 years to pay up at an interest rate of four tenths of one percent. The French owed twice as much and were to pay it back at an interest of 1.6 percent. Great Britain had the biggest debt of all: $4,600,000,000, to be amortized in a similar period at 3.3 percent.

Since Europe was ruined, these debts could not realistically be paid. The ruling class in Britain and other countries passed the bill to the working class in the form of savage wage cuts that led to a sharp upswing in the class struggle. In order to pay their bills, the French and British ruling class exerted brutal pressure on the defeated Germans. They intended to pay the United States out of reparation funds squeezed from the German people. But bleeding, shattered, starving Germany could not pay.

Within one year the German payments stopped. The Dawes Commission looked into the situation and decided to reduce the amount paid to a more "lenient" sum: $500,000.000 in gold, payable by 1925, followed by an increasing amount thereafter. As a guarantee of payment, Germany's railroads, controlled revenues and large-scale industries were placed under international control. The author of this plan, Charles G. Dawes, was given a Nobel Prize in 1925, but the plan collapsed immediately.

In 1928 Germany ceased to make any payments. Another committee of experts was formed under Owen D. Young. It proposed that Germany liquidate its debts in 59 years. During the first 37 years the annual payments were to be $512,500,000; after that, "only" $391,250,000. The total amount was twenty-seven and a half billions. The only problem that the authors overlooked was that it is not possible to squeeze blood from a stone.

In 1931, President Hoover had to face the facts and announced a moratorium on all foreign debts owed to the U.S. government. The economic impact of the reparations mandated by the Treaty caused chaos and misery on an unprecedented scale. These conditions ultimately led to the rise of Adolf Hitler who seized power in Germany in 1933. The United States Senate did not ratify the Treaty of Versailles; instead, the United States signed separate peace treaties with Germany and her allies. But the power of the U.S.A. was enormously reinforced by its intervention in the War.

By 1934 all the foreign debtors, except Finland, had ceased to make payments of either principal or interest. From 1920 to 1932 the total payments on the consolidated principal amounted to $583,000,000. All these payments were made in gold or its equivalent in international exchange. In this way, the United States accumulated the biggest stock of gold ever held by a national treasury in the whole of human history. Other nations were forced off the gold standard as a result of this huge drain. This opened the door to a chain of competitive devaluations that seriously aggravated the Great Depression of the 1930s.

CHAPTER FORTY-THREE

The Russian Revolution

In March 1917, demonstrations in Petrograd culminated in the overthrow of Tsar Nicholas II. The workers and soldiers organized themselves in soviets –democratically elected action committees. The appointment of the Provisional Government, dominated by bourgeois liberals and politicians of the old regime, solved nothing. Power was really in the hands of the workers and the Petrograd Soviet. This confused and chaotic situation of dual power could not last. The bourgeois Provisional Government could neither end the war, nor solve any other of the pressing problems of the Russian workers and peasants. As a result, discontentment grew and the government became more and more unpopular.

Inside the soviets, the Bolshevik party, led by Vladimir Ilyich Lenin and Leon Trotsky, began to gain an echo. By the autumn of 1917 they had won an overwhelming majority in the Soviets and were in a position to take power. The triumph of the Bolsheviks in November (October according to the old pre-Revolutionary calendar) was a turning point in world history. Here, for the first time – if we exclude that glorious episode that was the Paris Commune – working people succeeded in overthrowing the old oppressive order and at least beginning the socialist transformation of society.

It is true that the Revolution later suffered a process of bureaucratic degeneration, as the result of being isolated under conditions of extreme backwardness. But at least the Russian workers showed that a socialist revolution was possible. As Rosa Luxemburg said: "They alone dared". The Bolshevik Revolution lighted a beacon that inspired hope in the hearts of millions of downtrodden and exploited people everywhere. Its echoes were heard far across the Atlantic in the United States.

If you ever visit Moscow and take a stroll around the Kremlin walls, you will find among the tombs of famous Russian revolutionaries the graves of two outstanding Americans – "Big" Bill Haywood and John Reed, the celebrated American writer and journalist who was the central character of the movie *Reds*. John Reed was active in the American labor and socialist movement before the First World War and is best remembered for his marvelous book about the Russian Revolution *Ten Days that Shook the World*, which Lenin himself described as a most truthful account of the October revolution. After Trotsky's monumental *History of the Russian Revolution* it is the best book one could read about this subject. Not only is this a great and truthful work of historical journalism. It is a remarkable human document in which every line is vibrant with the excitement of the moment:

"It is still fashionable, after a whole year of the Soviet Government, to speak of the Bolshevik insurrection as an 'adventure.' Adventure it was, and one of the most marvellous mankind ever embarked upon, sweeping into history at the head of the toiling masses, and staking everything on their vast and simple desires. Already the machinery had been set up by which the land of the great estates could be distributed among the peasants. The Factory-Shop Committees and the Trade Unions were there to put into operation workers' control of industry. In every village, town, city, district and province there were Soviets of Workers', Soldiers' and Peasants' Deputies, prepared to assume the task of local administration.

"No matter what one thinks of Bolshevism, it is undeniable that the Russian Revolution is one of the great events of human history, and the rise of the Bolsheviki a phenomenon of world-wide importance. Just as historians search the records for the minutest details of the story of the Paris Commune, so they will want to know what happened in Petrograd in November, 1917, the spirit which animated the people, and how the leaders looked, talked and acted. It is with this in view that I have written this book.

"In the struggle my sympathies were not neutral. But in telling the story of those great days I have tried to see events with the eye of a conscientious reporter, interested in setting down the truth." (*Ten Days that Shook the World*, preface)

What a refreshing change from the kind of book that now floods onto the market every day, written by allegedly "objective" and "scholarly" authors whose only intention is to blacken the name of the Russian Revolution, to bury it under a heap of lies and calumnies and thereby to convince the new generation that revolution is a very bad thing. What concerns these "impartial" hypocrites, of course, is not so much what happened in Russia almost a century ago, but what might happen in America tomorrow.

The modern American who wishes to understand the Russian Revolution could do no better than to read this marvellous book. John Reed was by no means an exception. Many Americans were inspired by the Russian Revolution at the time. And despite what happened subsequently, it remains a source of infinite inspiration and hope for the human race. Future generations of Americans will look back with infinite gratitude and affection to people like John Reed who were prepared to face slander, isolation, persecution and worse to defend the cause of socialism and justice.

CHAPTER FORTY-FOUR

White Terror in the U.S.A.

John dos Passos' U.S.A. is yet another socialist American literary masterpiece. It comprises three novels The *42nd Parallel, 1919,* and *The Big Money.* The second of these novels expresses with extraordinary vividness the nature and atmosphere of the period that followed the Russian Revolution. It is an extraordinary work, written in a highly original form, combining newspaper headlines and telegraphic episodes with real-life and fictional stories. Although in later life dos Passos went to the right, he wrote a book that really gives a flavour of the times.

The notorious Versailles Treaty that set the seal on Germany's defeat in 1919 was put together by the U.S.A., Britain and France. As an example of cynical power politics and imperialist robbery it is perhaps without parallel. With the sureness of touch of a master artist, dos Passos conveys the essence of the wheeling and dealing of the great imperialist powers and the sheer hypocrisy of the leaders of the "civilized Christian world":

"Clemenceau,
Lloyd George,
Woodrow Wilson.
Three old men shuffling the pack,
dealing out the cards:

Rhineland, Danzig, the Polish Corridor, the Ruhr, self-determination of small
nations, the Saar, League of Nations, mandates, the Mespot, Freedom of the Seas,
Transjordania, Shantung, Fiume, and the Island of Yap: machinegun fire and arson
starvation, lice, cholera, typhus;
oil was trumps. […]"

"On June 28 the Treaty of Versailles was ready and Wilson had to go back home to explain to the politicians, who'd been ganging up on him meanwhile in the Senate and House, and to sober public opinion and to his father's God how he'd let himself be trimmed and how far he'd made the world safe for democracy and the New Freedom."

Whether it is Germany in 1919 or Iraq in 2004, the diplomatic representatives of the great powers never admit that their activities are dictated by crude economic interests (*oil was – and is – trumps*). Their motivations are always pure and noble (*"making the world safe for democracy")*. And just as the monstrous Treaty of Versailles, which was supposed to make the world safe for peace, made the world a lot more unsafe and guaranteed the Second World War, so the present wars waged by the U.S.A. in Afghanistan and Iraq to "make the world a safer place" only render it far more unstable, unsafe and dangerous than before. George W. Bush also believes fervently in the God of his fathers, to whom he prays while ordering the bombing of Iraqi cities and inflicting machine-gun fire, arson, starvation and disease on millions of people. Meanwhile, behind all the rhetoric, oil is still trumps.

The description of the class struggle in the U.S.A. in the stormy years after the First World War in Dos Passos' book is outstanding in its raw and uncompromising realism. These were the years when the bosses and the government, fearing the effect of the Russian revolution on the American working class resorted to the methods of lynch law and mob rule to crush the labor movement. The year 1919, which gives Dos Passos' book its name, was a high point in the class struggle in the U.S.A. The war, as we have seen, was a time when the bosses were making easy profits. The coming of peace was marked by more difficult conditions. The party was over for the capitalists.

As in other countries, the American bosses tried to pass the bill for post-war read-justments to the workers. As a result, an epidemic of strikes and labor disputes broke out involving, at one time or another, 4,160,000 workers. In April 1922, there was the first coal mining strike in American history in which both the bituminous and anthracite coalfields were involved. More than half a million miners struck against sweeping reductions in wages. The strike lasted four months and ended in victory for the miners.

The repression against the labor movement had begun during the War when many were sent to prison, including socialist veteran Eugene Debs, now an old man. His only offence was that he had opposed the war. This gentle old man of American socialism was sentenced to ten years in a federal penitentiary. After the War, that fine Christian humanitarian Woodrow Wilson, out of spite, refused to pardon him. President Harding finally released him, after he had spent three years in prison.

Congress passed draconic espionage and sedition laws. The Postmaster General was given autocratic powers of censorship over written or printed matter sent through the mail. Socialist publications like the *Milwaukee Leader* and *The Masses* were excluded from the mail – a measure intended to bankrupt them. As if that was not enough, Congressman Victor L. Berger, the editor of the *Leader*, was given a twenty-year prison sentence. All these measures were in direct violation of the First Amendment of the

Constitution, which guarantees all American citizens freedom of speech and of the press. More than fifteen hundred people were dragged before the courts for disloyal utterances.

State repression reached a feverish peak after the War. Terrified of the events in Russia, and fearful that revolution would spread to the United States, the ruling class unleashed a white terror against the American labor movement. When the AFL unions, which had grown to a membership of five million by 1920, organized a wave of strikes to combat the post-war inflation, corporate leaders denounced them as "radicals, connected with Bolshevism, aided by Hun money." Given the record of the moderate AFL leadership, this was ironic. But as always the ruling class was not afraid of the leaders of the unions but of the masses that were behind them.

A wave of violence was unleashed against the strikers, of whom twenty were killed. The strikes were defeated. Thousands of spies were hired to infiltrate the unions and identify labor leaders who were fired and blacklisted right across the U.S.A. The bosses attempted to destroy the unions by forcing the workers to sign "yellow dog" contracts, promising not to join unions. It is an indication of how far back we have been thrown that such contracts still exist in the U.S. at the beginning of the 21st Century. And this is regarded as acceptable in a supposedly democratic country! A mood of hysteria was created that fed the flames of lynch law. *The Washington Post* reported approvingly that when an irate citizen shot someone who had criticized a patriotic pageant, "the crowd burst into cheering and hand clapping." (P.N. Carroll and D.W. Noble, *The Free and the Unfree, a New History of the United States*, p. 331.)

In Indiana it took a jury just two minutes to acquit another patriotic citizen who killed a man for saying "to hell with the United States". In Connecticut a salesman for a clothing company was sentenced to prison for calling Lenin "one of the brainiest men in the world." As usual, the most violent expressions of hate were reserved for the religiously minded. Billy Sunday, the nation's most powerful evangelists, said: "If I had my way with those ornery, wild-eyed socialists, I would stand them before a firing squad." (ibid.) Senator McKellar of Tennessee was much more moderate. He merely advocated the establishment of a penal colony on Guam for political prisoners. The senator was a man ahead of his times. It took another 85 years for his ideal to be realized by another great democrat and patriot, George W. Bush. However, some of his contemporaries had a good crack at it.

The Attorney General, A. Mitchell Palmer, set in motion widespread raids, breaking into private homes and union halls without even the pretence of a warrant. On Palmer's initiative, a special anti-radical division was set up under a young officer by the name of J. Edgar Hoover. Thousands of suspected radicals were arrested, held without bail, denied access to lawyers, and often brutally beaten after being marched in chains through the streets. Most were later released. But not all were so lucky. In Massachusetts two anarchists, Nicola Sacco and Bartolomeo Vancetti, were convicted on a murder charge. The trial was clearly politically motivated. Judge Thayer who presided, declared that he wanted to get "those anarchist bastards". Despite a huge international campaign to save them, Sacco and Vancetti were executed – two more martyrs to the cause of American labor. They were not the only ones.

In his book *1919*, John dos Passos recounts the story of the brutal lynching of War veteran and Wobbly Wesley Everett is one of the most moving episodes of the work:

"Armistice Day was raw and cold; the mist rolled in from Puget Sound and dripped from the dark boughs of the spruces and the shiny storefronts of the town. Warren O. Grimm commanded the Centralia section of the parade.

The ex-soldiers were in their uniforms. When the parade passed by the union hall without halting, the loggers inside breathed easier, but on the way back the parade halted in front of the hall. Somebody whistled through his fingers. Somebody yelled, 'Let's go ... at 'em boys'. They ran towards the wobbly hall. Three men crashed through the door. A rifle spoke. Rifles cracked on the hills back of the town, roared in the back of the hall.

"Grimm and an ex-soldier were hit.

"The parade broke in disorder, but the men with rifles formed again and rushed the hall. They found a few unarmed men hiding in an old icebox, a boy in the stairs with his arms over his head.

"Wesley Everest shot the magazine of his rifle out, dropped it and ran for the woods. As he ran he broke through the crowd in the back of the hall, held them off with a blue automatic, scaled a fence, doubled down an alley and through the back street. The mob followed. They dropped the coils of rope they had with them to lynch Britt Smith the IWW secretary. It was Wesley Everest's drawing them off that Kept them from lynching Britt Smith right there.

"Stopping once or twice to hold the mob off with some scattered shots, Wesley Everest ran for the river, started to wade across, up to his waist in water he stopped and turned.

"Wesley Everest turned to face the mob with a funny quiet smile on his face. He'd lost his hat and his hair dripped with water and sweat. They started to rush him.

"'Stand back,' he shouted, 'if there's bulls [police] in the crowd I'll submit to arrest.'

"The mob was at him. He shot from the hip four times, then his gun jammed. He tugged at the trigger, and taking cool aim shot the foremost of them dead. It was Dale Hubbard, another ex-soldier, nephew of one of the big lumbermen of Centralia.

"Then he threw his empty gun away and fought with his hands. The mob had him. A man bashed his teeth in with the butt of a shotgun. Somebody brought a rope and they started to hang him. A woman elbowed through the crowd and pulled the rope off his neck.

"'You haven't the guts to hang a man in the daytime' was what Wesley Everest said.

"They took him to the jail and threw him on the floor. Meanwhile they were putting the other loggers through the third degree.

"That night the city lights were turned off. A mob smashed in the outer door of the jail. 'Don't shoot, boys, here's your man,' said the guard. Wesley Everest met them on his feet, 'Tell the boys I did my best,' he whispered to the men in the other cells.

"They took him off in a limousine to the Chehalis River Bridge. As Wesley Everest lay stunned in the bottom of the car, a Centralia businessman cut his penis and testicles off with a razor. Wesley Everest gave a great scream of pain. Somebody has remembered that after a while he whispered, 'For God's sake, men, shoot me ... don't let me suffer like this. Then they hanged him from the bridge in the glare headlights."

Having described this bloody lynching in merciless detail, dos Passos reverts to a cold and crushing irony:

"The coroner at his inquest thought it was a great joke. He reported that Wesley Everest had broken out of jail and run to the Chehalis River Bridge and tied a rope around his neck and jumped off, finding the rope too short he'd climbed and fastened on a longer one, had jumped off again, broke his neck and shot himself full of holes.

"They jammed the mangled wreckage into a packing box and buried it.

"Nobody knows where they buried the body of Wesley Everest, but the six loggers they caught they buried in Walla Walla Penitentiary."

CHAPTER FORTY-FIVE

"Happy Days are Here Again"

"The American Plan; automotive prosperity seeping down
From above; it turned out there were strings to it.
But that five dollars a day
paid to good, clean American workmen
who didn't drink or smoke cigarettes or read or think,
and who didn't commit adultery
and whose wives didn't take in boarders,
made America once more the Yukon of the sweated
workers of the world;
made all the tin lizzies and the automotive age, and
incidentally,
made Henry Ford the automobilieer, the admirer of Edison,
the birdlover,
the great American of his time."
(John dos Passos, *The Big Money*.)

The so-called "Golden Twenties" witnessed a boom that was very similar to the boom of the 1990s through which we have just passed. Production soared to dizzy heights, the stock exchange still higher. President Coolidge believed fervently in the supreme wisdom of the market and its invisible hand. The business of government was to do nothing, to allow business a free hand and all would be well. For a time it seemed to work. No attempt was made to control speculation, which soared to the sky and beyond. Big fortunes were made, and as long as the money kept rolling in, why ask awkward questions? The same mood of what we now know as *"irrational exuberance"* has existed in every boom in capitalism from the Dutch tulip speculation of the 17th century to the new technology boom of the 1990s. And they all end the same way.

In the boom of the 1920s the illusion was created that wealth could be plucked out of thin air. In the stock exchange, money seemed to beget money in a miraculous and mysterious process. As a matter of fact, the boom of the 1920s, like any other boom under capitalism, was based on the super-exploitation of the working class. Between 1925 and 1929, the number of manufacturing establishments in the U.S.A. increased from 183,000 to 206,000 and the value of their output rose from $60 billion to $68 billion.

J.K. Galbraith comments:

"The Federal Reserve index of industrial production which had averaged only 67 in 1921 (1923-5 = 100) had risen to 110 by July 1928, and it reached 126 in June 1929. In 1926, 4,301,000 automobiles were produced. Three years later, in 1929, production had increased by over a million to 5,358,000, a figure which compares very decently with the 5,700,000 new car registrations of the opulent year of 1953. Business earnings were rising rapidly, and it was a good time to be in business." (J.K. Galbraith, *The Great Crash 1929*, p. 31.)

This is the real secret of the boom of the 1920s – the extraction of bigger and bigger amounts of surplus value from the sweat and nervous strain of the workers. Workers in the mass production industries – steel, auto, rubber, textiles, oil, chemicals, etc., – were unorganized, atomized and at the mercy of the employers. They were deprived of all rights and open to the most vicious kind of exploitation.

Anyone who stood up for the workers' rights ran the risk of being accused of being a Communist, a Red, or a Bolshevik. Harry M. Daugherty, head of the Justice Department in the corruption-ridden Harding administration, was put on trial on charges of conspiracy to defraud the federal government. Incredibly, he blamed his downfall on a Red plot: "I was the first public official that was thrown to the wolves by the Red borers of America." In his book *The Inside Story of the Harding Tragedy*, Daugherty wrote:

"I believed then, as I firmly believe now, that Soviet Russia is the enemy of mankind. That unless the forces of civilization stamp out this nest of vipers who have enslaved a hundred and sixty million human beings, our social system as well as our form of government will perish from the poison that is being poured into our vitals."

There is a surprising degree of unanimity on this question that extends right across the spectrum of opinion in the community of red-blooded, freedom-loving American entrepreneurs. The following is another good example from an impeccable source: "We must keep America whole and safe and unspoiled. We must keep the worker away from Red literature and Red ruses; we must see that his mind remains healthy." This ringing endorsement of the free market economy was the work of Al Capone, the notorious gangster, while awaiting trial. But Mr. Capone's touching faith in the market economy was misplaced. Even when he was speaking, America had already entered the Great Depression of the 1930s.

There is always a speculative element in every boom. Demand increases, the market expands, credit is needed for new investment, banks lend money as if there were no tomorrow. Prices rise in step with demand, and wages follow. Real estate prices soar along with the stock markets. Industrial production reaches dizzying heights and there is the beginning of what is now called over-investment, but which is more properly termed over-production. The whole thing is reaching its limits, but nobody knows or cares. Paradoxically, it is precisely at the apex of a boom when it is on the point of collapsing, that the illusion is strongest that the boom will last forever, and that the boom-slump cycle is a thing of the past. Then comes the collapse. In the language of Marxist dialectics, everything turns into its opposite: all the factors that created the upswing now push the whole thing downwards. Cause becomes effect and effect cause. The result is a slump.

Marx explains that the ultimate cause of every real capitalist crisis is overproduction. The automobile tire industry in the U.S.A. had expanded far more than the demand for tires. Shoe factories had a productive capacity about twice the shoe-purchasing requirements of the country. Two-thirds of the potential capacity of the flour industry was not needed. It would have been possible to close about 40 percent of the U.S. steel industry and nobody (except the sacked workers) would have noticed the difference. And so on. When the stock market finally collapsed in October 1929, it was not, as is generally assumed, the cause of the Great Depression, but only a symptom of the underlying problems of the real economy, and a warning of worse to come.

CHAPTER FORTY-SIX

The Great Crash – Then and Now

On 4 December 1928, President Coolidge delivered his state of the Union speech to the nation. In it we read the following:

"'No Congress of the United States ever assembled, on surveying the state of the Union, has met with a more pleasing prospect than that which appears at the present time. In the domestic field there is tranquillity and contentment ... and the highest record of years of prosperity. In the foreign field there is peace, the goodwill which comes from mutual understanding... ' He told the legislators that they and the country might 'regard the present with satisfaction and anticipate the future with optimism'. And breaking sharply with the most ancient of our political conventions, he omitted to attribute this well-being to the excellence of the administration which he headed. 'The main source of these unexampled blessings lies in the integrity and character of the American people."

As late as March 1929, when Hoover took over the Presidency, he was still singing the same song: "We are a happy people – the statistics prove it. We have more cars, more bathtubs, oil furnaces, silk stockings, bank accounts, than any other people on earth." Then in October 1929 the stock market collapsed. Industrial production fell by 50 percent and national income fell from $82 billion to $40 billion in just four years. Unemployment soared from two million in 1928 to three million in 1929, four million in 1930, seven million in 1931, twelve million in 1932 and 15 million in 1933.

The optimistic speeches of America's leaders on the eve of the collapse have been frequently quoted as proof of the stupidity and short sightedness of Coolidge, Hoover and their contemporaries who failed to foresee the Great Crash of 1929 or to take measures to prevent it. The comforting assumptions are that a) slumps are produced by the stupidity or mistakes of governments and leaders, and that b) our present governments and leaders are much cleverer than Coolidge and will not make the same mistakes again. Unfortunately, both assumptions are false. The history of the past 200 years should be enough to convince any reasonable person that the boom-slump cycle is something inherent to the capitalist system and not an accident caused by clumsy behavior. As sure as night follows day, a period of boom will be followed by a slump. Only the timing, duration and depth of the slump is unpredictable. But slumps under capitalism cannot be avoided.

It is true that the capitalists have evolved a number of mechanisms for postponing a slump, but the problem is that usually the very act of postponing it makes it all the more severe when it finally arrives. Chief among these mechanisms is credit, which, as Marx explained long ago, is a way by which the market ("demand") is extended beyond its natural limits. This can work for a time, but only at the cost of increased levels of indebtedness. This means that the market is expanded today at the cost of undermining it tomorrow. The central problem is not abolished but aggravated in the long run.

The idea has often been repeated that "we have learned from history" and that therefore a repeat of 1929 is not possible. This is an excessively optimistic view of things.

Hegel was much more realistic when he wrote that anyone who studies history can only conclude that nobody has ever learned anything from it. He said that precisely because the same situations continually repeat themselves in history in general, and we might add, in economic history in particular. There are many striking similarities between the boom of the second half of the 1920s and the boom of the second half of the 1990s. Then too the economists and politicians assured us that the boom-slump cycle had been vanquished forever. Marx had been consigned once and for all to the dustbin of history. Once again, they were all merrily plunging into a speculative orgy that drove the stock markets to unprecedented heights. Then came the fall.

It is true that so far, the fall has not been as steep as in 1929. Indeed it has been one of the mildest on record. But the story is not yet ended. The boom of the 1990s, like the boom of the 1920s, was based on a speculative bubble of vast proportions. That bubble has not yet been entirely burst. In fact, they are currently busy reflating it. The astronomical levels reached by the housing market internationally is a symptom of this fact. It bears an uncanny resemblance to the property boom in the 1920s, the bursting of which was one of the things that led to the collapse of 1929. Alan Greenspan long ago referred to the "irrational exuberance" of the boom of the 1990s. But he is doing nothing to restrain this exuberance, which poses a serious threat to the future prospects of both the U.S. and world economy. The longer the bubble is allowed to inflate, the more painful the final reckoning will be. This is what J.K. Galbraith has to say on this subject:

"A bubble can easily be punctured. But to incise it with a needle so that it subsides gradually is a task of no small delicacy. Among those who sensed what was happening in early 1929, there was some hope but no confidence that the boom could be made to subside. The real choice was between an immediate and deliberately engineered collapse and a more serious disaster later on. Someone would certainly be blamed for the ultimate collapse when it came. There was no question whatever as to who would be blamed should the boom be deliberately deflated (For nearly a decade the Federal Reserve authorities had been denying their responsibility for the deflation of 1920-1.) The eventual disaster also had the inestimable advantage of allowing a few more days, weeks, or months of life. One may doubt if at any time in early 1929 the problem was ever framed in terms of quite such stark alternatives. But however disguised or evaded, these were the choices which haunted every serious conference on what to do about the market." (J.K. Galbraith, op. cit., p. 52.)

These lines could have been written yesterday. They are a graphic warning of just how little the economists and politicians have learned from the past, and just how little they can control the boom-slump cycle. Contrary to the received wisdom, a repeat of 1929 at some stage is not at all ruled out. In fact, it is implicit in the whole situation.

CHAPTER FORTY-SEVEN

The New Deal

The Stock Market crash in 1929 and the ensuing economic slump punctured the dream of never-ending prosperity and pushed millions into poverty. Construction and housing stagnated after 1929, joining declines in the agriculture, mining and petroleum industries. Overproduction dragged down prices and profits. Wages did not rise fast enough to enable consumers to purchase all the new homes and home products offered for sale. Foreign trade was constrained by growing protectionism in the industrialized world. The Stock Market Crash led to a collapse of consumer confidence and led to a crisis of the financial institutions. Investment slumped. The economy sank into a severe depression, referred to by Americans as the "Great Depression". This was characterized by high levels of unemployment, negligible investment, and falling prices and wages. Millions of Americans were out of work and living precariously on public or private charity. When Russia invited Americans to apply for six thousand skilled jobs in 1931 it received a hundred thousand applications. Millions of Americans were reduced to penury. A survey in New York City in 1932 concluded that 20 percent of the children were suffering from malnutrition.

A report in a Chicago newspaper graphically describes the conditions: "Around the truck which was unloading garbage and other refuse, were about thirty-five men, women, and children. As soon as the truck pulled away from the pile, all of them started digging with sticks, some with their hands, grabbing bits of food and vegetables."

John Steinbeck was the author of novels depicting the lives and struggles of ordinary working Americans during the Great Depression – *The Grapes of Wrath, Cannery Row,* of *Mice and Men. The Grapes of Wrath* was published in 1939, when America had still not emerged from the Great Depression and millions were living in dire poverty. Steinbeck's poignant description of the conditions of the hungry and downtrodden, and their struggle to maintain human dignity, won him the Pulitzer in 1940.

In this novel Steinbeck vividly describes the ruthlessness of the big corporations that sent in the bulldozers to demolish the smallholdings and cabins that represented so much hope and so many years of labor. Men, women and children were evicted overnight and transformed from small farmers into propertyless vagrants. The most remarkable thing about this novel is that it does not seem to be a description of the masses written from without. The author has succeeded in getting under the skin of the "Okies", and expressing, in their own words and language the innermost thoughts, feelings and aspirations of the people. Here, for example, is how they see the police:

"'What'd the deputy say?' Huston asked.

"'Well, the deputy got mad. An' he says: "You goddamn reds is all the time stirrin' up trouble," he says. "You better come along with me." So he takes this little guy in, an' they give him sixty days in jail for vagrancy.'

"'How'd they do that if he had a job?' asked Timothy Wallace.

The tubby man laughed. 'You know better'n that,' he said. 'You know a vagrant is anybody a cop don't like. An' that's why they hate this here camp. No cops can get in. This here's United States, not California'."

Tom Joad expressed the voice of the underdog: "They're a-workin' away at our spirits. They're a tryin' to make us cringe an' crawl like a whipped bitch. They tryin' to break us. Why, Jesus Christ, Ma, they comes a time when the on'y way a fella can keep his decency is by takin' a sock at a cop. They're workin' on our decency."

In a situation where millions were going hungry, Hoover decided that relief was exclusively a matter for the local and state authorities. This worthy representative of big business, a millionaire himself, was concerned lest federal relief should corrupt the American character and undermine the spirit of free enterprise. For Hoover and the Establishment there was no problem: the market would sort things out in the long run. But as the English economist Keynes pointed out, in the long run we are all dead.

There was a sharp increase of political ferment and discontent among the workers of America. At that time many of the strategists of Capital feared a socialist uprising in the U.S.A. In order to prevent revolution from below, as so often happened in history, the more far-seeing sector of the U.S. ruling class decided to launch a program of reforms from above. In this way the idea of the New Deal was born. The Democratic President Franklin D. Roosevelt was elected in 1932. He implemented a number of programs to relieve the plight of the poor and unemployed. Over the past twenty years, historians have emphasized the "revolutionary" legislation of the Roosevelt administration. However, at the time, he was bitterly attacked by Conservative businessmen as a revolutionary and a Communist.

F.D. Roosevelt was no radical but the son of a wealthy patrician family and a relative of Theodore Roosevelt. Actually, he was attempting to combat the spread of Communism in the U.S.A. and save the capitalist system from revolution. He probably saved the American ruling class from the threat of social revolution, which was closer then than at any other time in American history. But the Establishment was too stupid to realize this. They distrusted Roosevelt and heaped abuse on him as a covert socialist and a dangerous radical. Roosevelt protested that this was a misunderstanding – and he was right. "I am fighting Communism, Huey Longism, Coughlinism, Townsendism," he declared. "I want to save our system: the Capitalist system." The difference is that he was a more competent defender of capitalism than his opponents. Roosevelt was smart enough to see that Hoover's policies would undermine capitalism in the U.S.A. quicker than anything else.

In the middle of a terrible agricultural crisis, Hoover had the brilliant idea of asking the farmers to reduce their crops, a piece of advice that rivals Marie Antoinette's "let them eat cake". Roosevelt correctly said that it was a "cruel joke" to advise the "farmers to allow 20 percent of their wheat to lie idle, to plough up every third row of cotton and shoot every tenth dairy cow." In order to defend the fundamentals of capitalism, Roosevelt was prepared to be flexible. In an emergency, he was prepared to resort to deficit financing to keep the level of unemployment within certain limits. But this policy has its limits. If it is continued for a long time it will have inflationary consequences. Therefore, as soon as there were signs of a modest economic recovery, Roosevelt cut back on state expenditure. This produced a sharp recession in 1937 and unemployment again doubled from five to ten million and remained high until the outbreak of War.

A whole mythology has grown up about the New Deal. Those who believe that capitalism can be reformed in such a way that it can avoid slumps and achieve social justice point to it as proof of their assertions. But in practice, Roosevelt's policies had at best only a marginal effect in pulling the U.S. economy out of the slump. The recovery, when it finally came, was not due to the New Deal but to the Second World War. The lowest point of the Great Depression was in 1933, but the U.S. economy showed very little improvement through the end of the decade, and remained grim until it was dramatically reshaped through America's arms program and participation in the Second World War, which had an even bigger effect than the previous one in stimulating the U.S. economy.

CHAPTER FORTY-EIGHT

The CIO and the Sit-In Strikes

Following the Great Crash of 1929, the bosses launched on a program of savage wage cuts. The AFL responded by announcing "no-strike" deals. This was supposed to be the result of a "gentleman's agreement" between the unions and the bosses. But in practice the unions conceded everything, the bosses nothing. From 1922 to 1929 the number of labor disputes diminished year after year. In 1929 there were only 903 labor disputes involving 203,000 workers. On September 1, 1929, noting with satisfaction that the number of strikes in the U.S.A. had gone down from 3,789 in 1916 to 629 in 1928, AFL President William Green asserted that "collective bargaining is coming to be accepted more and more as a preventative of labor disputes."

Weakness invites aggression. In June-July 1930, 60 corporations and industries announced wage cuts, and the AFL did nothing about it. The result was a rapid decline in union membership. In 1929 only one in five industrial workers belonged to a union in the U.S.A. Of those who did, nearly half were either building or transport workers. By 1931 the AFL was losing 7,000 members a week, and from a high of 4,029,000 in 1920, fell to 2,127,000 in 1933. This is a fitting epitaph on the supposedly "realistic" policies of "unionism pure and simple".

These were years of violent class struggle in the U.S.A. As Art Preis recalled in his book *Labor's Giant Step*: "Almost all picket lines were crushed with bloody violence by police, deputies, troops and armed professional strike-breakers." The mass demonstrations of unemployed workers organized by the Communist Party were broken up violently by the police, with many jailed, wounded or killed. On March 7, 1932 a demonstration of unemployed demanding work at the Ford Rouge Plant was dispersed with machine-guns, leaving four dead and many wounded. On the direct orders of President Hoover, General Douglas MacArthur, riding a white horse at the head of his troops, attacked a demonstration of 25,000 unemployed war veterans and their families with tear gas, gunfire and bayonets. Such "incidents" were common throughout the 1930s – including under Roosevelt's "New Deal". In 1937, for example, ten people were killed and 80 wounded in a Memorial Day clash between police and members of the Steel Workers Organizing Committee at a plant of the Republican Steel Co. in South Chicago.

Several AFL unions established the Committee for Industrial Organization (CIO) to organize the unorganized industries. This organization effort had great success in the rubber, steel, and automobile industries. The internal dispute over organizing these industries continued and, in 1938, the AFL expelled the unions, which formed its own federation and called itself the Congress of Industrial Organizations. John L. Lewis of the United Mine Workers became the organization's first president. The formation of the CIO was labor's giant step. Overnight the unorganized were orga-nized. It is not generally realized that the Trotskyists – especially in Minneapolis – helped lead the big Teamsters strikes, which led to the formation of the CIO. People like Farrell Dobbs played a key role, all the more extraordinary given that he had voted Republican in the most recent elections. As a result of the experience of the class struggle he went straight from Republicanism to revolution. This little detail shows how fast moods can change.

Most people believe that it was the French workers who invented the method of factory occupations during the 1930s. Not so! The American workers in the early 1930s developed a powerful movement known in the U.S.A. as *the sit-down strikes*. It involved employees going to their workplaces and then refusing to work. That is a factory occupation in all but name. The first successful sit-down strike happened in Flint, Michigan in 1937 when the United Auto Workers at a GM factory stopped production. This controversial method proved effective, yet controversial among management and some labor leaders. In the first large sit-down strike the United Rubber Workers (CIO) won recognition from the Goodyear Tire and Rubber Co. But not every strike ended in victory. The five week long "Little Steel" strike was broken when Inland Steel workers returned to work without even having won union recognition.

The militancy of the CIO had dramatic results. It quickly reversed the decline in union membership and led to the organization of new layers who showed great energy and élan. Very soon the CIO had gained two million new members. The mass factory occupations were illegal, but the workers newly awakened to the struggle were determined to fight for their rights. One worker recalled the tremendous spirit of class solidarity:

"It was like we was soldiers, holding the fort. It was like war. The guys became my buddies." And it was war: class war. The big corporations like General Motors and Ford spent millions of dollars a year on spies and private police to fight the strikers. But the workers' organization, class consciousness and discipline defeated the bosses and their hired gunmen.

CHAPTER FORTY-NINE

America and the Second World War

Marx explained long ago that capitalism develops as a world economic system. Today nobody can doubt the correctness of this statement. In 1935 Roosevelt stated: "Foreign markets must be regained if America's producers are to rebuild a full and enduring domestic prosperity for our people." That is the reason why the U.S.A. was compelled to participate in the world, despite the objections of the isolationists.

Since the First World War, America's position as the most powerful and wealthy imperialist power had been clear to all. So when in 1939 a new conflict broke out between the old imperialist powers of Europe, it was only a matter of time before the U.S.A. would have to be involved. After some early ambiguity, Roosevelt came down decisively in favour of using America's colossal military, industrial and economic power to enhance its position as the leading capitalist nation on earth.

Paradoxically, until the 1930s, the main antagonism on a world scale was between the rising power of the U.S.A. and the old imperial master of the planet, Great Britain. Trotsky had even posed the possibility of war between the two if the U.S.A. insisted on boosting its naval strength to the point of challenging Britain's dominance of the seas. In the end, however, it was the threat to American commercial interests posed by Japan and Germany that decided the issue. In particular, the clash of interests of the U.S.A. and Japan in Asia and the Pacific was decisive. Japan was challenging the Open Door policy of the United States in China and Germany was making a similar challenge in Europe. Even more threatening was the expansion of Japanese and German interests in Latin America.

Roosevelt attempted to modify the Neutrality Acts in order to prepare for war, but was thwarted at every step by the powerful isolationist lobby. However, the outbreak of war in Europe gave him an excuse to embark on a major program of rearmament with the approval of a budget of $18 billion in 1940. By September Congress was ready to approve the first peacetime conscription Act. All that was missing was the necessary incident that could ignite a mood of mass indignation leading to a declaration of war. At the time of the election of 1940, the polls indicated that the majority of the U.S. public was still opposed to intervention. Roosevelt played along with the general mood: "I have said this before, but I shall say it again and again. Your boys are not going to be sent into any foreign wars."

No sooner had he been re-elected, however, Roosevelt took steps to involve America in the war. He persuaded Congress to approve a Lease Lend Act to send arms and supplies to Britain. He ordered the navy to attack German submarines that interfered with the shipment of these supplies. He announced on the radio: "America has been attacked by German rattlesnakes of the seas." These were concrete steps in the direction of war.

The decisive turning point was the Japanese attack on Pearl Harbor on December 7th, 1941. This was precisely the incident that Roosevelt needed. In fact, it is perfectly obvious that he brought it about deliberately. For the whole of the previous year, Roosevelt and his Secretary of State, Cordell Hull, had refused to sell crucial resources, notably oil and steel, to Japan. This embargo convinced the war party in

Tokyo that war with the United States was inevitable. The war party demanded immediate action to secure the economic supplies denied to them by the U.S.A. This led inexorably to the attack on Pearl Harbour. U.S. intelligence had cracked the Japanese secret codes and therefore knew about the Japanese plans. Roosevelt and Hull were also well aware of the consequences of their embargo and their refusal to negotiate. The American fleet at Pearl Harbor was an obvious target. Yet strangely, when the Japanese attacked, the American commanders were completely unprepared.

Pearl Harbour was the excuse Roosevelt was looking for. He demanded that the Congress recognize that a state of war existed with Japan, and who could argue? Yet as late as 1945, 80 percent of Americans consulted in a poll considered that Roosevelt had violated his 1940 pledge to keep America out of the war. Pearl Harbor was worth more than ten divisions to Roosevelt.

CHAPTER FIFTY

Russia and the War

The policies and tactics of the British and American ruling class in the Second World War were not at all dictated by a love of democracy or hatred of fascism, as the official propaganda wants us to believe, but by class interests. When Hitler invaded the U.S.S.R. in 1941, the British ruling class calculated that the Soviet Union would be defeated by Germany, but that in the process Germany would be so enfeebled that it would be possible to step in and kill two birds with one stone. It is likely that the strategists in Washington were thinking on more or less similar lines. But like Hitler, the British and U.S. ruling circles had miscalculated. Instead of being defeated by Nazi Germany, the Soviet Union fought back and inflicted a decisive defeat on Hitler's armies.

The defenders of capitalism can never admit the real reason for this extraordinary victory, but it is a self-evident fact: *the existence of a nationalized planned economy gave the U.S.S.R. an enormous advantage in the war.* Despite the criminal policies of Stalin, which nearly brought about the collapse of the U.S.S.R. at the beginning of the war, the Soviet Union was able to swiftly recover and rebuild its industrial and military capacity. The truth is that the war against Hitler in Europe was fought mainly by the U.S.S.R. and the Red Army. For most of the war the British and

Americans were mere spectators. Following the invasion of the Soviet Union in the summer of 1941, Moscow repeatedly demanded the opening of a second front against Germany. But Churchill was in no hurry to oblige them. The reason for this was not so much military as political.

The Soviet working class was fighting to defend what remained of the gains of the October Revolution. Despite the monstrous crimes of Stalin and the Bureaucracy, the nationalized planned economy represented an enormous historic conquest. Compared with the barbarism of fascism – the distilled essence of imperialism and monopoly capitalism, these were things worth fighting and dying for. The working people of the U.S.S.R. did both on the most appalling scale.

In 1943 alone, the U.S.S.R. produced 130,000 pieces of artillery, 24,000 tanks and self-propelled guns, 29,900 combat aircraft. The Nazis, with all the huge resources of Europe behind them, also stepped up production, turning out 73,000 pieces of artillery, 10,700 tanks and assault guns and 19,300 combat aircraft. (See V. Sipols, *The Road to a Great Victory*, p. 132.) These figures speak for themselves. *The U.S.S.R., by mobilizing the immense power of a planned economy, managed to out-produce and outgun the mighty Wehrmacht.* That is the secret of its success.

To some extent the same was true of the United States. The need to mobilize all the productive forces of the U.S.A. for the war effort made it necessary to introduce at least some measures of central control and planning. This was, of course, not socialism but "state capitalism". Roosevelt appointed a War Resources Board with a prominent representative of big business at its head, Edward Stettinius of U.S. Steel. His ideal was not a workers' democracy but an economy run by a handful of big corporations operating without price competition within the parameters of objectives laid down by the state: a kind of "managed capitalism".

It goes without saying that a genuine planned economy is not possible under capitalism. Nevertheless, we are entitled to ask the following question to the defenders of market economics and free enterprise: if the capitalist system is so superior, when America (and Britain) had its back to the wall, when economic efficiency and production were a matter of life and death, did your government simply rely on the laws of the free market? *It did not. It introduced elements of central planning, state control and even nationalization. Why? The answer is very clear: because this gave better results!*

And we are entitled to ask another, even more interesting question: if a semi-planned economy could give such good results in time of war, *why cannot a genuine socialist planned economy, combined with democratic control and administration by the workers themselves, not give even better results in time of peace?*

CHAPTER FIFTY-ONE

The Turn of the Tide

The real turning point of the War was the Soviet counteroffensive in 1942, culminating in the Battle of Stalingrad and later in the even more decisive Battle of Kursk. After a ferocious battle lasting one week, the German resistance collapsed. To the fury of Hitler, who had ordered the Sixth Army to "fight to the death," General Paulus surrendered to the Soviet army. Even Churchill, that rabid anti-Communist, was compelled to admit that the Red Army had "torn the guts out of the German army" at Stalingrad.

Throughout the war, the Russians were demanding that the Allies open a second front against Germany in Europe. This was resisted particularly by Churchill. Churchill wanted to confine the Allies' war to the Mediterranean, partly with an eye on the Suez Canal and the route to British India, and partly because he was contemplating an invasion of the Balkans to bloc the Red Army's advance there. In other words, his calculations were based exclusively on the strategic interests of British imperialism and the need to defend the British Empire. In addition, Churchill had still not entirely given up the hope that Russia and Germany would exhaust themselves, creating a stalemate in the east.

The conflicts between Churchill and Roosevelt on the question of D-day were of a political and not a military character. The interests of U.S. imperialism and British imperialism were entirely contradictory in this respect. Washington, while formally the ally of London, was all the time aiming to use the war to weaken the position of Britain in the world and particularly to break its stranglehold on India and Africa. At the same time it was concerned to halt the advance of the Red Army and gain control over a weakened Europe after the war. That explains the haste of the Americans to open the second front in Europe and Churchill's lack of enthusiasm for it. Harry Hopkins, Roosevelt's main diplomatic representative, complained that Churchill's delaying tactics had "lengthened the timing of the war."

In the end, Churchill's calculations backfired. The Red Army defeated the Wehrmacht and embarked on the most spectacular advance in military history. They took control of Eastern Europe and held onto it. The landlords and capitalists of Poland, Hungary and the other countries of the region had collaborated with the Nazis and fled together with them.

Trotsky once said that to kill a tiger one requires a shotgun, but to kill a flea, a thumbnail is sufficient. The Stalinists liquidated capitalism in Eastern Europe but they did not introduce socialism. These regimes began where the Russian revolution ended – as bureaucratically deformed workers' states. The expropriation of the capitalists and landlords was undoubtedly a progressive task, but it was carried out bureaucratically, from above, without the democratic participation and control of the working class.

The regimes that emerged from this were a bureaucratic and totalitarian caricature of socialism. Unlike the Russian workers' state established by the Bolsheviks in 1917, they offered no attraction to the workers of Western Europe. With the exception of Czechoslovakia, the bourgeoisie of Eastern Europe had been very weak before the War. The

U.S. imperialists attempted to strengthen the bourgeois elements and gain control of Eastern Europe by offering them Marshall Aid. Stalin understood the manoeuvre and gave the order. The Stalinists took power by expelling the bourgeois elements from the coalitions and nationalizing the means of production.

CHAPTER FIFTY-TWO

Origins of the Cold War

President Roosevelt died on April 12, 1945 and was replaced by Vice President Truman. Many people have assumed that Roosevelt was less anti-Communist than his successor. But this is not the case. The reason why Roosevelt did not want an immediate clash with Moscow was that it did not suit the interests of American imperialism to break with Moscow *at that point in time*. In addition to the considerations already mentioned, the Americans had another reason for not sharing Churchill's enthusiasm for a "crusade against Bolshevism" – or, at least, the timing. The Americans'main preoccupation was the war in the Pacific, where they were still locked in a life-or-death struggle with Japanese imperialism.

The problem was that the U.S.S.R. had a huge army in the heart of Europe. Only the possession of nuclear weapons gave the U.S.A. a potential advantage, since the U.S.S.R. did not yet have the atom bomb. But the bomb had not yet been tested, and there was no guarantee that it would work. The Americans tested the first atom bomb on June 16, 1945 at the very time the wartime Allies were meeting in Berlin to discuss the post-war situation.

Truman and Churchill were informed that the test had been successful and wasted no time in letting Stalin know all about it. They hoped to use the threat of nuclear devastation to tip the balance of the negotiations in their favor. Some have maintained that the Cold War did not begin until 1947, but in fact it began immediately after the surrender of Japan, and was prepared even before that. D.F. Fleming states: "President Truman was ready to begin it before he had been in office two weeks." (D.F. Fleming, *The Cold War and its Origins*, 1917-1960, Vol. 1, p. 268.)

The possession of the atom bomb gave Truman a sense of superiority, which he did not feel the need to hide. James F. Burns, director of the U.S. war mobilization department, assured Truman that possession of the atom bomb would put the U.S.A. in a position "to dictate our own terms at the end of the war." (Harry S. Truman, Memoirs, vol. I, *Year of Destiny*, New York, p. 87.)

As usual, Churchill was the first to foment an anti-Communist crusade. This rabid reactionary and warmonger did everything in his power to push the Americans into a conflict with Russia. Describing his mood at this time, General Allen Brooke, the Chief of the British Imperial General Staff, noted in his diary that "*he was always seeing himself capable of eliminating all the Russian centres of industry and population* [...]" (Arthur Bryant, *Triumph in the West*, 1943-1946, London, 1959. p. 478.) But the British working class had had enough of Churchill. They had had enough of war too, and certainly had no desire to engage in a new war, least of all against the Soviet Union. In the 1945 general election they kicked Churchill and the Conservatives out of power and voted massively for a Labour government.

In any case, Britain was already reduced to the role of a secondary power, a mere satellite of the U.S.A. – a role that has continued to the present day. The Americans did not pay much attention to Churchill's raving because they still had unfinished business in the Pacific. They needed the help of the Soviet Union to defeat Japan, and therefore were not in a hurry to bring about a premature confrontation with the Russians in Europe. That could wait until Japan had surrendered.

CHAPTER FIFTY-THREE

The Defeat of Japan

All the peoples paid a terrible price for the War. Britain's casualties totalled 370,000, the U.S.A., 300,000. But the Soviet Union lost a staggering 27 millions – about half of all the casualties of the Second World War. According to one estimate, even before the Normandy landings, 90 percent of all young men between the age of 18 and 21 in the Soviet Union had already been killed. These chilling figures accurately express the real situation. They show that the people of the Soviet Union suffered a disproportionate number of casualties, because the main front in Europe was the eastern front.

Western historians, motivated rather by political considerations than historical truth, have systematically minimized the role of the Soviet Union in the Second World War. This systematic campaign of distortion has increased a hundred-fold since the fall of the Berlin Wall. The defenders of capitalism are not willing to acknowledge the achievements of the nationalized planned economy in the U.S.S.R.. They cannot admit that the spectacular military victory over Hitler's Germany was due precisely to this.

In order to belittle the role of the U.S.S.R. in the war, they exaggerate the importance of things like American Lease-Lend to the Soviet Union. This falsification is easy to answer. The fact is that the Red Army had halted the

German advance and begun to counterattack by the end of 1941 in the Battle of Moscow – before any supplies had reached the U.S.S.R. from the U.S.A., Britain or Canada.

These supplies came mainly in the period 1943-5, that is, at a period when the Soviet economy was already producing more military hardware than the German war machine. They accounted only for a fraction of Soviet war production: two percent of artillery, ten percent of tanks and twelve percent of aircraft. In no sense can this be considered decisive to the Soviet war effort as a whole. Its importance was marginal.

The real reasons for the marvellous achievements of the Soviet Union in the Second World War was something the Western historians are never prepared to admit – *firstly, the superiority of a nationalized economy and central planning, and secondly, the determination of the Soviet working class to defend what remained of the conquests of the October Revolution against fascism and imperialism.*

This was no thanks to Stalin and the bureaucracy, who had placed the U.S.S.R. in extreme danger by their criminal and irresponsible policy before the War, but in spite of them. The Soviet workers, despite all the crimes of Stalin and the bureaucracy, rallied to the defence of the U.S.S.R. and fought like tigers. This was what ultimately guaranteed victory.

The role of the U.S.S.R. in the defeat of Japan has always been overlooked. Actually, it was quite a significant one. Americas war in the Pacific had resolved itself into a bloody slogging match to wrest control of one coral atoll after another from Japanese control. What is never mentioned is that the Japanese had a powerful land army in Manchuria, the Kwantung army. Its total strength was up to a million men. It had 1,215 tanks, 6,640 guns and mortars and 1,907 combat aircraft.

This formidable fighting force was faced by 1,185,000

Soviet troops stationed in the Soviet Far East. These were reinforced with additional forces after the surrender of Germany and when the offensive began on August 9 totalled 1,747,000 troops, 5,250 tanks and self-propelled guns, 29,835 guns and mortars and 5,171 combat aircraft. In a campaign lasting just six days the Red Army smashed the Japanese forces and advanced through Manchuria with lightning speed. The Soviet forces entered Korea and the South Sakhalin and Kurile Islands and were in striking distance of Japan itself.

On August 6, Truman ordered the U.S. Air Force to drop an atom bomb on Hiroshima. Three days later, the very day the Soviet army began its offensive, they dropped a second bomb on Nagasaki. They did this despite the fact that these were civilian cities with no military value and the Japanese were already defeated and suing for peace. The fact is that these atom bombs were intended as a warning to the U.S.S.R. not to continue the Red Army's advance, otherwise they could have occupied Japan. The use of the atom bomb was a political act. It was intended to show Stalin that the

U.S.A. now possessed a terrible new weapon of mass destruction and was prepared to use it against civilian populations. There was an implicit threat: what we have done to Hiroshima and Nagasaki we can do to Moscow and Leningrad.

Once Japan had surrendered, Washington's attitude to Moscow changed immediately. The whole shape of the post-war world was now determined. The world would be dominated by two great giants: mighty U.S. imperialism on the one hand and mighty Russian Stalinism on the other. They represented two fundamentally opposed socio-economic systems with antagonistic interests. A titanic struggle between them was inevitable.

The American imperialists now felt themselves masters

of the world. They had suffered relatively little from the war. Their productive base was intact, whereas most of Europe's industry lay in a heap of smouldering rubble. Two thirds of all the available gold in the world was in Fort Knox. The U.S.A. had a huge army and a monopoly of nuclear weapons. They could impose their conditions on the rest of the world. Only the Soviet Union stood in their way. The arrogance of American power was put into words by the managing director of *The New York Times* Neil MacNeil, who wrote that "both the United States and the world need peace based on American principles – a *Pax Americana* [...] We should accept an American peace. We should accept nothing less." (Neil MacNeil, *An American Peace*, New York, 1944, p. 264.)

CHAPTER FIFTY-FOUR

The Post-War Economic Upswing

The period after the Second World War was completely different to the period that followed the First World War. After 1945 there was a remarkable upswing of the productive forces in the U.S.A. and internationally. What were the basic reasons for the developments of the post-Second World War economy? In 1938, Leon Trotsky had predicted that the war would end with a revolutionary wave. In fact there were a whole series of revolutionary explosions after 1943, in Italy, France, Greece, and even Denmark. Unfortunately, the Stalinists and the social democrats, in Britain and Western Europe succeeded in diverting this revolutionary movement into safe reformist channels, and the revolutionary potential was wasted. This created the *political* climate for a recovery of capitalism.

The effects of the war, in the destruction of consumer and capital goods, created a big market (war has effects similar to, but deeper than, a slump in the destruction of capital). These effects, according to United Nations' statisticians, only disappeared in 1958. Moreover, during the war a whole series of new avenues of investment were opened up as a by-product of arms production – plastics, aluminium, rockets, electronics, atomic energy and its by-products.

The growth of these new industries provided the basis

for an enormous increase in productive investment after the war. The increasing output of the newer industries-chemicals, artificial fibers, synthetic rubber, plastics, rapid rise in light metals, aluminum, magnesium, electric household equipment, natural gas, electric energy, together with the building activity caused by post-war reconstruction, provided the basis for a huge boom.

However, a key role was played by the U.S.A. America had emerged virtually unscathed from the War, while her main competitors – Britain, France, Germany, Japan – were either severely damaged or completely shattered. Two-thirds of the world's gold was in the vaults of Fort Knox. The U.S.A. was therefore able to dictate terms to the rest of the Western world. The Bretton-Woods agreement established the dollar as the world currency, which further assisted the growth of world trade.

The war had created enormous amounts of fictitious capital, created by the armaments expenditure, which amount to 10 per cent of the national income in Britain and America. But in a situation of a gigantic upswing of the productive forces, nobody was worried about the danger of inflation. On the contrary, everybody wanted to get hold of dollars (the pound sterling was now reduced to a secondary currency, reflecting the decline of Britain as a world power). The dollar was considered to be "as good as gold."

Fear of revolution and "Communism" compelled Washington to intervene decisively to save the European capitalists. The Marshall Plan and other economic aid played a key role in assisting the recovery of Western Europe. This in turn provided new markets for the mighty productive capacity of the U.S.A. The increasing trade, especially in capital goods and engineering products, between the capitalist countries, consequent on the increased economic investment, in its turn acted as a spur.

State intervention also played a role in stimulating economic activity, especially in countries like Britain where the post-War Labour government carried out a policy of nationalization and reforms. A new world order was gradually taking shape. The old empires ruled by Britain, France, Holland and Belgium, had been shaken to their foundations by the war and the Japanese conquests in Asia. One by one, the old colonial masters were being driven out by national liberation movements. This provided new opportunities for U.S. imperialism to muscle in on the new markets in Asia, Africa and the Middle East, elbowing their European rivals to one side.

The new market for capital and engineering products gave the local bourgeoisie the opportunity to develop industry on a greater scale than ever before. All these factors interacted on one another. The increased demand for raw materials, through the development of industry in the metropolitan countries in its turn, reacted on the undeveloped countries and vice-versa. All these factors explain the increase in production since the war. But the decisive factor was the increased scope for capital investment, which is the main engine of capitalist development.

CHAPTER FIFTY-FIVE

America After 1945

For all these reasons, after the Second World War, America experienced a period of tremendous and sustained economic growth that set its stamp on her entire development. It shaped the consciousness of its people in a decisive way. For decades, American capitalism seemed to be "delivering the goods". The economy was growing rapidly and the recessions were so shallow and fleeting that they were barely noticed. Living standards were increasing. There was an abundance of things like refrigerators, televisions, telephones and cars that made people feel prosperous.

The feeling that "we have never had it so good" was reinforced by what Americans could see in the rest of the world. Whenever anybody complained, the defenders of the established order could point triumphantly to Stalinist Russia, that monstrous bureaucratic and totalitarian caricature of socialism and say: "You want socialism? That's socialism for you -dictatorship and the rule of an autocratic bureaucracy! You will be slaves of the state. Is that what you want?" And even the most critical American worker would shake his or her head and conclude that the devil they knew was probably a lot better than the one they didn't.

In case they were not completely convinced, however, a little coercion could be brought to bear. It was not as severe as the white terror that followed the First World War. That was not necessary, given the full employment and rising living standards. But during what was known as the Cold War, state repression was unleashed in quite a ruthless manner. It was known as the McCarthy era.

On February 9, 1950 Senator Joseph R. McCarthy of Wisconsin claimed that there were no fewer than two hundred Communists in the State Department. This outrageous allegation unleashed a witch-hunt against everyone who was even slightly "tainted" with left wing, progressive or even vaguely democratic opinions in public life. The hysteria that accompanied this campaign closely resembled the kind of pathological collective hysteria of the notorious Salem witch trials of the 17th century. This comparison was made explicit in Arthur Miller's famous play *The Crucible*.

In fact, the witch hunting of the American Left had commenced a couple of years earlier. After 1945 the American ruling class lived in dread of Communism and revolution, and launched a "Reds under the bed" campaign, using the House of Un-American Committee (HUAC) to grill suspects. Prominent among the interrogators was an ambitious young Republican congressman, Richard Milhous Nixon (later dubbed "Tricky Dicky") who was out to make a name for himself as a notorious red-baiter. He subsequently became President, only to be removed for crooked practices following the Watergate scandal.

The power behind the scenes of these witch-hunts was FBI chief and ultra-reactionary, J. Edgar Hoover, who for years ran a state within the state, acting as a law unto himself, scorning all the principles of democratic government, and imitating the conduct of the Mafia that he was supposed to be fighting. This Paragon of Public Virtue said in March 1947: "Communism, in reality, is not a political party. It reveals a conditions akin to a disease that spreads like an epidemic and like an epidemic a quarantine is necessary to keep it from infecting this nation." (Quoted in Jeremy Isaacs and Taylor Downing, *Cold War*, p. 109.)

Since his death, Hoover has been exposed as a corrupt gangster who used extortion and blackmail to exert unconstitutional control over elected politicians while he extolled the virtues of American democracy, and secretly led a luxurious and degenerate lifestyle while he delivered lectures on the need for puritanical morals. These were the kind of heroes who led the crusade against Communism in the U.S.A.

Obsessed with his hatred of Communism and radicals, Hoover ordered his agents to use illegal means: wiretaps, break-ins, phone intercepts and bugging of private homes to get incriminating evidence. Neighbors were encouraged to spy on neighbors; parents were asked to spy on their children, and children on their parents. When defence lawyers exposed these illegal practices and used this to get cases thrown out, Hoover launched an attack on the National Lawyers' Guild, which he accused of being a Communist front (!).

One of the first great achievements of the witch-hunt was to send to the electric chair a young electrical engineer, Julius Rosenberg, and his wife Ethel. They were charged with passing atomic secrets to the Soviet Union. The evidence against Rosenberg came largely from his brother-in-law David Greenglass, who had been part of a wartime spy network. Though interrogated by the FBI, Julius Rosenberg refused to give information or name any other agents. So the FBI arrested his wife, Ethel, although she was clearly not a spy, in order to break her husband. It did not work. He remained silent.

Rosenberg was found guilty of passing secrets to the Russians. Spying in wartime is punishable by death, but when Rosenberg passed secrets to Russia, it was an ally of the U.S.A. But despite pleas for clemency, among others from Albert Einstein and Pope Pius XII, both Julius and Ethel Rosenberg were sent to the electric chair. What is interesting is the conduct of the judicial system in this case. The judges were clearly intimidated to the point where they did not dare defy the general hysteria. Arthur Kinoy, the Rosenberg's lawyer, reports the words of one such judge:

"Judge Frank looked at us and he said something that we have never, never forgotten. He said, 'If I were as young as you are, I would be sitting there saying the same things you're saying, arguing the same points you're arguing, making the same argument that these planned executions are invalid. But when you are as old as I am, you will understand why I cannot do it.'And he stands up, turns his back to us, and walks away, and we were devastated. We began to sense something which in later years we understood so clearly. That was that Jerome Frank, as the leading liberal judge, was terrorized himself and frightened by the atmosphere of fear in the country. That if he as a liberal would do something to save Julius and Ethel Rosenberg's life, he would be charged as a commie." (Quoted in Jeremy Isaacs and Taylor Downing, *Cold War*, p. 113.)

The tentacles of the witch hunters extended into every branch of public life. Given the importance of the film industry in American life, Hollywood became a key target. Hoover established an extensive network of spies and informers, chief among whom was a second-rate actor in B-movies called Ronald Reagan. Based in Los Angeles, Reagan was President of the Screen Actors' Guild. He used his position to pass on information about his colleagues to Hoover. This was the start of a promising political career that ended in the White House. When he died recently, there was flood of laudatory obituaries, praising the former

President for his great intellect and ability and attributing to him the posthumous title of "the man who defeated Communism."

Although he could be accused of many things (bad acting, lack of principles, cowardice, dishonesty, ignorance, provincial narrow-mindedness, disloyalty towards friends and colleagues etc.) no serious person could ever accuse Ronald Reagan of possessing either *intellect* or *ability*. As a matter of historical record, the U.S.S.R. (which, in the period under consideration, had very little in common with Communism) collapsed because of its internal contradictions and this had nothing to do with the intellect or abilities of Ronald Reagan.

In 1951, the HUAC launched an all-out offensive against Hollywood. Prominent actors and film directors were grilled by the HUAC, in scenes reminiscent of the Inquisition. The only way to escape from this torture was to incriminate others. Some brave souls refused. The great German composer Hans Eisler, who had fled to America from Nazi persecution and wrote distinguished film scores, when he was accused of being the "Marx of the music world", answered that he was flattered by the comparison, and was deported for his courage.

However, others were not so courageous. The bosses of the big Hollywood studios pledged not to employ anybody who had ever been a Communist or had refused under oath to declare that they had never been a Communist. Many of the big names in Hollywood decided that discretion was the better part of valor and collaborated in the dirty name of denouncing their fellow actors. Elia Kazan, the famous director who introduced Marlon Brando to the cinema, named eleven former Communists to the HUAC. Jerome Robbins, the successful Broadway and Hollywood choreographer also co-operated with the Inquisition, as did Sterling Hayden. But the man who broke the record for denunciation was screenwriter Martin Berkeley, who named no fewer than 162 Hollywood artists as Communists, past or present.

The consequences for those so-named were dire. They would be sacked and never work again in any studio in Hollywood or any other part of the U.S.A. They would immediately lose their livelihood and reputation and be treated as outcasts and pariahs. About 250 Hollywood personalities were blacklisted in this way in the early 1950s. Some just disappeared. Others went into exile. A few continued to work under assumed names, like Dalton Trumbo, author of *Johnny Got His Gun*, who caused the whole industry considerable embarrassment when he actually won an Oscar in 1956 for a screenplay written under the name of Robert Rich. One group of blacklisted filmmakers and actors made the marvellous film "Salt of the Earth", brilliantly depicting the class struggle in the silver mines of New Mexico.

Among the victims of McCarthyism were some of the most talented directors, writers and performers in America. Some did not work again till the 1960s. The great Negro singer Paul Robeson was savagely persecuted. The legendary Charles Chaplin, although British by birth and nationality, had lived in the U.S.A. for over 30 years. He had learned while in England that he would be denounced as a Communist and decided to live the rest of his life outside the U.S.A. He did not return to the U.S.A. until 1972 and then only briefly to accept a special Academy Award. American culture was the real loser.

The place of talented people was taken by hacks who were prepared to write third-rate trash like *I was a Communist for the FBI*, which won an Oscar for the best documentary (this shows how much an Oscar is really worth). Other gems of the period included *My Son John*, which depicts a nice young American boy, who, unknown to his parents, becomes a Communist, and *I Married a Communist*, which depicts a nice American girl who married one, *Evil Epidemic*, in honor of J. Edgar Hoover, and so on.

The health of the American cinema industry was in good hands. The Motion Picture Alliance for the Preservation of American Ideals was presided by good old John Wayne. This fearless, clean-living cowboy of the silver screen was always speaking lines like "a man's gotta do what a man's gotta do." In this case what a man like John Wayne had to do was to betray his friends and colleagues and throw them to the wolves. This did not require much courage but definitely did one's career no harm.

Other heroes of the same kind were Clark Gable (*"Frankly, my dear, I don't give a damn"*), Gary Cooper and John Ford, who were all on the executive committee of the MPAPA. The presence of the last two named is perhaps ironical, since the celebrated film *High Noon,* starring Gary Cooper and directed by John Ford, has been widely interpreted as a criticism of McCarthyism in the guise of a Western.

The witch hunters then turned their unwelcome attentions to American education. The worthy senator from Wisconsin discovered that American colleges and universities were hotbeds of Red subversion. Formally, there was no black list as in Hollywood, but in practice anyone involved in political activity of the "wrong sort" would not easily get a job in academia. J. Edgar Hoover, whose educational qualifications were somewhat comparable to those of Conan the Barbarian, complained that American schools were in the hands of *"Reducators"*. The latter were *"tearing down respect for agencies of government, belittling tradition and moral customs and* [...] *creating doubts in the validity of the American way of life."*

The ruling class let these mad dogs off the leash to snap

and snarl to their heart's content. It was useful to have such people intimidate the Left. But the real Establishment had no intention of handing power to the mad dogs. In the end McCarthy overreached himself when he began to interfere with the most sensitive part of the state, the armed forces. In a series of sensational television interviews in 1954, McCarthy accused *the U.S. Army* of being infiltrated by Communists. That was too much. Having made use of the Senator's services, the Establishment unceremoni-ously ditched him. The Senate voted to condemn him for bringing it into disrepute. He was politically a dead man.

CHAPTER FIFTY-SIX

The Unions After 1945

Many European leftists regard Americans as hopelessly reactionary. This view demonstrates a lamentable ignorance of American history. I hope that this short study will serve at least partially to correct the error. Americans are neither more nor less revolutionary than anybody else. What is true, as Marx pointed out long ago, is that social being determines consciousness. For several decades after 1945, for the special reasons that we have outlined above, capitalism entered into a phase of upswing. It was the greatest economic fireworks display in history. The main beneficiary was the U.S.A. The living standards of most Americans increased (some more than others, it is true). This was the material basis for a major psychological change. The idea was widely accepted that capitalism was "delivering the goods". Workers are generally very practical people, and pragmatism has sunk deeper roots in America than any other country. "If it ain't broke, don't fix it" is a wise old American saying.

Under these conditions the old revolutionary traditions of U.S. labor, old traditions that went back to the Knights of Labor, passing through the Labor Uprising of 1877, the Chicago Martyrs, the Wobblies, and the class struggles of the 1920s and 1930s, receded from the collective consciousness and were largely forgotten. The new generation knew little of them. In that sense, the knot of history was broken. There is no automatic mechanism whereby the traditions of the working class, the lessons of past victories and defeats can be transmitted from one generation to another. The only mechanism that can fulfil this role is the revolutionary party. The absence of a Marxist revolutionary party with deep roots in the working class in America is a serious problem. It means that the class can only learn through its own experience: this is a slow and painful process that can take decades. This is a situation that must be remedied in the coming period.

Although politically speaking the American workers are not as educated as their European counterparts and lack a class party through which to express their interests and aspirations, even in a distorted and incomplete manner, this by no means signifies that they lack class-consciousness. What they lack in political organization they have made up for in terms of industrial organization and militancy. On the industrial front the American workers have had a tradition that is second to none. It is true that, as in Europe, the American unions are under attack and the control of a bureaucracy that does its best to suffocate the militancy of the rank and file. The capitalist class does its best to corrupt and bribe the union tops. Through the bureaucracy of the unions, the influence of bourgeois ideology, class collaboration and so on, can percolate down into the working class. In particular, the leaders of the big unions are linked to the Democrats, just as the British union leaders were linked to the Liberals in the 19th century. But this situation was the logical consequence of the long years of economic upswing and prosperity. It did not survive in Britain, and will not survive the new period of storm and stress into which we are now heading in the United States.

The traditions of the CIO in its early years are something that the new generation of young Americans should take time out to study. They were reflected very poorly in the big Hollywood movie *Hoffa*, and much better in the earlier and lesser-known film called *FIST* – the only decent film Sylvester Stallone ever made. The main thing to see is that this is not ancient history. The class struggle did not cease in the 1930s but has continued, with ebbs and flows, ever since. The American workers have always had a good union tradition, and as a matter of fact, the number of strikes actually increased in the years after the Second World War. From 1936 through 1955, there was a staggering total of 78,798 strikes in the United States, involving 42,366,000 strikers. The breakdown was as follows:

Number of Strikes and Strikers (By Decades)

Years	*Number of Strikes*	*Number of Strikers*
1923-32	9,658	3,952,000
1936-45	35,519	15,856,000
1946-55	43,279	26,510,000

In order to curb union militancy, the bosses and the government introduced the anti-union Taft-Hartley Act in 1947. Yet in 1949 there were major strikes in the coal and steel industries; 1952, was a year of coal and steel strikes; and 1959, the year of the 116-day steel strike, the largest strike of all-time in the United States as measured by total workdays on strike.

Big business and its state were, and remain, bitterly hostile to trade unionism. Although unions are no longer illegal, the state does not hesitate to invoke anti-union legislation whenever it suits the bosses to do so. The national emergency machinery provided under the Taft-Hartley Act for the investigation of disputes threatening to "imperil national health or safety" was invoked by the President in 23 situations from the time of its enactment in 1947 through 1963 – and is still called upon today.

This is not ancient history. Taft-Hartley is alive and well

and still used for busting unions in the U.S.A. President Ronald Reagan fired most of the nation's air traffic controllers for striking illegally and ordered their union, the Professional Air Traffic Controllers Association, decertified. 13,000 air traffic controllers defied the return-to-work order. Subsequently 400,000 unionists participated in the largest labor rally in American history which was held in Washington in protest against the policies of the Reagan administration. More recently still, George W. Bush used Taft-Hartley against the longshoremen of the ILWU.

In addition, there are other laws that are regularly invoked by the legal establishment to prevent the workers from using their legitimate right to strike. In the war between Labor and Capital, the state is not impartial now any more than it was in the past! The fight for union rights, against unjust anti-union laws is a burning need for the American working class. This fact also shows the utter futility of trying to separate trade unionism from politics.

If anyone believes the class struggle is dead in the U.S.A. I advise him or her to look at experience of strikes such as that of the miners in 1989. In April of that year the United Mine Workers (UMW) called a strike against the Pittston Coal Group for unfair labor practices. These miners had worked 14 months without a contract before the UMW called the strike. Among the practices cited by UMW were the discontinuing of medical benefits for pensioners, widows, and the disabled; refusal to contribute to a benefit trust established in 1950 for miners who retired before 1974; and refusing to bargain in good faith. Miners in Virginia, Kentucky and West Virginia struck against Pittston.

The miners and their families engaged in an inspiring civil disobedience campaign against the company. In the time-honoured tradition of the American bosses, the strike was met with calculated violence, as state troopers were called out to arrest striking miners. The miners fought back courageously with dynamite. Despite the enormous importance of this strike, the "free press" of the U.S.A. made practically no mention of it, preferring to give a great deal of coverage to another miners' strike – *in Russia*!

The movement of the American working class to fight for its own interests continues – as the recent disputes at UPS and on the West Coast docks shows very clearly. If there have not been more strikes and if the living standards and conditions of the workers have not kept pace with the huger increase in profits, it was due to a failure of the leadership of the unions, not the workers. In recent years the trade unions have hit difficulties as a result of this. As in other countries, the unions in the United States have become heavily bureaucratized and the leaders were out of touch with the problems of ordinary workers.

The rundown of heavy industries in the North and East – the traditional base of unionism – has led to a fall in membership. Yet the leadership proved incapable of responding to the challenge posed by Big Business to the union movement. With the development of new industries in the South and West, millions of workers in the United States are now unorganized. The task of organizing them into unions is perhaps the most pressing need at the present time. In order to solve this problem, the unions must go back to their roots, to the militant traditions of the CIO when they organized the unorganized in the stormy years of the 1930s. When that happens, we shall discover that those formerly inert and "backward" layers will be among the most militant and revolutionary in the whole union movement.

The unions have always been the basic organizations of the class. They are on the front line in the defence of the most basic rights of the working class. Without the day-to-day struggle for advance under capitalism, the socialist transformation of society would be utopia. Therefore the struggle to transform the unions, to democratize them at all levels and make them genuinely responsive to the wishes and aspirations of working people, to turn them into genuine organs of struggle, is a prior condition for the fight for a socialist America, in which the unions will play the role that was envisaged for them by the pioneers of Labor – as the basic organizations for running the economy in an industrial democracy.

CHAPTER FIFTY-SEVEN

Vietnam

The war in Vietnam, which completely transformed the situation in the U.S.A., did not begin in a planned way. The U.S.A. was sucked into it almost by accident. It began with a covert operation, the sending of officers and "advisers" to prop up an unpopular and corrupt government against its own people. This is the usual style of U.S. imperialism! The regime of Ngo Dinh Diem was guilty of vicious repression in South Vietnam. Buddhist monks burned themselves alive in protest. Finally, Diem was assassinated by his own generals.

Three weeks later, the President of the U.S.A. suffered the same fate. Kennedy was succeeded by his Vice President, Lyndon B. Johnson, who immediately announced that he was "not going to lose Vietnam". "Win the war!" was his clear instruction. But despite all its tremendous wealth and military firepower, the U.S.A. did not win the war. On the contrary, Vietnam was the first war America ever lost. Korea was a draw. But in the steamy jungles and swamps of Vietnam, the Americans suffered a bitter defeat at the hands of a barefoot army.

In order to step up its military activities in Vietnam (as usual) an incident was required. This was (as usual) manufactured in the so-called Bay of Tonkin incident. It was alleged that a U.S. warship, the *Maddox*, had been fired upon by North Vietnamese naval vessels in the Gulf of Tonkin. For years it was believed that the

U.S. navy had been the target of unprovoked "Communist aggression". That was completely untrue. Even at the time, the captain of the *Maddox* admitted that none of his crew had made "actual visual sightings" of North Vietnamese naval vessels, and not one sailor either on the *Maddox* or the *Turner Joy* had actually heard North Vietnamese gunfire. The opening of the Hanoi archives has proven conclusively that the North Vietnamese did not fire on the American ships, which were actually inside Vietnamese territorial water at the time. Yet the American public was persuaded to back a foreign war on the basis of false information – and not for the last time, as we know.

The very next day Lyndon Johnson ordered the bombing of North Vietnamese naval bases and an oil depot. It was the start of a huge campaign of bombing that caused havoc in Vietnam, killing a large number of civilians and destroying its industry and infrastructure. On television, President Johnson declared: "Repeated acts of violence against the armed forces of the United States must be met not only with alert defense but with positive reply. That reply is being given as I speak to you tonight." (Quoted in Jeremy Isaacs and Taylor Downing, *Cold War*, p. 216.)

There was not a word of truth in any of this. Johnson and co. had decided to send U.S. troops to Vietnam and that was that. In the same way, George W. Bush and his friends decided long before 11 September to invade Iraq and lied through their teeth about the alleged weapons of mass destruction that were supposed to pose a deadly threat to American security to sell it to the public.

In the years that followed, high explosives, napalm and cluster bombs rained down on Vietnam. The U.S. Air Force dropped toxic chemicals, including the notorious agent orange on forests, allegedly to kill the vegetation and deny shelter to the Vietnamese guerrillas. A total of 18 million gallons of herbicide were dropped. Even today U.S. servicemen are dying from the effects of just handling these toxic agents, especially cancer. One shudders to think of the effects they had on the Vietnamese men, women and children on whom they were dropped. Tests have shown that the South Vietnamese have levels of dioxin three times higher than those in U.S. citizens. It will take many years to flush these toxins out of the fragile ecosystem. This was chemical warfare pursued with a vengeance!

In all, the U.S. dropped more tons of explosives on Vietnam than were dropped by all sides in the Second World War. After bombing one village to rubble, one U.S. officer was quoted as saying: "We had to destroy the town in order to save it." They are still "destroying towns in order to save them" today. Ask the inhabitants of Fallujah. And the tactic of dropping tons of poisonous chemicals still continues in Colombia, where herbicides are being used in the so-called war against drugs. The damage to people, vegetation and wild life will be the same as in Vietnam. But nobody talks about that.

The name of this particular operation was "Rolling Thunder". There must be somebody in the Pentagon, some frustrated poet, whose sole function is to think up picturesque names for such acts of barbarity. Lately we had "Operation Shock and Awe". It is a pity such talented people were not around at the time of the fall of the Roman Empire, or Attila the Hun might have called his activities: "Operation Sweetness and Light". No matter what the name was, it did not succeed. Once an entire people stands up and says "no!" to a foreign invader, no amount of troops, guns, bombs or chemical agents will make any difference, as George W. Bush will learn to his cost in Iraq. The Vietnamese continued to resist. More and more U.S. troops had to be sent in and more and more body bags were being flown home.

At first the U.S. authorities simply hid the facts of the growing escalation from the American public. They continued to lie and deceive with the active assistance of what is known in some quarters as the free press. But as Abe Lincoln pointed out: you can fool some of the people all the time, and all of the people some of the time, but you cannot fool all of the people all of the time. Slowly, by degrees, and not all at the same time, the people of the United States became aware of what the true situation was.

The suffering of the Vietnamese population will never be fully known. Apart from the huge number killed and maimed, the war caused many other human casualties. The relentless bombing, shelling and defoliation drove tens of thousands of peasants from the countryside to the outskirts of the big cities where they lived in humiliating poverty. The traditional structures of Vietnamese village life were shattered. Young girls became prostitutes for the U.S. soldiers.

A drug culture flourished, which later fed back into the cities of the U.S.A., with devastating results. In 1971 the Pentagon calculated that nearly 30 percent of the U.S. troops in Vietnam had taken heroin or opium, while smoking marijuana was commonplace. Attempts to stamp out the drug trade met with the opposition of the South Vietnamese puppet regime, which was heavily involved in it. That was an indication of the rottenness of the regime the U.S.A. was trying to prop up.

By the end of 1967 the U.S. was spending $20 billion a year on the Vietnam War, which contributed massively to a balance of payments deficit of $7 billion. By the end of 1968, the number of U.S. troops in Vietnam was over 500,000. Towards the end of the war, the U.S. troops in Vietnam were completely demoralized. They understood the situation, that they were fighting an unwinnable war. The Vietnamese were fighting a just war of national liberation, while the U.S. army was a hated army of foreign occupation. In any army there is an element of killers and sadists, and in such a situation atrocities and brutality against civilians became routine. Eventually, these horrors became known at home, with the massacre at My Lai among the most infamous. The supposed moral justification for the war was blasted to pieces – just as in Iraq today.

In January 1968, President Johnson announced that the U.S.A. was winning the war. This was immediately blown apart by the Tet offensive. The Vietnamese mounted simultaneous attacks in more than a hundred cities. In Saigon a sapper unit even managed to penetrate the U.S. embassy compound. These events were shown all over America on the television screens to a shocked public. This cruelly exposed the fact that for all its military might, the U.S.A. had not succeeded. The war finished Johnson's political career. Richard Nixon, the Republican candidate, defeated L.B.J.'s Vice President Hubert Humphrey in the Presidential elections of November 1968.

CHAPTER FIFTY-EIGHT

The Anti-Vietnam War Movement

While these dramatic events were unfolding, on the other side of the world, France was facing revolution. In May 1968 the French working class staged the biggest revolutionary general strike in history. Ten million workers occupied the factories, while the students demonstrated on the streets of Paris, built barricades and fought with the police. The general mood of radicalization naturally affected the youth first. The youth of America was mobilizing for Civil Rights and against the Vietnam War. Already in October 1967 anti-war protesters organized a huge march. For the first time since 1930 the Federal government called in armed troops to defend the capital. The kids tried to fraternize with the troops, but that night the troops attacked the demonstrators, kicking and clubbing them with extreme violence. One eyewitness spoke of "troops and marshals advancing, cracking heads, bashing skulls."

This was a good lesson in the realities of bourgeois state power. Engels and Lenin explained that the state in the last analysis is "armed bodies of men". Its whole purpose is to keep the majority under control by means of organized violence or the threat of violence. The rest is just show. The pent-up tensions of American society, which exposed deep unresolved contradictions, were about to erupt in a most violent way. Dramatic events were being prepared. The broad sweep of the Civil Rights movement had shaken America from top to bottom. The assassination of black leader Martin Luther King sparked-off mass rioting in a hundred cities. There were more than 20,000 arrests and fifty deaths. 75,000 troops were called out to keep order. King's death meant that the leadership of the black movement passed to more radical elements. The Black Panthers, who embraced Marxism and advocated the united struggle of the black and white poor, were organizing military training in the ghetto of Oakland, California. People were calling openly for revolution. The assassination of Robert Kennedy underlined the general mood of violence and social tension.

A million students and faculty members were boycotting classes in protest at the war. Things came to a head with the Democratic Party convention in Chicago, where the Party was to choose its Presidential candidate. Mayor Richard J. Daley announced: "As long as I am mayor, there will be law and order on the streets". He gave the Chicago police the order to shoot to kill. When thousands of demonstrators descended on the city, they were brutally attacked by the police. The demonstrators were infiltrated by 200 plainclothes policemen. Demonstrators, newsmen and passers-by were all clubbed and beaten. So much tear gas was thrown that it entered the ventilation system of the hotel where Humphrey was giving his acceptance speech, with predictable results. He commented bitterly: "Chicago was a catastrophe. My wife and I went home heartbroken, broken and beaten." Some of the demonstrators went home rather more broken and beaten than Mr. Humphrey.

CHAPTER FIFTY-NINE

'A Nation on the Edge of Chaos'

The election of Richard Nixon signified the continuation of the war. It also signified the continuation of the anti-war movement. Nixon authorized the extension of the war into Cambodia, where the U.S. Air Force staged an even more vicious bombing campaign than in Vietnam. The massive destruction and loss of life caused by this bombing was the real explanation for the fanatical hatred of the Americans and their Cambodian allies that motivated the later brutal conduct of the Khmer Rouge, ending in the "Killing Fields", and a new period of chaos, death and bloodshed.

The student protests against the war led to the shooting of students at Kent State and Jackson State Universities. This poured petrol on the flames. Five hundred universities closed in protest. *"Four dead in Ohio"* sang the rock group Crosby, Stills, Nash and Young. There was a general outcry. Meanwhile, an increasingly paranoid President authorized wiretaps, surveillance, and "surreptitious entry" – a euphemism for burglary – against the leaders of the anti-war movement. This was the slippery slope that led the Nixon administration to Watergate.

Nixon was re-elected, just as George W. Bush was re-elected. But his troubles had only just begun. He tried to force Hanoi to come to terms by stepping up the bombing of the North. For twelve days over Christmas, the North was battered by wave after wave of B-52 bombers. Still Nixon spoke of "peace with honor". The people of Vietnam still faced two more gruelling years of war, but in reality the will to fight on the part of the Southern army and the U.S. troops in Vietnam had collapsed. In early 1975 the North launched another offensive, leading to the fall of the cities of Hue and Da Nang. First there was military rout, then political collapse. The American stooge Thieu fled. Within days the Vietnamese Liberation Army entered Saigon. The world was witness to the incredible scenes of panic as the last remaining American personnel had to scramble into helicopters from the roof of the embassy building in Saigon.

The Vietnam War was not only the greatest military defeat in American history. It had a profound effect on American society. The truth is that U.S. imperialism was defeated, not in the swamps and jungles of Vietnam, but in the cities, campuses and streets of the U.S.A. From a military point of view, there was no reason why the U.S.A. should not have won the war – in time. But the colossal drain of the war had a revolutionary effect on American society. In fact, if a revolutionary party had existed in the U.S.A. at that time, it would have been on the brink of a social revolution. This is not an exaggeration. A presidential commission set up to investigate the shootings in Ohio, concluded: *"The crisis has its roots in a division of American society as deep as any since the Civil War. A nation driven to use the weapons of war upon its youth is a nation on the edge of chaos."* The word *"chaos"* must here be understood as a synonym for *revolution.*

The explosive mood of discontent was not confined to the students, as has often been maintained. The student youth is always a sensitive barometer reflecting deep moods of discontent in the bowels of society. The wind always blows through the tops of the trees first. A radicalization of the students is an anticipation of a later revolutionary movement in society as a whole. That was true of the first Russian revolution, which commenced with student agitation against the war with Japan and ended with the revolution of 1905. The student demonstrations in Paris in May 1968 did not cause the general strike, as many have believed. It merely acted as the catalyst for moods of discontent that had been accumulating silently over a long period of time. In the same way, the student agitation in the U.S.A. was the expression of a general mood of dissatisfaction and discontent, which had not yet surfaced but which was being prepared.

It is no accident that the movement of the black Americans reached its most explosive point at the same time, and found its expression in the Black Panthers, the most conscious, courageous and consistently revolutionary of all the tendencies in the black community (along with Malcolm X before his death). They were seen as a particularly dangerous threat by the Establishment because they had moved beyond black nationalism towards Marxism and were advocating the revolutionary unity of black and white workers – an absolutely correct policy. For this they were deliberately targeted by the state and systematically exterminated.

But the greatest danger to the state came from within the state. The U.S. troops in Vietnam were not only completely demoralized by this time. They were in a state of open revolt. There were many cases of mutiny, and also of the killing of officers by their own troops. A new verb entered into the English language at this time: "fragging". This is derived from "fragmentation grenade" A soldier would pass the officer's mess or quarters and casually lob a grenade in, killing and wounding those inside. *The fact is that the U.S. government had to withdraw the troops from Vietnam, or else face a general revolt.* One American general, commenting on the state of the U.S. troops in Vietnam, said that there was only one possible historical analogy, and that was the morale of the Petrograd garrison in 1917. That is correct. If there had been an American equivalent of the Bolshevik Party, which would have had cells in the army, the analogy could have been carried to its logical and successful conclusion.

CHAPTER SIXTY

Intervention in Latin America

For more than a century, the U.S.A. regarded Latin America and the Caribbean as its own back yard. In 1954, the CIA organized the overthrow of the democratically-elected government of President Jacobo Arbenz Guzman in Guatemala. Arbenz was a reformist leader who had intervened in labor disputes between the U.S.-owned United Fruit Company. The latter had considerable influence in Washington, where one of its directors had been U.S. Secretary of State, John Foster Dulles. His brother, Allen Dulles, by a fortunate coincidence, was head of the CIA. By an even more fortunate coincidence, the latter was a former member of the company's board of trustees.

With a little friendly encouragement from United Fruit, the Eisenhower administration approved a secret plan to depose Arbenz, now dubbed "Red Jacobo". In fact, Arbenz was never a Communist, although he had been supported in the election by the Left Parties in Guatemala. But Arbenz was carrying out a land reform. He had nationalized 400,000 acres of uncultivated private land, much of it belonging to United Fruit. That was sufficient for Washington. The U.S. ambassador wrote to John Foster Dulles: "If the President is not a Communist, he will do until one comes along." (Quoted in Jeremy Isaacs and Taylor Downing, *Cold War*, p. 185.)

In June 1954, an army of Guatemalan anti-Communist exiles, armed and trained by the CIA, crossed the frontier. Prior to this, the CIA had subverted the officers of the Guatemalan army, who defected to the rebels. Arbenz was forced into exile and a right wing U.S. puppet, Colonel Castillo Armas, was installed in power. His junta immediately reversed the land reform and evicted 500,000 peasants from the land they had occupied.

A nightmare began for the people of Guatemala, which has lasted till the present day. The junta unleashed a white terror, killing hundreds of left wingers, union leaders and peasants. The Eisenhower administration, however, was euphoric. Guatemala was considered to be pacified. Central America was safe for United Fruit. But this was an overly optimistic assessment. Guatemala and the whole of Central America was plunged into instability. Castillo Armas was murdered by unknown assassins three years later. Guatemala suffered years of civil war, resulting in genocidal slaughter.

The Guatemalan incident shows just how far the government of the U.S.A. is controlled by the big corporations like United Fruit and just how far the foreign policy of the U.S.A. is dictated by big business interests. There is an uncanny resemblance between these events and the events leading to the invasions of Afghanistan and Iraq, and the ongoing U.S. intrigues within Venezuela.

CHAPTER SIXTY-ONE

The U.S.A. and Cuba

In 1898 the U.S.A. invaded Cuba, allegedly to free it from Spanish rule. But, as the people of Iraq have discovered, such "liberators" tend to hang around for a long time after the "liberation". In the decades after driving out the Spaniards, Cuba was virtually bought up by American companies. Unlike Puerto Rico, the island could not be directly annexed, since this was ruled out under an amendment signed by the U.S.A. at the time of Cuba's "independence". But there was nothing to prevent U.S. businessmen from buying up most of the land and industry. In this way, Cuba's so-called independence became a fiction. U.S. business ruled there with the collusion of corrupt puppet governments like that of the dictator Fulgencio Batista y Zaldivar, who ruled the island directly or indirectly for 25 years until he was overthrown by the Cuban revolution in 1959.

Fidel Castro organized a guerrilla struggle against Batista's increasingly unpopular and corrupt regime. After two years his government collapsed like a house of cards. A general strike by the workers of Havana dealt the regime the final death-blow. On January 8, 1959, Castro led his guerrilla forces into Havana, after Batista had fled to Miami. At that time, his program went no further than democracy and land reform. It did not include proposals to nationalize U.S. property. Moscow adopted a cautious attitude. The Cuban "Communists" had supported the dictator Batista.

The initial program of the Cuban revolution was therefore not socialist but national-democratic. But all history shows that under modern conditions the national-democratic program cannot be carried out under capitalism. Either the revolution is prepared to go beyond the limits of capitalism, or it is doomed. The Cuban revolution is a classical case. The U.S. companies in Cuba tried to sabotage Castro's land reform, just as United Fruit had done in Guatemala. In response, Castro leaned on Moscow for support. The Russians signed a trade agreement with Cuba and Washington responded by imposing an economic blockade and stopped buying Cuban sugar. This was a blatant act of aggression against a sovereign state. Since sugar was Cuba's main export, it would have meant the swift strangulation of its economy.

When the Soviet Union agreed to buy Cuban sugar, Washington responded by refusing to sell petroleum products to Cuba. This was really an act of economic war. The Cubans replied by nationalizing U.S. businesses. Almost overnight, capitalism was abolished in Cuba. Eisenhower reacted by approving yet another covert program of action by the CIA, on the lines of the one that successfully destabilized the Arbenz government. But this time the result was very different.

The CIA trained a force of anti-Castro Cuban guerrillas in the jungles of Guatemala. Eisenhower also endorsed a plan for an amphibious landing by these forces, backed by the CIA, which they hoped would lead to a nation-wide uprising against Castro. These plans, hatched by Eisenhower and Allen Dulles, were passed on to the new president, John Kennedy, on the day before his inauguration in January 1961. He was apparently surprised by the scale of the operation but supported it anyway.

Despite the attempts to present Kennedy as a progressive president, he acted no differently than his predecessors. He kept the plans for the invasion secret and lied about them in public. Three days before the invasion was due to start, he told a press conference: there would not be "under any conditions an intervention in Cuba by United States armed forces." But privately he told his aides: "The minute I land one marine, we're in this thing up to our necks […] I'm not going to risk an American Hungary." (Quoted in Jeremy Isaacs and Taylor Downing, *Cold War*, p. 189.)

The reference to Hungary is instructive. In October 1956 there was a popular uprising in Hungary, which was put down by the Russians with extreme violence. Kennedy's words reveal the real situation and intentions of the U.S. imperialists in Cuba. They understood that, like in Hungary, they would be faced with the opposition of the majority of the population, and that, like in Hungary, they would have to wade through a sea of blood to obtain their objectives. They were quite prepared to do this.

The only problem is that they were defeated. The reactionary rabble that landed was immediately routed by Castro's forces. The Bay of Pigs episode was one of the most humiliating defeats suffered by U.S. imperialism in its history. After only three days of fighting, the remaining counterrevolutionary forces surrendered. More than a hundred of these bandits had been killed. Only fourteen were picked up by the U.S. Navy.

U.S. imperialism has never forgiven Cuba for this humiliation. It has maintained its criminal blockade. Although this has failed in its objective, it has caused a lot of suffering for the people of Cuba. The CIA has carried on a policy of terrorism against Cuba for decades, including numerous plans to assassinate Fidel Castro. But the Cuban revolution remains a source of hope and inspiration to the oppressed and downtrodden peoples of Central and South America and the Caribbean.

CHAPTER SIXTY-TWO

From Chile to Nicaragua

In 1970 the socialist Salvador Allende was elected in Chile. Once again the CIA began a campaign of destabilization, backing the right wing in its attempts to overthrow a democratically elected reformist president. On September 11, 1974, they finally succeeded, by using the services of general Augusto Pinochet to overthrow the government. Allende was either murdered or committed suicide. In the bloody dictatorship that followed, thousands of people were arrested, savagely tortured, murdered or were simply "disappeared" – all with the complicity of the CIA and Washington.

A similar story unfolded later in Nicaragua, where a left-wing guerrilla movement overthrew the dictatorship of general Anastasio Somoza. The Somoza family had ruled Nicaragua, the largest country in Central America, for decades. They had enriched themselves by plundering the country's wealth mercilessly with the wholehearted backing of the U.S.A. Franklin D. Roosevelt once commented about the founder of this dynasty of scoundrels: *"I know he's a son of a bitch, but he's our son of a bitch."*

In 1977, there was a national uprising against this rotten and corrupt dictatorship. After a bloody civil war costing nearly 50,000 lives, the Somoza regime was overthrown. As in Cuba, a general strike in Managua put paid to the dictatorship. Somoza fled to Paraguay, where he was later murdered. The Sandinista government began a program of agrarian reform, as in Cuba. But unlike Cuba they failed to expropriate the capitalists. This was a mistake that cost them dearly.

It is not possible to make half a revolution. The Nicaraguan capitalists organized a campaign of sabotage directed against the government with the active support of Washington. But this was only the tip of the iceberg. In November 1981 the U.S. National Security Council authorized substantial funds to assist the extreme right wing counter-revolutionary insurgency of the Contras. With CIA arms, funds and training, a small counterrevolutionary army grew from a few hundred in 1981 to about 15,000 in the mid-1980s.

The stated objective of the NSC was "to eliminate Cuban / Soviet influence in the region" and, in the longer term, to "build politically stable governments able to stand such influences." Heavy pressure was put on the Sandinista government: the U.S. Navy patrolled Nicaragua's coast, U.S. aircraft violated its air space, and the U.S. Army staged manoeuvres in Honduras just over the border. As a result of this com-bined internal and external pressure, in the end the Sandinista government fell and was replaced with a bourgeois government more to Washington's liking.

In El Salvador, another dictatorial regime was faced with a guerrilla war that had lasted for many years. President Reagan increased the U.S. military aid to the ruling junta from $36 million to $197 million in 1984. The junta used the most savage methods to defeat the opposition, sending death squads into the villages to torture and murder any peasants suspected of sympathies with the guerrillas. Tens of thousands of people were killed or just went "missing". Almost one in five of the population fled abroad to escape.

In El Salvador U.S. imperialism preferred a bloody right wing dictatorship to the victory of a popular insurrection. Likewise in Argentina, when the brutal military junta seized power in 1976, Washington supported the generals and had excellent relations with the dictatorship until it invaded the Falkland Islands, provoking a clash with British imperialism, the U.S.A.'s main European ally. With extreme reluctance, Reagan was forced to support Thatcher against his old friend Galtieri. But this decision was made purely for political convenience, not out of hatred for dictatorship and love of democracy.

Now Washington is faced with a new problem: the Venezuelan revolution. The people of Venezuela, after decades of oppression and exploitation at the hands of a corrupt and degenerate oligarchy of landlords, bankers and capitalists backed by U.S. imperialism, have begun to shake off the old despotism and move to take control of their own lives and destinies. As in Cuba, this revolutionary movement poses a mortal threat to U.S. imperialism because of the example it gives to millions of workers and peasants in Latin America.

With monotonous predictability, Washington has organized a plan to destabilize the democratically-elected government of Hugo Chavez. It has backed a coup, which failed, then a bosses' lockout thinly disguised as a "general strike", which also failed. Finally, it backed a recall referendum, which also failed. Chavez has won every election or referendum in the last six years with big majorities, yet the lie machine in Washington continues to churn out the legend that he is a "dictator".

In their hostility to the Venezuelan revolution, there was no difference between Bush and Kerry in the 2004 presidential elections. If anything, Kerry's statements on Venezuela were more aggressive than those of Bush. This fact only serves to underline the extremely reactionary nature of U.S. policy in Latin America. U.S. imperialism is the declared enemy of democracy and progress throughout the entire continent. Everywhere and at all times it has allied itself with the forces of reaction, the oligarchies, the thieves, the cut-throats, the torturers, and the dictators, against the people.

CHAPTER SIXTY-THREE

Dynamite in the Foundations

On the eve of the Second World War, Leon Trotsky made a very perceptive prediction. He predicted that U.S. imperialism would emerge victorious from the War and would become the decisive force in the planet. But he added that it would have dynamite built into its foundations. Decades later this remarkable prediction has come true. America has inherited the role of world policeman that was once held by Britain. But Britain had that position in a different period, when capitalism was in its phase of historical ascent. At that time Britain could make considerable profits out of its imperial possessions, despite the overheads involved in maintaining direct military-bureaucratic rule. But now all that has changed.

The U.S.A. has taken over the mantle of British imperialism at a time when the capitalist system is in decline. There is a general crisis, reflected in turbulence everywhere. Wars, uprisings and terrorism are on the order of the day. The U.S.A. finds itself sucked into one foreign adventure after another. This supposes a never-ending and ultimately unsustainable drain on its resources. Whereas Britain succeeded in plundering its colonies and enriching itself with the proceeds, America's war in Iraq is costing it, on a conservative estimate, one billion dollars a week. Even the richest power on earth cannot sustain such a tremendous hemorrhage for long. The U.S. military is also increasingly over-extended, with long deployments and "stop loss" orders driving down recruitment and re-enlistments. The problem is that to withdraw will be even more costly. But sooner or later, withdraw they must.

The Bush Administration has learned nothing from the experience of Vietnam. It is said that the manifest destiny of the United States is to be involved in Latin America. But the people of the United States can have no interest in plundering the peoples of the rest of the continent for the benefit of the bank balances of wealthy and irresponsible U.S. corporations. The criminal activities of these corporations, and the oligarchies and dictators backed by them, are continually destabilizing the Continent. This instability must sooner or later affect the United States.

Everywhere, the people are rising against oppression. The success of the revolution in any important country in Latin America will have the most profound effects in the U.S.A., where the largest and most rapidly growing part of the minority population is of Hispanic origin. Instead of intervening against the revolution in South America, the U.S. imperialists would be fighting revolution at home.

CHAPTER SIXTY-FOUR

The Dictatorship of Big Business

> *"All governments are more or less combinations against the people. . .and as rulers have no more virtue than the ruled. . . the power of government can only be kept within its constituted bounds by the display of a power equal to itself, the collected sentiment of the people."* (Benjamin Franklin, in a *Philadelphia Aurora* editorial 1794.)

Human consciousness always lags behind the march of history. Tradition, habit and routine weighs heavily on the minds of men and women and it is always comforting to look back to a supposedly happier past. Mythology is a powerful force and not only in religion. Ideas can persist long after the material causes that gave birth to them have disappeared.

Nowadays, nothing is left of the old democratic and egalitarian America of which de Tocqueville wrote. Yet in the United States today many people still believe that it is possible to get rich by working hard, and that the old "frontier spirit" can still triumph over adversity. This is pure mythology, but it is in the interests of those who rule America to foster the myth. In the United States and on a world scale, we see a huge and growing gap between rich and poor. The class divide, which according to the official theories should have disappeared long ago, or at least been reduced to insignificance, has reached unheard of proportions. It does not diminish, but rather increases in times of economic boom. Today, the richest 20 percent of Americans own half the country's wealth, while the poorest 20 percent own barely 4 percent.

In that epoch-making document *The Communist Manifesto*, Marx and Engels predicted that free competition would inevitably end in monopoly. For a long time the official economists tried to deny that the concentration of capital predicted by Marx had taken place. Particularly in the last two decades they insisted that the tendency would be in the opposite direction, that is, towards small enterprises, in which the small businessman would come into his own. They even coined a phrase: "small is beautiful".

How absurdly inappropriate these words sound now! The process of the concentration of capital has everywhere reached unheard-of levels. The whole of world trade is now dominated by no more than 200 giant companies – most of them based in the U.S.A., where this process has gone furthest of all. Today, the lives and destinies of millions of Americans are in the hands of a tiny handful of corporations, which in turn are in practice run by tiny handfuls of super-rich executives. The sole purpose of this new caste of robber barons is to enrich themselves, and to increase the power of their respective companies. The interests of the vast majority of U.S. citizens are of little interest to them, while those of the inhabitants of the rest of the globe are of no interest at all.

In his recent best seller *Stupid White Men*, Michael Moore gives some very telling facts about the world we now live in:

From 1979 until now, the richest 1 percent in the country have seen their wages increase by 157 percent; those of you in the bottom 20 percent are actually making $100 *less* a year (adjusted for inflation) than you were at the dawn of the Reagan era.

The world's richest two hundred companies have seen their profits grow by 362.4 percent since 1983; their combined sales are now higher than the combined gross domestic product of all but ten nations on earth.

In the most recent year for which there are figures, forty-four of the top eighty-two companies in the United States did not pay the standard rate of 35 percent in taxes that corporations are expected to pay. In fact, 17 percent of them paid NO taxes at all – and seven of those, including General Motors, played the tax code like a harp, juggling business expenses and tax credits until the government actually owed *them* millions of dollars!

Another 1,279 corporations with assets of $250 million or more also paid NO taxes and reported 'no income' for 1995 (the most recent year for which statistics were available)." (Michael Moore, *Stupid White Men*, pp. 52-3.)

These ladies and gentlemen (for there are quite a few females among them now) are the real rulers of America. The famous democracy of which de Tocqueville wrote has become just a cover for the dictatorship of the big corporations. It really matters little who the people of America elect into the White House or Capitol Hill, since all the important decisions are taken behind closed doors by these tiny, unrepresentative cliques that are in practice responsible only to themselves.

The vested interests of this ruling stratum are backed up by the most powerful military machine in history. It claims the right to intervene everywhere, to topple legally-elected governments, to launch wars and civil wars, to bomb and destroy supposedly sovereign states, without let or hindrance. Is it any wonder why *this* America has earned the hatred of millions of people throughout the world? This is really not hard to understand. Yet this is not the real America, or the real people of America who fought British imperialism to win their freedom and then fought a Civil

War to extend that freedom (at least on paper) to the black slaves.

Illusions die hard. To many Americans, the U.S.A. despite everything remains the land of the brave and the home of the free. They cannot understand why it is that the U.S.A. is so unloved by the rest of the world. Yet slowly but surely a realization is dawning that all is not well with America. A recent survey by *Business Week* revealed that seventy four percent of Americans thought that big business had too much power over their lives. The rest of this interesting survey also showed that beneath the surface of calm and contentment, there is a growing feeling of dissatisfaction with the present state of affairs. The massive demonstrations that began five years ago in Seattle served notice on the ruling class of the U.S.A. that something is beginning to stir. This is just the beginning.

CHAPTER SIXTY-FIVE

Growing Discontent

> *"The spirit of resistance to government is so valuable on certain occasions, that I wish it always to be kept alive. It will often be exercised when wrong, but better so than not to be exercised at all. I like a little rebellion now and then"*. (Thomas Jefferson, letter to Abigail Adams, 1787.)

The long years of economic upswing that followed the Second World War cut across the revolutionary movement that was developing in the 1930s in the United States and to some extent blunted the class consciousness of the proletariat. But now the world crisis of capitalism is affecting the U.S.A. in a serious way. Millions are threatened with closures and sackings. This represents a fundamental change. The U.S.A. has not experienced sustained unemployment at the 2000 level since the 1960s. The rate of unemployment now stands at around 5.4 percent with no improvement in sight. The economy must create 150,000 new job positions each month just to keep pace with the growing workforce, yet most months it does not achieve even this paltry figure. Moreover, workers who have lost their jobs have had more trouble finding new ones. A recent article in *The New York Times* (November 28, 2002) pointed out that the proportion of those who have been out of work for more than 27 weeks is very high:

"Now, about 800,000 more workers have been out of work for six months or longer, compared with the number in 2000. That is why extending unemployment benefits is so important.

"In addition, the number of part-time workers who would like full-time work has risen by one million. And the increase in the labor force has slowed markedly because many more people have stopped looking for jobs. They do not show up in the unemployment data. In the recessions of the early 1980s and 1990s, the labor force grew far more rapidly, pushing up the unemployment rate."

The boom of the 1990s meant a certain amelioration for many workers and "middle class" people and fabulous fortunes for a small minority. Even at this time the rich gained much more than the poor, whose position improved far more slowly. But since the recession that began four years ago, family incomes are once again falling across the board (even during the so-called recovery). And they are falling most rapidly for those in the bottom 20 or 30 percent. Inequality is increasing, and the contrast between the fat cats at the top and the "have-nots" at the bottom is more glaring than ever.

The wealthy find ways of avoiding the payment of taxes, and the burden of taxation falls heavily on the shoulders of the "middle class" and the working poor. A good example of this is the estate tax, which is overwhelmingly, a tax on the wealthy. In 1999, only the top two percent of estates paid any tax at all. Paul Krugman in an article in *The New York Times* (October 20, 2002.) with the significant title "The Class Wars: The End of Middle Class America", writes:

"Income inequality in America has now returned to the levels of the 1920s. Inherited wealth doesn't yet play a big part in our society, but given time – and the repeal of the estate tax – we will grow ourselves a hereditary elite just as set apart from the concerns of ordinary Americans [...] And the new elite, like the old, will have enormous political power."

Even those who still retain their jobs are unhappy. They have little confidence in the future. Nobody feels secure any more. There is a new volatility and a mood of criticism and discontent at all levels. There is a huge and growing alienation between the people of America and those who rule their lives. And a growing number of Americans are becoming aware of this state of affairs and are dissatisfied with it. Maybe they do not know exactly what they want, but they certainly know what they do not want. The sense of alienation is reflected in the large number of people who do not vote in elections.

There is a groundswell of discontent that comes from the very heart of America. Millions of ordinary men and women are unhappy with the kind of lives they are leading: the long hours, the remorseless pressure, the dictatorial attitudes of management, the chronic insecurity. These moods are beginning to affect even the formerly affluent layers of the working "middle class". And even at a higher level, there are those who are beginning to question the values of a society where the laws of the jungle are held up as a model: dog-eat-dog! Each man for himself and let the devil take the hindmost! Is this what life in the 21st century is really all about?

A few years ago, economist J. K. Galbraith wrote a book called *The Policy of Contentment,* in which he issued a warning to America: "Recession and depression made worse by long-run economic desuetude, the danger implicit in an autonomous military power and growing unrest in the urban slums caused by worsening deprivation and hopelessness have been cited as separate prospects. All could in fact, come together. A deep recession could cause stronger discontent in the areas of urban disaster in the aftermath of some military misadventure in which, in the nature of the modern armed forces, the unfortunate were disproportionately engaged." (J. K. Galbraith, *The Policy of Contentment*, pp. 172-3.)

So far, America has avoided the kind of deep recession predicted by Galbraith. But postponement does not signify avoidance. The present rally of the U.S. economy, based as it is on consumption and debt rather than productive investment, may not be long-lasting and may well be just the prelude to an even steeper fall. In any case, the future of the capitalist economy, both in the U.S.A. and on a world scale has a sombre aspect. New shocks are inevitable, with unforeseen consequences.

The point is that nobody can control the forces that have been unleashed on a global scale over the past ten or twenty years. The fundamental contradictions of capitalism have not been abolished, as some American economists have claimed, but only reproduced on a far vaster scale than ever before. There is no law that says that these market forces will achieve some kind of automatic equilibrium. On the contrary, the anarchic, unplanned character of capitalism must manifest itself in the most tremendous convulsions. Globalization will manifest itself as a global crisis of capitalism – in fact, it is already doing so. George Soros, who is certainly no Marxist but is an expert on the workings of world market, has pointed out that the market does not operate like a pendulum but rather like a wrecking ball – demolishing anything that gets in its way. We have already seen the results of this wrecking ball in the economic meltdown of Argentina. It will not be the last case.

CHAPTER SIXTY-SIX

The Rotten Heart of Corporate America

The Enron scandal, and the tidal wave of corporate scandals that followed it, completely exposed the lie that the market economy is the most efficient system, the best way to avoid bureaucracy and corruption, and that it is somehow "more democratic" and allows more people a say on how things are run. The fact of the matter is that inside the big corporations in the U.S.A. corruption is rife, tyranny reigns, and the jobs, lives and pensions of millions are in the hands of powerful and despotic minorities of super-rich executives.

It is entirely untrue that the present system works well because it rewards efficiency. There is precious little reward for the vast majority of American workers who are obliged to work long hours under remorseless pressure to earn enough for their families' needs. All too often, they have to take two or three jobs to make ends meet – while others languish on the unemployment line or fall off the social radar as they are no longer even counted as "looking for work". In the last twenty years, produc-tivity in the U.S.A. has been hugely increased and vast profits have been made out of squeezing the U.S. workforce. The working week has been lengthened inexorably from 40 to over 50 hours on average. People are feeling the strain. It is undermining their physical and mental health and ruining their family life. This is increasingly the case, not only with blue-collar workers but also with professional people and lower management. What keeps them going is not free choice or incentive to "get on", but relentless pressure to get results (i.e. profits for the bosses), and fear of losing their jobs and homes.

On the other hand, it is equally untrue that the top executives of the big corporations are guided by the principle of greater rewards for greater results. On the contrary, over the past decades, the CEOs have consistently rewarded themselves with the most staggering sums of money, bearing no relation to performance or productivity. Vast fortunes have been made, and are still being made, by people who do next to nothing (and sometimes nothing at all). Even in the present recession, when company profits are falling and workers are sacked or told to make sacrifices, the fat cats continue to plunder the wealth of America in the most shameless manner.

Quite apart from their huge salaries – which are quite unrelated to performance – the CEOs receive a wide range of perks, amounting to corruption on a grand scale. The best example is the notorious system of stock options. Thus, although AOL-Time-Warner executives were "punished" by the non-payment of bonuses, they nevertheless received stock options valued at around $40 million a head. Many American workers would be very pleased to receive such "punishment" during a recession, or for that matter even during a boom.

There is also a wide range of perks that do not appear in the normal surveys of bosses' earnings. Coca-Cola demands that both its boss and his wife always travel in the company's jet – a privilege that cost the company $103, 898 last year alone. At AOL Time Warner, Gerald Levin and Richard Parkins, his appointed successor, each got

$97,500 in "financial services" (for "tax return preparation and financial planning", the company explained – whatever that might mean). True, some of them have now taken "pay cuts". What do these "cuts" consist of? Stanford Weill, the chief executive of Citigroup, took an 83 percent pay cut recently, which left the poor fellow with a miserable $36.1 million. *The Economist* (6/4/02) commented:

"One worry is that executive pay has risen to such heights that the bad times look rather like the good times used to: the median total compensation in the Mercer survey [a recent survey of 100 big companies by William M. Mercer and the *Wall Street Journal*] was still $2.16 million. Nor has pay fallen by nearly as much as profits have done. The total compensation of chief executives is down by 2.9 percent on a year ago, but after-tax profits fell by nearly 50 percent last year among the companies included in the S&P 500. Some components of bosses' pay such as basic salaries actually rose healthily on the back of this dreadful performance."

The Economist continues: "Some of the financial services that American companies offer to their top chaps would put regular banks out of business. Compaq, a computer maker, has agreed to forgive a $5 million (!) loan it extended to its boss, Michael Capellas, and is providing him with a new loan to help with the tax bill. Bernie Ebbers, the chief executive of WorldCom, a troubled telecom firm, borrowed a princely $341m. From his employer, on which he is paying a little over 2 percent on interest."

When they are employed, these executives, responsible in reality to nobody, enrich themselves shamelessly out of the profits that are the unpaid wages of the working class. It is a condemnation of the system that when layoffs are announced, the value of the stock invariably goes up. When a worker is sacked (which these people rarely are) or retires, they receive a very meager compensation – if they get anything at all. But these ladies and gentlemen continue to act like leeches even when they are formally retired.

"On top of his pension, worth around $9 million a year, Jack Welch, the retired boss of General Electric, is 'required' under the terms of his contract to consult with the company for the rest of his life, for which he will charge a daily [yes, that's right, daily] rate of $17,000." (Ibid.)

What exactly this "consultation" consists of is not mentioned. But the general picture is pretty clear. What we have here is not the picture of the go-getting, self-made American entrepreneur, so assiduously cultivated by the advocates of capitalism, but the exact opposite. This is a picture of unqualified and unrestrained plunder of the American economy by a tiny, unrepresentative and above all, unproductive corporate drones. Comfortably installed in their shiny glass towers, utterly remote from the workforce and the American people, at the head of vast and servile corporate bureaucracies, they quietly determine the fate of millions, both in the U.S.A. and on a global scale. This is the real face of corporate America and the reality of the so-called free market economy. Enron was just the tip of a very large, ugly and dangerous iceberg.

In case anyone thinks that this is just Marxist exaggeration and alarmism, let us leave the last word to that champion of the free market economy, *The Economist*, which we have already quoted. It predicts that on present trends, "by 2021 there will emerge a big American company where the boss is paid more than the firm's entire sales. If that is market forces at work, then market forces had better be ignored."

CHAPTER SIXTY-SEVEN

Socialism and Democracy

The idea that socialism and democracy are somehow incompatible is yet another falsehood. On this question, the defenders of capitalism behave like a squid that defends itself by squirting a large quantity of ink to confuse its enemy. The fact of the matter is this: that the democracy in the U.S.A. is a cover for the dictatorship of a handful of powerful corporations run by tiny cliques of non-elected and irresponsible people. The latter do not only own and control the wealth of America. They also control its press, television and all other means of moulding and conditioning public opinion. While in theory there are two parties, everyone knows that the difference between the Democrans and Republicrats is minimal.

Stalinist Russia was a one-party dictatorship (something that neither Marx nor Lenin ever advocated). America boasts a pluralistic democracy. In this democracy everyone can say what they want (well, almost), as long as the banks and big corporations decide what happen. Elections take place regularly, but in fact the electorate have no real choice. Both Democrats and Republicans stand for the interests of big business. There is no real difference between them: what small differences used to exist in the past have all but disappeared. In order to get elected at all, one has to be either a billionaire, or else have access to vast sums of money.

And as the proverb goes: "He who pays the piper calls the tune". The Enron scandal merely confirmed what everyone already knew: that the great majority of senators and congressmen and women are in the pockets of big business. No wonder millions of U.S. citizens feel disenfranchised and do not bother to vote.

Marxists stand for democracy. But we advocate a genuine democracy, not a fraudulent caricature. And the first condition for the introduction of democracy in the U.S.A. is the overthrow of the dictatorship of big business. The power of the big banks and corporations must be broken, and the commanding heights of the economy nationalized, under the democratic control and administration of the workers themselves. There would be plenty of scope for personal initiative!

The talents of the engineers, managers, scientists and technicians would play a crucial role in a socialist planned economy. Once private profit was no longer the overriding principle, the way would be open for an unprecedented boom in inventions, innovations of all kinds. Above all, the men and women on the shop floor would be encouraged to participate in discussions and debates on how to improve working practices and conditions. In this way, everyone would have a stake in the running of society. Decision-making would no longer be the privilege of a few wealthy executives, but the common property of all Americans.

In what way does this idea contradict the traditional and dearly held American ideals of democracy and individual rights? It does not contradict them at all, but reaffirms them and takes them to a qualitatively higher level. In fact, at the moment there is really very little scope for the free development of the individual in the U.S.A. of the giant corporations. None of the important decisions affecting the lives of the people are taken by the people. They are not even being taken on Capitol Hill, but by unseen individuals behind locked doors on Wall Street, in the Pentagon, the State Department, and above all in the boardrooms of the giant corporations that really rule the U.S.A.

CHAPTER SIXTY-EIGHT

The Future of Democracy

> *"This country, with its institutions, belongs to the people who inhabit it. Whenever they shall grow weary of the existing government, they can exercise their constitutional right of amending it, or their revolutionary right to dismember or overthrow it."* (Abraham Lincoln, April 4, 1861.)

The celebrated American sociologist C. Wright Mills coined the phrase "the military industrial complex" to describe the union between big business, government and the military that runs the U.S.A. today. The modern American state is a vast bureaucratic monster that exists not to serve the people but to lord it over them in the interests of the big companies that really rule America. When Thomas Jefferson was made the first Secretary of State, he had just five employees to man his office. Now the state bureaucracy numbers a huge army of hundreds of thousands of bureaucrats. Though they talk incessantly about "cutting government down to size", all administrations have added to this monster, increasing its size and power constantly, at tremendous cost to the economy. "Cheap government" has become a hollow phrase from the distant past. In present-day America, the bureaucratic monster of big business is indissolubly linked to the bureaucratic monster of the state. That is what the Military-Industrial Complex means.

Most people in the U.S.A. nowadays take democracy for granted. But this is a dangerous misconception. The history of the United States shows that the common people have always had to struggle to win even the most elementary rights, and that democracy is a very fragile plant. Whenever the ruling oligarchy feels itself challenged it immediately takes steps to limit or even cancel those hard-won democratic rights enshrined in the Constitution and the Bill of Rights. It should be added that the Constitution itself has a number of defects from a strictly democratic standpoint. The powers given to the President are truly immense. Section One of Article Two says simply: "The executive power shall be vested in a President of the United States of America." The President is commander in chief of the armed forces. He has powers to make treaties with the concurrence of the Senate and to make appointments of public officials and employees.

Theoretically, the powers of the executive are limited by a complicated system of checks and balances. But the fact is that the powers of the President have never been used to their full extent. They are important reserve powers that, under certain conditions could be used to carry through a legal coup and institute a Presidential dictatorship (i.e., the possibility of a socialist majority in Congress that wanted to nationalize the big corporations). This possibility is never considered because it has never been seen, but it is a real danger.

In any situation deemed by the ruling elite to constitute a national emergency it would be possible for the President, with the connivance of a majority of Congress, to virtually set aside the Constitution, vote unlimited authority to the President, and adjourn *sine die*. This may seem unlikely, but if we look at the recent trends we can see an increasing tendency to encroach upon the democratic rights of American citizens and grant ever-greater power to the state and its organs of repression. Some even say that the Constitution itself has already been turned into a dead letter.

Real power lies in the hands of a tiny number of boards of directors of the big corporations and banks. These faceless men and women are, in practice, elected by nobody and responsible to nobody. Yet they wield more real power than millions of ordinary Americans. With billions of dollars to play with, they can, and do, buy congressmen and women, judges, lawyers, newspaper editors, parties and Presidents. They decide what you can read, hear on the radio or see on television. Their psychology is that of Commodore Vanderbilt: "*Law? What law? Hain't I got the Power?*"

What is the attitude of Marxists to democracy? In the first place, we stand for the defense of all the democratic conquests that were won through the struggle of the working class in the past. The working class needs freedom to develop its organizations: the unions, shop stewards committees and all the other things that represent the embryo of a new society within the womb of the old. We need the maximum freedom of speech, of assembly, and of the press; freedom to strike, demonstrate and agitate in favor of socialism. We must therefore fight any attempt by the dictatorship of big business to cancel or restrict any of these rights. We will make use of every democratic channel; that is open to us to put our case before the people.

We will fight for the creation of a mass party of labor that will fight for the interests of the working class and all oppressed people, and will stand for the nationalization of the big corporations under workers' control and management. Once we have broken the stranglehold of the Democrats over the unions, it will be possible to fight and win elections in a cause that will inspire millions of people with hope. The working class, together with the small farmers, the unemployed, and other non-exploitative sections of society, constitute the decisive majority of the population, will respond enthusiastically, once they see they have a real alternative. It is entirely possible that a Labor Party could win a majority. But in that case, we have to ask ourselves how the big banks and corporations that really run America would react.

All history shows that no ruling class has ever given up its power, wealth and privileges without a fight, and that has normally meant a fight with no holds barred. We must be prepared to deal with a slaveholders' rebellion in the same way that Abraham Lincoln did. Therefore, while accepting the need to fight to win the majority through elections, we understand that in the last analysis the decisive conflict will be fought outside Congress: in the streets and factories, in the farms, schools and universities.

The power of the American working class is colossal. Not a light bulb shines, not a telephone rings, not a wheel turns without the kind permission of the workers. This is potentially such a tremendous power that no force can resist it, as long as the working class is organized, mobilized and united in the struggle to change society. The resistance of the present day slaveholders can be swiftly overcome and reduced to nothing, on one condition: that the workers are determined to fight to the end.

CHAPTER SIXTY-NINE

Is Bureaucracy Inevitable?

It is frequently asserted that private ownership is superior to nationalized enterprises because it permits private initiative. But in practice, the big corporations that dominate the U.S. economy are extremely bureaucratic, inefficient and corrupt. They do not allow much room for initiative – at least as far as the big majority of the workforce is concerned. They are fundamentally undemocratic, being run by a handful of super-rich executives whose main aim in life is to make themselves even more wealthy.

The general public good is of no concern to such individuals, except inasmuch as bad publicity may harm sales, and therefore profits. The solution to this problem, however, is not to act in the public interest, but to pay for the services of a slick public relations department which is used to present the company's image in the most favorable light –that is to say, to mislead and deceive the public. The case of Enron is an excellent example of the reality of U.S. corporate practice. It should be noted that this company was so closely connected with the U.S. government at the highest levels that it proved almost impossible to investigate its activities and even now the whole truth has not come out. And there are many more Enrons which have not yet been exposed.

No less an authority than the classical bourgeois

economist Adam Smith already warned of the dangers of monopoly, when he wrote: "The directors of such [joint-stock] companies [.] being the managers rather of other people's money than of their own, it cannot be well expected that they should watch over it with the same anxious vigilance with which the partners in a private company frequently watch over their own [.] *Negligence and profusion, therefore, must always prevail, more or less, in the management of the affairs of such a company.*" (Adam Smith, *Wealth of Nations*, part 3, p. 112.)

The solution to this problem cannot be a return to the era of small businesses, as some people advocate. That period has been relegated to history and will not return. The modern capitalist economy is entirely dominated by big monopolies, and nothing can reverse that tendency. Anyone who doubts this has only to examine the history of anti-trust legislation in the U.S.A. There have been laws against monopolies for a very long time, yet their practical effect has been negligible. Witness the recent tussle between Bill Gates and the Federal authorities. No one doubts that Mr. Gates has created the world's biggest monopoly, and that this is harming the progress of technology in a most vital area. Yet in practice, it is proving impossible to reverse the position.

Since it is not possible to halt the inevitable tendency towards monopolization, there remains only one alternative: to bring these giant corporations – which are at present responsible to nobody but themselves – under democratic control. But here we come up against an insurmountable difficulty. It is not possible to control what you do not own. The answer is very clear: in order to control the monopolies, it is necessary to take them out of private hands altogether –that is, to nationalize them. Only then would it be possible to ensure that the key points of the economy are the servants of society, not its master.

But would this not create the danger of a bureaucracy, as existed in Stalinist Russia? This seems to be a very serious objection, but actually it is not. The bureaucratic degeneration of the Russian revolution was not the result of nationalization, but of the isolation of the revolution under conditions of frightful backwardness. It should not be forgotten that in 1917 Russia was an extremely backward semi-feudal country. Out of a total population of 150 million, there were only four million industrial workers. In a remarkably short space of time, the nationalized planned economy transformed Russia from a backward country like Pakistan is today into the second most powerful nation on earth. For several decades the U.S.S.R. achieved economic results that have never been equalled by any other country. Nor should we forget the fact that its economy suffered the most terrible devastation in the Second World War when 27 million Soviet citizens perished.

It is not possible to understand what happened in the Soviet Union without considering these facts. Nor is it reasonable to draw an analogy between the fate of the nationalized planned economy in backward Russia and the prospects for a socialist planned economy in the United States. *Bureaucracy is a product of economic and cultural backwardness.* It is not difficult to prove this. If one considers the state of affairs in those countries which are sometimes referred to as the "Third World" – the states of Africa, Asia and Latin America, then it immediately becomes obvious that bureaucracy is a feature common to every single one of them – whether the means of production are nationalized or not (and even in the advanced capitalist countries it is to be seen).

It is possible to draw a graph showing that the degree of bureaucratization of a given society is in inverse proportion to the level of its economic and cultural development. The same is true of phenomena like corruption, inefficiency and red tape that are usually connected with bureaucracy. Society tends to free itself of these things to the degree that it lifts itself out of a low level of economic and technological development, and raises the cultural level of the population.

Of course, where a bureaucracy becomes an entrenched ruling caste as happened in Russia after the death of Lenin, it can hang onto its power and privileges even when the level of economic and cultural development renders it entirely superfluous. But in that case, the bureaucracy will suffocate and destroy the nationalized planned economy – which is precisely what occurred in the Soviet Union. But that is exactly the point. The existence of the bureaucracy in Russia was not only not the product of the nationalized planned economy, but was in complete antagonism to it. Trotsky explained that a nationalized planned economy requires democracy as the human body requires oxygen.

Without democracy and the control and administration of society by the working class, the planned economy eventually seized up, clogged and obstructed by the suffocating control of the bureaucracy.

CHAPTER SEVENTY

What About Russia?

Ah, but the Soviet Union collapsed. Doesn't that prove that socialism has failed? Yes, the Soviet Union collapsed after decades of bureaucratic and totalitarian rule, which completely negated the regime of workers' democracy established in 1917. As early as 1936, Leon Trotsky predicted that the Stalinist bureaucracy that usurped power after Lenin's death, would not be satisfied with its legal and illegal privileges, but would inevitably strive to replace the nationalized planned economy by privately owned monopolies. The capitalist counter-revolution in Russia, however, offers no way forward to the peoples of the former U.S.S.R.. It has been accompanied by a horrific collapse of the Russian economy, living standards and culture, as Trotsky predicted. If there is a country in the world where capitalism stands condemned, that country is Russia.

The prolongation of senile capitalism threatens the future of human culture, civilization, democracy, perhaps even the survival of humanity itself. The world is crying out for a fundamental social and economic transformation. The only hope for humanity consists in the radical abolition of capitalism and the establishment of a harmonious system of production and distribution based on the common ownership of the means of production under democratic workers' control and administration.

The enormous potential of a nationalized planned economy was demonstrated by the Soviet Union, before, during and in the first 25 years after the Second World War. Despite all the efforts of the bourgeoisie and its hired prostitutes to deny it, the fact is that the U.S.S.R. (and later China) showed that it is possible to run an economy without private capitalists, bankers, speculators and landlords, and that such an economy can obtain spectacular results.

The future socialist planned economy of the U.S.A. will not be based on backwardness, as was the regime established by the Bolshevik Party of Lenin and Trotsky in November 1917. It will be as different from Russia as computer science is from the wooden plough. American socialism from the very beginning will draw on the colossal advances of industry, science and technology, which will become the servants of human needs, not the slaves of the profit motive. Once the vast productive capacity of the U.S.A. is organized on the basis of a rational plan, the sky will be the limit.

This is not just a theoretical assertion. It has already been proved in practice, and not only in Russia. As we have seen, during the Second World War, when elements of a planned economy and state control were introduced in the U.S.A., the economy grew rapidly and unemployment all but disappeared. That gives us just a glimpse of the tremendous potential that a socialist planned economy in America would unleash. Of course, this was not socialism. The basic levers of the economy remained in the hands of private capitalists. Real planning is not possible under capitalism. And the nationalized industries were run by bureaucrats. But despite these limitations, even these elements of a planned economy gave serious results for a time.

The elements of planning, even on a capitalist basis, gave better results than the free-for-all of the market economy. Just imagine the results that would be possible in a real socialist planned economy in which the benefits of a central plan would be combined with the democratic control and administration of the working people themselves. On the basis of a modern, technologically advanced economy, rational planning will spur production to an unprecedented level.

CHAPTER SEVENTY-ONE

The Soul of America

In the first part of *Reason in Revolt*, a reference is made to the contradiction between the marvellous advances of science and the extraordinary lag in human consciousness. This contradiction is particularly striking in the United States. In the country that has done more than any other to advance the cause of science in the past period, the overwhelming majority of people in the U.S.A. believe in god, or are religious in some way. Thirty six percent of Americans think the Bible is the literal world of god, and half believe that America enjoys divine protection. After September 11, 78 percent thought that the influence of religion on public life was growing. Books on the apocalypse became best sellers. This situation is quite different to that of most European countries, where organized religion is dying on its feet (although there is still plenty of superstition and mysticism around).

Strangely enough, the Founding Fathers were not at all religious. These true sons of the 18th century Enlightenment expressed themselves in the most scathing terms about religion in general and Christianity in particular. Founding Fathers George Washington & John Adams, in a diplomatic message to Malta, wrote: "The United States is in no way founded upon the Christian religion." John Adams, in a letter to Thomas Jefferson, went even further when he wrote: "This would be the best of all possible worlds, if there were no religion in it."

Thomas Jefferson, in 1814, commented: "In every country and in every age, the priest has been hostile to liberty. He is always in alliance with the despot, abetting his abuses in return for protection to his own." And the same Thomas Jefferson wrote in 1823: "The day will come when the mystical generation of Jesus by the Supreme Being as his father, in the womb of a virgin, will be classed with the fable of the generation of Minerva in the brain of Jupiter." He added: "I do not find in orthodox Christianity one redeeming feature."

Things were no better with Abraham Lincoln, who was also openly irreligious: "The Bible is not my book, and Christianity is not my religion," he said. "I could never give assent to the long, complicated statements of Christian dogma." These views were the natural outcome of the rationalist philosophy that represented the most advanced philosophical ideas of the 18th century Enlightenment. The rejection of religion was always the first step towards a rational view of nature and society. It was the beginning of all modern progress, the basis of both the American and the French revolutions. And it was equally the starting point for the development of modern science and technology, the true foundation for America's greatness. Nowadays the degree of scientific and technological advance in the U.S.A. is unequalled by any other country. Here we have a tantalizing glimpse of the future – the staggering potential of human development. But we also see a contradiction. Side by side with the most advanced ideas we see the persistence of ideas that have been handed down, unchanged, from a remote and barbarous past.

The reason for the persistence of religious belief is that men and women feel that their lives are under the control of strange unseen forces. They do not feel in control of their own destinies, as really free human beings should. And in fact, our lives really are determined by forces not under our control. The wild swings of "market forces" on a world scale determine whether millions of people will have a job or not. The equally wild gyrations of the stock markets can ruin millions of families in a matter of days or even hours. There is a general instability and volatility throughout the world that expresses itself in unending wars, terrorist outrages and other barbarities. This creates a general climate of fear and uncertainty. It is what is called *the new world order*.

In its period of ascent, capitalism based itself on rationalism. That is just what is expressed in the ideas of the Founding Fathers reproduced above. In general, when a particular socio-economic system is in a state of collapse, its decline is expressed in a general crisis of morality, the family, beliefs and so on. The ideology of the ruling elite becomes increasingly decrepit, its values rotten. People no longer believe in the old ways and the old "ideals" are met with scepticism and irony. Eventually a new set of ideals emerge and a new ideology that reflects the standpoint of the rising revolutionary class. In the 18th century that was the bourgeoisie, which generally adopted a rationalist standpoint. In the 21st century, it is the working class, which must stand on the basis of scientific socialism – Marxism.

In general, when society enters – as capitalism has undoubtedly entered – into a phase of terminal decline, one can react in one of two ways. One response is to turn inwards, try to escape from a horrific reality by closing all the doors and windows and shutting one's eyes to what is happening in the world outside. The problem with this is that the world outside has an uncomfortable way of intruding into the life of even the most private persons. Sooner or later it will come knocking at your door, and usually at a most uncivilized hour. There is really no escape.

The second way is to look reality squarely in the face, to try to understand it and thus prepare to change it. Hegel said long ago that true freedom is the recognition of necessity, that is to say, if we want to change the circumstances in which we live, we must first understand them. Marxism provides us with a wonderful tool to help us to grasp the nature of the world we live in and to make us understand where we have come from and where we are going to. Unlike religion, which offers the consolation of a vision of future happiness and fulfilment beyond the grave, Marxism directs our eyes, not to heaven, but to the present life and helps us to understand the apparently mysterious forces that determine our fate.

Since *Reason in Revolt* first appeared, there have been a number of other spectacular advances in science – notably the mapping of the human genome. These results have completely demolished the positions of genetic determinism that we criticized in *Reason in Revolt*. It has also cut the ground from under the feet of the racist "theories" put forward by certain writers in the U.S.A. who attempted to enlist the service of genetics to peddle their reactionary pseudo-scientific "theories", that black people are genetically predisposed to ignorance and poverty.

They have also dealt a mortal blow to the nonsense of the Creationists who want to reject Darwinism in favor of the first chapters of Genesis, and impose this on American schools.

For many Americans, Marxism is a closed book because it is seen as anti-religious. After all, did Marx not describe religion as the "opium of the people"? As a matter of fact, just before these famous words, Marx wrote: "*Religious* distress is at the same time the *expression* of real distress and the *protest* against real distress." In essence, religion is an expression of a desire for a better world and a belief that there must be something more to life than the vale of tears through which we pass in the all-too-brief interval from cradle to grave.

Many people are discontented with their lives. It is not just a question of material poverty – although that exists in the U.S.A. as in all other countries. It is also a question of spiritual poverty: the emptiness of people's lives, the mind-deadening routine of work that is just so many hours out of one's life; the alienation that divides men and women from each other; the absence of human relations and solidarity that is deliberately fostered in a society that proudly proclaims the laws of the jungle and the so-called survival of the fittest (read: wealthiest); the mind-numbing banality of a commercialized "culture". In this kind of world the question we should be asking ourselves is not: "is there a life after death" but rather "is there a life *before* death?"

The capitalist system is a monstrously oppressive and inhuman system, which means untold misery, disease, oppression and death for millions of people in the world. It is surely the duty of any humane person to support the fight against such a system. However, in order to fight effectively, it is necessary to work out a serious program, policy and perspective that can guarantee success. We believe that only Marxism (scientific socialism) provides such a perspective.

The problem a Marxist has with religion is basically this: We believe that men and women should fight to transform their lives and to create a genuinely human society which would permit the human race to lift itself up to its true stature. We believe that human beings have only one life, and should dedicate themselves to making this life beautiful and self-fulfilling. If you like, *we are fighting for a paradise on this earth, because we do not think there is any other*.

Although from a philosophical point of view, Marxism is incompatible with religion, it goes without saying that we are opposed to any idea of prohibiting or repressing religion. We stand for the complete freedom of the individual to hold any religious belief, or none at all. What we do say is that there should be a strict separation between church and state. The churches must not be supported directly or indirectly by taxes or exemption therefrom, nor should religion be taught in state schools. If people want religion, they should maintain their churches exclusively through the contributions of the congregation and preach their doctrines in their own time.

To the degree that men and women are able to take control of their lives and develop themselves as free human beings, I believe that interest in religion – that is, the search for consolation in an afterlife – will decline naturally of itself. Of course, you may disagree with this prediction. Time will tell which of us is right. In the meantime, disagreements on such matters should not prevent all honest Christians from joining hands with the Marxists in the struggle for a new and better world.

CHAPTER SEVENTY-TWO

Religion and Revolution

Christianity itself began as a revolutionary movement about 2000 years ago when the early Christians organized a mass movement of the poorest and most downtrodden sections of society. It is not an accident that the Romans accused the Christians of being a movement of slaves and women. The early Christians were also communists, as you will know from the Acts of the Apostles. Christ himself worked among the poor and dispossessed and frequently attacked the rich. He said that it is easier for a camel to pass through the eye of a needle than a rich man to enter the Kingdom of God. There are many such expressions in the Bible.

The communism of the early Christians is also shown by the fact that in their communities all wealth was held in common. Anyone who wished to join had first to give up all his or her worldly goods. Of course, this communism had a somewhat naive and primitive character. This is no reflection on the men and women of that time, who were very courageous people who were not afraid to sacrifice their lives in the struggle against the monstrous Roman slave state. But the real achievement of communism (that is, a classless society) was impossible at that time because the material conditions for it were absent.

Marx and Engels for the first time gave communism a scientific character. They explained that the real emancipation of the masses depends on the level of development of the productive forces (industry, agriculture, science and technology) which will create the necessary conditions for a general reduction of the working day and access to culture for all, as the only way of transforming the way people think and behave towards each other.

The material conditions at the time of early Christianity were not sufficiently advanced to permit such a development, and therefore the communism of the early Christians remained on a primitive level – the level of consumption (the sharing out of food, clothes, etc.) and not real communism which is based on the collective ownership of the means of production.

However, the revolutionary traditions of early Christianity bear absolutely no relation to the present situation. Ever since the 4th Century AD, when the Christian movement was hijacked by the state and turned into an instrument of the oppressors, the Christian Church has been on the side of the rich and powerful against the poor and oppressed. Today the main churches are extremely wealthy institutions, closely linked to big business. The Vatican owns a big bank and possesses enormous wealth and power, the Church of England is the biggest landowner in Britain, and so on.

Politically, the churches have systematically backed reaction. Catholic priests blessed the armies of Franco in their campaign to crush the Spanish workers and peasants. The Pope in effect backed Hitler and Mussolini. Finally, in the U.S.A. today, the religious right, backed by millions of dollars, is conducting a campaign in favour of all manner of reactionary causes. It has at its disposal television and radio stations, where religious charlatans make a fortune by playing on people's fear and superstition.

The Kingdom of God may be reserved for the poor, but

these ladies and gentlemen have ensured for themselves a very comfortable life on this earth. Jesus' first act on entering Jerusalem was to drive the moneychangers out of the Temple. But those who presume to speak in his name almost always take the side of the rich and powerful against the poor and oppressed of this earth. They are often the most fervent advocates of welfare cuts and other policies directed against the most defenceless sections of society, such as single parents. Christ defended the woman taken in adultery, but the latter-day Pharisees line up to stone the poor and defenceless.

For such "religious" people, we have nothing but contempt. But for those honest Christians who wish to join us in the fight to change society, we extend a warm and fraternal welcome. We may disagree about philosophy, but we can agree that the present society is unworthy of humanity and ought to be changed. And we know that many devoted and self-sacrificing class fighters in the U.S.A. are practicing Christians. This has always been the case, as we see from the following extract from *The Jungle*, that great socialist novel by Upton Sinclair:

"'I am not defending the Vatican,' exclaimed Lucas vehemently. 'I am defending the word of God – which is one long cry of the human spirit for deliverance from the sway of oppression. Take the twenty-fourth chapter of the Book of Job, which I am accustomed to quote in my addresses as 'the Bible upon the Beef trust'; or take the words of Isaiah – or of the Master Himself. Not the elegant prince of our debauched and vicious art, not the jewelled idol of our society churches – but the Jesus of the awful reality, the man of sorrow and pain, the outcast, despised of the world, who had nowhere to lay His head - '

"'I will grant you Jesus,' interrupted the other.

"Well then,' cried Lucas, 'and why should Jesus have nothing to do with His Church –why should His words

His life be of no authority among those who profess to adore Him? Here is a man who was the world's first revolutionist, the true founder of the socialist movement; a man whose whole being was one flame of hatred for wealth, and all that wealth stands for – for the pride of and the luxury of wealth, and the tyranny of wealth; who was Himself a beggar and a tramp, a man of the people, an associate of saloon-keepers and women of the town; who again and again, in the most explicit language, denounced wealth and the holding of wealth: 'Lay not up for yourselves treasures on earth!" "Sell that ye have and give alms!" – "Blessed are ye poor, for yours is the kingdom of heaven!" – "Woe unto you that are rich, for ye have received your consolation!" – "Verily, I say unto you, that a rich man shall hardly enter into the kingdom of heaven!" Who denounced in unmeasured terms the exploiters of His own time: "Woe unto you, scribes and Pharisees, hypocrites!" – "Woe unto you also, you lawyers!" – "Ye serpents, ye generation of vipers, how can ye escape the damnation of hell?" Who drove out the businessmen and brokers from the temple with a whip!' Who was crucified – think of it – for an incendiary and a disturber of the social order! And this man they have made into the high priest of property and smug respectability, a divine sanction of all the horrors and abominations of modern commercial civilization! Jewelled images are made of Him, sensual priests burn incense to Him, and modern pirates of industry bring their dollars, wrung from the toil of helpless women and children, and build temples to Him, and sit in cushioned seats and listen to His teachings expounded by doctors of dusty divinity."

The voice of revolt of the oppressed against injustice and oppression has spoken in this kind of language for at least 2,000 years. What is important is not the language but the meaning. What is important is not the form but the content. The original message of the Christian movement 2,000 years ago was both revolutionary and communist. As has been explained, nobody could be a Christian unless they first gave up all their worldly wealth, renounced private property and embraced the doctrine of the universal brotherhood (and sisterhood) and equality of all. That revolutionary message was restated by the left wing of the Puritans in the 16th and 17th centuries. It has resurfaced many times since, as an expression of the instinctive revolutionism of the masses. Marxism takes as its starting point this instinctive revolutionism but gives it a scientific and rounded-out expression.

Our first task is to unite to put an end to the dictatorship of Capital that keeps the human race in a state of slavery. Socialism will permit the free development of human beings, without the constraint of material needs. As far as the future of religion is concerned, one can say the following: socialism, being based upon full human freedom, will never try to prohibit people from thinking and believing in any way they choose. People should be allowed to hold any religious beliefs they wish – or none at all.

As we have already pointed out above, religion must, of course, be completely separated from the state. Those who wish to practice religion must pay for it out of their own pockets. And there is no place at all for religion in the schools. Once we have established a genuinely free society in which men and women take control of their own lives and destinies, in which they are able to develop to the full all their physical and mental abilities and relate to each other in a really human manner, we believe there will be no room left for the superstitions of the past, and these will gradually disappear.

You do not agree? Well, that is your right. But first of all, let us agree to combine all our forces in a mighty movement dedicated to driving the moneychangers out of the temple, or rather, out of our homes, streets and workplaces. Let us cleanse this society of all oppression, exploitation and injustice. Then we can let the future take care of itself.

CHAPTER SEVENTY-THREE

The Philosophy of the Future

Marxism is a philosophy, but it is quite unlike other philosophies. Dialectical materialism is both a powerful methodological tool to understand the workings of nature, thought and human society and a guide to action. As the young Marx put it: "philosophers have only interpreted the world in various ways – the point is, however, to change it."

Now, it may be that you are quite happy with the world in which we live, and do not wish to change it. In that case, you may find this essay educational, or at least entertaining. But you will not have understood it, basically because we will be talking mutually unintelligible languages. However, if ever there was a time when Americans should be seriously re-examining their view of the world and their place in it, that time is now. And in order to obtain a rational insight into this world an understanding of Marxist philosophy is of great importance.

The most essential feature of dialectical materialism is its dynamic character. It sees the world as an ever-changing process, driven by internal contradictions, in which sooner or later things change into their opposite. Moreover, the line of development is not a smooth, linear process, but a line that is periodically interrupted by sudden leaps, explosions that transform quantity into quality. This is an accurate picture of both processes we see in nature and in the process of social development we call history.

Most people imagine that the kind of world into which they are born is something fixed and immutable. They rarely question its values, its morality, its religion, its political and state institutions. This mental inertia, reinforced by the dead weight of tradition, customs, habit and routine, is a powerful cement that permits a given socio-economic order to continue to exist long after it has lost its rational basis. In the U.S.A., perhaps more than any other country in the world, this inertia exercises a major role and prevents people from realizing what is happening to them.

In actual fact, societies are not immutable. The whole of history teaches us that. Socio-economic systems, like individual men and women, are born, mature, reach a high point in their development, and then at a certain point enter into a phase of decline and decay. When a form of society ceases to play a progressive role (which, in the last analysis, is that point where it is unable to develop the productive forces as it did in the past), people can feel it. It manifests itself in all manner of ways – not only in the economic field. The old morality begins to break down. There is a crisis of the family and personal relations, a growing lack of solidarity and social cohesion, a rise of crime and violence. People no longer believe in the old religions and turn in the direction of mysticism, superstition and exotic sects. We have seen these things many times in history, and we are seeing the same things now – even in the U.S.A.

We are living at a time when many people have begun to ask questions about the world in which they live, and to ask questions is never a bad thing. The terrible events of September 11, 2001 have caused many Americans to think seriously about matters in which they previously showed little interest. They have suddenly realized that all is not well with the world, and that America is deeply involved in a worldwide crisis from which no one can escape, and in which no-one is safe. The destruction of the twin towers cast a dark shadow over America. For a time, Bush and the most reactionary wing of the ruling class have had things all their own way. But this situation will not last forever. Sooner or later the thick fog of propaganda and lies will dissipate and people will become aware of the real state of affairs both in the U.S.A. and on a world scale.

Although many people feel in their innermost being that something is going badly wrong, they find no logical explanation for it. That is not surprising. The entire way in which they have been taught to think from their earliest years conditions them to reject any suggestion that there is something fundamentally wrong with the society in which they live. They will close their eyes and try to avoid drawing uncomfortable conclusions for as long as they can.

This is quite natural. It is very hard for people to question the beliefs they have been brought up with. But sooner or later, events catch up with them – cataclysmic events that compel them to re-think many things that they previously took for granted. And when such a moment arrives, the same people who stubbornly refused to consider new ideas, will eagerly examine what only yesterday they regarded as heresies, and find in them the explanations and alternatives for which they were searching.

Today, Marxism is seen as such a heresy. Every hand is raised against it. It is said to have no basis, to have failed, to be out of date. But if this is really the case, then why do the apologists of capitalism still persist in attacking it? Surely, if it is so dead and irrelevant, they should just ignore it. The power of Marxist ideas is precisely that they – and they alone – can provide a coherent, rigorous, and, yes, scientific explanation of the most important phenomena of the world in which we live.

It is a matter of great regret that so many people,

especially in the U.S.A., have the same attitude towards Marxism as the representatives of the Roman Catholic Church had towards Galileo's telescope. When Galileo begged them to look with their own eyes and examine the evidence, they stubbornly refused to do so. They just "knew" that Galileo was wrong, and that was that. In the same way, many people "just know" that Marxism is wrong, and do not see any reason to investigate the matter any further. But if Marxism is wrong, by studying it, you will be more firmly convinced of its erroneousness. You have nothing to lose, and will have added to your store of knowledge. But the author of these lines is firmly convinced that if more people only took the trouble to read the original works of Marx, Engels, Lenin and Trotsky, they would soon convince themselves that Marxism really does have a lot of important things to say – and that these things are of great relevance to the modern world.

CHAPTER SEVENTY-FOUR

No More War!

After 1945 the United Nations was set up, supposedly to guarantee world peace. But today, six decades after D-Day, the world is anything but a peaceful place. One war succeeds another in one country after another, on one continent after another. In the modern epoch wars are the expression of the unbearable contradictions that flow from the capitalist system itself. The entire world is dominated by a handful of super-rich nations, which in turn are dominated by a handful of super-rich and powerful corporations and banks. The actions of these are determined – as they were always determined – by the greed for rent, interest and profit, for markets, raw materials and spheres of influence. In the Second World War, fifty-five million men, women and children perished. Millions more will perish in the coming years and decades, not just in wars and other military conflicts, but from starvation and epidemics like malaria, AIDS and simple diseases caused by the lack of clean drinking water.

The worst thing about all this is that it is objectively unnecessary. In the first decade of the 21st century, when science and technology have performed unheard-of miracles, the majority of the human race faces a grinding struggle to survive. The gap between rich and poor has widened into an abyss, and at the same time the gap between the so-called rich and poor nations has never been greater.

These facts lie behind the tensions and antagonisms that create wars, ethnic strife, terrorism, and all the other horrors that afflict our tortured and turbulent planet. As long as these central contradictions are not resolved, wars and other violent conflicts will continue to sow death and destruction. It is useless to bemoan the results of war, as moralists and pacifists do. It is necessary to diagnose the source of the illness and prescribe a cure.

At bottom, the worldwide turbulence is a reflection of the crisis of a bankrupt socio-economic system that has long ago outlived its usefulness and become a colossal brake on the development of human culture and civilization. A system that subordinates everything to the greed of a handful of super-rich barons in control of huge and irresponsible corporations can only signify endless crises, hunger, disease, misery and wars. In order that humankind might live, this outmoded system must be abolished. There is no other way forward.

In place of the anarchy of capitalist production, what is needed is a planned economy, democratically run by the working class. On that basis, it will be possible in a relatively short time to abolish hunger, homelessness, misery and illiteracy and all the other elements of barbarism that make life a hell on earth for countless millions of people. In place of the old strife and rivalry between nations it will be possible to unite the productive forces of the whole planet in a socialist commonwealth, where wars will be consigned, along with slavery, feudalism and cannibalism, to a museum of barbarous relics of the past.

CHAPTER SEVENTY-FIVE

The Sky is the Limit

The development of the productive forces in the U.S.A. over the past century has reached vertiginous heights. Industry, agriculture, science and technique have all been developed to the point where it would easily be possible to make a gigantic leap forward. The productive potential of the U.S.A. alone – if it were harnessed in a rational, democratic plan of production – would be sufficient to eradicate poverty, illiteracy and disease on a world scale.

However, here too we stumble on a dialectical contradiction. In the first decade of the 21st century, millions of people are living on the brink of starvation. A hundred million children each year are born, live and die on the streets and they do not know what it is to live in a house. And the worst thing about this is that, for the first time in history, we can say that none of this is necessary. The terrible suffering, the colossal waste of human resources, all these things could be avoided by taking relatively simple steps.

There is no real objective reason why the world in the 21st century is in the state that it is. We are not faced with some vast, incomprehensible catastrophe, the nature and causes of which we are ignorant, and which we are powerless to resolve. All the contradictions we see on a world scale are only a reflection of the impasse of the capitalist system, a system that subordinates the interests of the millions to the rapacious greed of a few.

In its day, capitalism played a revolutionary role. It freed the productive forces from all the petty restrictions imposed by feudalism. It broke down the narrow local barriers, tithes, tolls and taxes that limited the free flow of goods, and established a national market, the prior condition for the establishment of the national state.

But now the capitalist system has itself become a barrier to the free development of the productive forces. Private ownership of the means of production is now a contradiction in terms, when the means of production have become gigantic corporations that straddle the continents and own greater wealth than many national states. And the national state itself has become as much of a barrier to the free development of the productive forces as were the old local feudal restrictions in the late Middle Ages. In order to break loose from these suffocating bonds, it is necessary to abolish private ownership of the means of production and the nation state. These reactionary barriers must be swept aside if the future of human progress is to be guaranteed.

Freed from the tyranny of the profit motive and a thousand other petty restrictions that cramp the development of the productive forces, science and technology would experience an explosive growth that would transform the lives of millions in a short space of time. The pioneers who opened up the West were inspired by a new and vast horizon of possibilities. But the advent of socialism would open up still vaster horizons for human development on a global scale. What tremendous new vistas would be opened up for humanity!

In recommending the ideas of Marxism to the American public, it is my fervent hope to convince the reader of the correctness and relevance of the ideas of Marx and Engels in the world of the 21st century. If I succeed even partly in convincing you, I will be very pleased. If not, I hope to have dispelled many misconceptions about Marxism and show that it at least has some interesting things to say about the world in which we live. In any event, I hope it will make people think more critically about our society, its present and its future.

Postscript

In addition to presenting Marxist ideas to the American public, and correcting at least some of the prejudices of Americans concerning Marxism, I hope that this short account will serve to correct some of the prejudices of non-American leftists about America. Even if I have not succeeded in this intention, I hope that at least people will begin to think more seriously about these matters – on both sides.

Those who wish to continue their studies of Marxism, and more importantly join in the historic struggle for socialism, can visit the *In Defence of Marxism* website at www.marxist.com and the *Socialist Appeal* magazine of the Workers International League in the U.S. at www.socialistappeal.org. These sites provide regular Marxist analysis of current events as well as historical and economic analysis, theory, and more. The *Youth for International Socialism* website at www.newyouth.com also provides a wealth of information and educational material for those wishing to learn more about Marxism and the struggle for socialism. Join us in the struggle for a better world!

APPENDIX I

If America Should Go Communist
By Leon Trotsky

Should America go communist as a result of the difficulties and problems that your capitalist social order is unable to solve, it will discover that communism, far from being an intolerable bureaucratic tyranny and individual regimentation, will be the means of greater individual liberty and shared abundance.

At present most Americans regard communism solely in the light of the experience of the Soviet Union. They fear lest Sovietism in America would produce the same material result as it has brought for the culturally backward peoples of the Soviet Union.

They fear lest communism should try to fit them to a bed of Procrustes, and they point to the bulwark of Anglo-Saxon conservatism as an insuperable obstacle even to possibly desirable reforms. They argue that Great Britain and Japan would undertake military intervention against the American soviets. They shudder lest Americans be regimented in their habits of dress and diet, be compelled to subsist on famine rations, be forced to read stereotyped official propaganda in the newspapers, be coerced to serve as rubber stamps for decisions arrived at without their active participation or be required to keep their thoughts to themselves and loudly praise their soviet leaders in public, through fear of imprisonment and exile.

They fear monetary inflation, bureaucratic tyranny and intolerable red tape in obtaining the necessities of life. They fear soulless standardization in the arts and sciences, as well as in the daily necessities of life. They fear that all political spontaneity and the presumed freedom of the press will be destroyed by the dictatorship of a monstrous bureaucracy. And they shudder at the thought of being forced into an uncomprehended glibness in Marxist dialectic and disciplined social philosophies. They fear, in a word, that Soviet America will become the counterpart of what they have been told Soviet Russia looks like.

Actually American soviets will be as different from the Russian soviets as the United States of President Roosevelt differs from the Russian Empire of Czar Nicholas II. Yet communism can come in America only through revolution, just as independence and democracy came in America. The American temperament is energetic and violent, and it will insist on breaking a good many dishes and upsetting a good many apple carts before communism is firmly established. Americans are enthusiasts and sportsmen before they are specialists and statesmen, and it would be contrary to the American tradition to make a major change without choosing sides and cracking heads.

However, the American communist revolution will be insignificant compared to the Bolshevik Revolution in Russia, in terms of your national wealth and population, no matter how great its comparative cost. That is because civil war of a revolutionary nature isn't fought by the handful of men at the top — the 5 or 10 percent who own nine-tenths of American wealth; this handful could recruit its counterrevolutionary armies only from among the lower middle classes. Even so, the revolution could easily attract them to its banner by showing that support of the soviets alone offers them the prospect of salvation.

Everybody below this group is already economically prepared for communism. The depression has ravaged your working class and has dealt a crushing blow to the farmers, who had already been injured by the long agricultural decline of the postwar decade. There is no reason why these groups should counterpose determined resistance to the revolution; they have nothing to lose, providing, of course, that the revolutionary leaders adopt a farsighted and moderate policy toward them.

Who else will fight against communism? Your corporal's guard of billionaires and multimillionaires? Your Mellons, Morgans, Fords and Rockefellers? They will cease struggling as soon as they fail to find other people to fight for them.

The American soviet government will take firm possession of the commanding heights of your business system: the banks, the key industries and the transportation and communication systems. It will then give the farmers, the small tradespeople and businessmen a good long time to think things over and see how well the nationalized section of industry is working.

Here is where the American soviets can produce real miracles. "Technocracy" can come true only under communism, when the dead hands of private property rights and private profits are lifted from your industrial system. The most daring proposals of the Hoover commission on standardization and rationalization will seem childish compared to the new possibilities let loose by American communism.

National industry will be organized along the line of the conveyor belt in your modern continuous-production automotive factories. Scientific planning can be lifted out of the individual factory and applied to your entire economic system. The results will be stupendous.

Costs of production will be cut to 20 percent, or less, of

their present figure. This, in turn, would rapidly increase your farmers' purchasing power.

To be sure, the American soviets would establish their own gigantic farm enterprises, as schools of voluntary collectivization. Your farmers could easily calculate whether it was to their individual advantage to remain as isolated links or to join the public chain.

The same method would be used to draw small businesses and industries into the national organization of industry. By soviet control of raw materials, credits and quotas of orders, these secondary industries could be kept solvent until they were gradually and without compulsion sucked into the socialized business system.

Without compulsion! The American soviets would not need to resort to the drastic measures that circumstances have often imposed upon the Russians. In the United States, through the science of publicity and advertising, you have means for winning the support of your middle class that were beyond the reach of the soviets of backward Russia with its vast majority of pauperized and illiterate peasants. This, in addition to your technical equipment and your wealth, is the greatest asset of your coming communist revolution. Your revolution will be smoother in character than ours; you will not waste your energies and resources in costly social conflicts after the main issues have been decided; and you will move ahead so much more rapidly in consequence.

Even the intensity and devotion of religious sentiment in America will not prove an obstacle to the revolution. If one assumes the perspective of soviets in America, none of the psychological brakes will prove firm enough to retard the pressure of the social crisis. This has been demonstrated more than once in history. Besides, it should not be forgotten that the Gospels themselves contain some pretty explosive aphorisms.

As to the comparatively few opponents of the soviet revolution, one can trust to American inventive genius. It may well be that you will take your unconvinced millionaires and send them to some picturesque island, rent-free for life, where they can do as they please.

You can do this safely, for you will not need to fear foreign interventions. Japan, Great Britain and the other capitalistic countries that intervened in Russia couldn't do anything but take American communism lying down. As a matter of fact, the victory of communism in America — the stronghold of capitalism — will cause communism to spread to other countries. Japan will probably have joined the communistic ranks even before the establishment of the American soviets. The same is true of Great Britain.

In any case, it would be a crazy idea to send His Britannic Majesty's fleet against Soviet America, even as a raid against the southern and more conservative half of your continent. It would be hopeless and would never get any farther than a second-rate military escapade.

Within a few weeks or months of the establishment of the American soviets, Pan-Americanism would be a political reality.

The governments of Central and South America would be pulled into your federation like iron filings to a magnet. So would Canada. The popular movements in these countries would be so strong that they would force this great unifying process within a short period and at insignificant costs. I am ready to bet that the first anniversary of the American soviets would find the Western Hemisphere transformed into the Soviet United States of North, Central and South America, with its capital at Panama. Thus for the first time the Monroe Doctrine would have a complete and positive meaning in world affairs, although not the one foreseen by its author.

In spite of the complaints of some of your archconservatives, Roosevelt is not preparing for a soviet transformation of the United States.

The NRA aims not to destroy but to strengthen the foundations of American capitalism by overcoming your business difficulties. Not the Blue Eagle but the difficulties that the Blue Eagle is powerless to overcome will bring about communism in America. The "radical" professors of your Brain Trust are not revolutionists: they are only frightened conservatives. Your president abhors "systems" and "generalities." But a soviet government is the greatest of all possible systems, a gigantic generality in action.

The average man doesn't like systems or generalities either. It is the task of your communist statesmen to make the system deliver the concrete goods that the average man desires: his food, cigars, amusements, his freedom to choose his own neckties, his own house and his own automobile. It will be easy to give him these comforts in Soviet America.

Most Americans have been misled by the fact that in the USSR we had to build whole new basic industries from the ground up. Such a thing could not happen in America, where you are already compelled to cut down on your farm area and to reduce your industrial production. As a matter of fact, your tremendous technological equipment has been paralyzed by the crisis and already clamors to be put to use. You will be able to make a rapid step-up of consumption by your people the starting point of your economic revival.

You are prepared to do this as is no other country. Nowhere else has the study of the internal market reached such intensity as in the United States. It has been done by your banks, trusts, individual businessmen, merchants, traveling salesmen and farmers as part of their stock-in-trade. Your soviet government will simply abolish all trade secrets, will combine all the findings of these researches for individual profit and will transform them into a scientific system of economic planning. In this your government will be helped by the existence of a large class of cultured and critical consumers. By combining the nationalized key industries, your private businesses and democratic consumer cooperation, you will quickly develop a highly flexible system for serving the needs of your population.

This system will be made to work not by bureaucracy and not by policemen but by cold, hard cash.

Your almighty dollar will play a principal part in making your new soviet system work. It is a great mistake to try to mix a "planned economy" with a "managed currency." Your money must act as regulator with which to measure the success or failure of your planning.

Your "radical" professors are dead wrong in their devotion to "managed money." It is an academic idea that could easily wreck your entire system of distribution and production. That is the great lesson to be derived from the Soviet Union, where bitter necessity has been converted into official virtue in the monetary realm.

There the lack of a stable gold ruble is one of the main causes of our many economic troubles and catastrophes. It is impossible to regulate wages, prices and quality of goods without a firm monetary system. An unstable ruble in a Soviet system is like having variable molds in a conveyor-belt factory. It won't work.

Only when socialism succeeds in substituting administrative control for money will it be possible to abandon a stable gold currency. Then money will become ordinary paper slips, like trolley or theater tickets. As socialism advances, these slips will also disappear, and control over individual consumption —whether by money or administration — will no longer be necessary when there is more than enough of everything for everybody!

Such a time has not yet come, though America will certainly reach it before any other country. Until then, the only way to reach such a state of development is to retain an effective regulator and measure for the working of your system. As a matter of fact, during the first few years a planned economy needs sound money even more than did old-fashioned capitalism. The professor who regulates the monetary unit with the aim of regulating the whole business system is like the man who tried to lift both his feet off the ground at the same time.

Soviet America will possess supplies of gold big enough to stabilize the dollar — a priceless asset. In Russia we have been expanding our industrial plant by 20 and 30 percent a year; but —owing to a weak ruble —we have not been able to distribute this increase effectively. This is partly because we have allowed our bureaucracy to subject our monetary system to administrative one-sidedness. You will be spared this evil. As a result you will greatly surpass us in both increased production and distribution, leading to a rapid advance in the comfort and welfare of your population.

In all this, you will not need to imitate our standardized production for our pitiable mass consumers. We have taken over from czarist Russia a pauper's heritage, a culturally undeveloped peasantry with a low standard of living. We had to build our factories and dams at the expense of our consumers. We have had continual monetary inflation and a monstrous bureaucracy.

Soviet America will not have to imitate our bureaucratic methods. Among us the lack of the bare necessities has caused an intense scramble for an extra loaf of bread, an extra yard of cloth by everyone. In this struggle our bureaucracy steps forward as a conciliator, as an all-powerful court of arbitration. You, on the other hand, are much wealthier and would have little difficulty in supplying all of your people with all of the necessities of life. Moreover, your needs, tastes and habits would never permit your bureaucracy to divide the national income. Instead, when you organize your society to produce for human needs rather than private profits, your entire population will group itself around new trends and groups, which will struggle with one another and prevent an overweening bureaucracy from imposing itself upon them.

You can thus avoid growth of bureaucratism by the practice of soviets, that is to say, democracy — the most flexible form of government yet developed. Soviet organization cannot achieve miracles but must simply reflect the will of the people. With us the soviets have been bureaucratized as a result of the political monopoly of a single party, which has itself become a bureaucracy. This situation resulted from the exceptional difficulties of socialist pioneering in a poor and backward country.

The American soviets will be full-blooded and vigorous, without need or opportunity for such measures as circumstances imposed upon Russia. Your unregenerate capitalists will, of course, find no place for themselves in the new setup. It is hard to imagine Henry Ford as the head of the Detroit Soviet.

Yet a wide struggle between interests, groups and ideas is not only conceivable — it is inevitable. One-year, five-year, ten-year plans of business development; schemes for national education; construction of new basic lines of transportation; the transformation of the farms; the program for improving the technological and cultural equipment of Latin America; a program for stratosphere communication; eugenics — all of these will arouse controversy, vigorous electoral struggle and passionate debate in the newspapers and at public meetings.

For Soviet America will not imitate the monopoly of the press by the heads of Soviet Russia's bureaucracy. While Soviet America would nationalize all printing plants, paper mills and means of distribution, this would be a purely negative measure. It would simply mean that private capital will no longer be allowed to decide what publications should be established, whether they should be progressive or reactionary, "wet" or "dry," puritanical or pornographic. Soviet America will have to find a new solution for the question of how the power of the press is to function in a socialist regime. It might be done on the basis of proportional representation for the votes in each soviet election.

Thus the right of each group of citizens to use the power of the press would depend on their numerical strength — the same principle being applied to the use of meeting halls, allotment of time on the air and so forth.

Thus the management and policy of publications would be decided not by individual checkbooks but by group ideas. This may take little account of numerically small but important groups, but it simply means that each new idea will be compelled, as throughout history, to prove its right to existence.

Rich Soviet America can set aside vast funds for research and invention, discoveries and experiments in every field. You won't neglect your bold architects and sculptors, your unconventional poets and audacious philosophers.

In fact, the Soviet Yankees of the future will give a lead to Europe in those very fields where Europe has hitherto been your master. Europeans have little conception of the power of technology to influence human destiny and have adopted an attitude of sneering superiority toward "Americanism," particularly since the crisis. Yet Americanism marks the true dividing line between the Middle Ages and the modern world.

Hitherto America's conquest of nature has been so violent and passionate that you have had no time to modernize your philosophies or to develop your own artistic forms. Hence you have been hostile to the doctrines of Hegel, Marx and Darwin. The burning of Darwin's works by the Baptists of Tennessee is only a clumsy reflection of the American dislike for the doctrines of evolution. This attitude is not confined to your pulpits. It is still part of your general mental makeup.

Your atheists as well as your Quakers are determined rationalists. And your rationalism itself is weakened by empiricism and moralism. It has none of the merciless vitality of the great European rationalists. So your philosophic method is even more antiquated than your economic system and your political institutions.

Today, quite unprepared, you are being forced to face those social contradictions that grow up unsuspected in every society. You have conquered nature by means of the tools that your inventive genius has created, only to find that your tools have all but destroyed you. Contrary to all your hopes and desires, your unheard-of wealth has produced unheard-of misfortunes. You have discovered that social development does not follow a simple formula. Hence you have been thrust into the school of the dialectic — to stay.

There is no turning back from it to the mode of thinking and acting prevalent in the seventeenth and eighteenth centuries.

While the romantic numskulls of Nazi Germany are dreaming of restoring the old race of Europe's Dark Forest to its original purity, or rather its original filth, you Americans, after taking a firm grip on your economic machinery and your culture, will apply genuine scientific methods to the problem of eugenics. Within a century, out of your melting pot of races there will come a new breed of men — the first worthy of the name of Man.

One final prophecy: In the third year of soviet rule in America, you will no longer chew gum!

August 17, 1934

APPENDIX II

Address of the International Working Men's Association to Abraham Lincoln, President of the United States of America (Drafted by Karl Marx)

Sir:

We congratulate the American people upon your re-election by a large majority. If resistance to the Slave Power was the reserved watchword of your first election, the triumphant war cry of your re-election is Death to Slavery.

From the commencement of the titanic American strife the workingmen of Europe felt instinctively that the star-spangled banner carried the destiny of their class. The contest for the territories which opened the dire epopee, was it not to decide whether the virgin soil of immense tracts should be wedded to the labor of the emigrant or prostituted by the tramp of the slave driver?

When an oligarchy of 300,000 slaveholders dared to inscribe, for the first time in the annals of the world, "slavery" on the banner of Armed Revolt, when on the very spots where hardly a century ago the idea of one great Democratic Republic had first sprung up, whence the first Declaration of the Rights of Man was issued, and the first impulse given to the European revolution of the eighteenth century; when on those very spots counterrevolution, with systematic thoroughness, gloried in rescinding "the ideas entertained at the time of the formation of the old constitution", and maintained slavery to be "a beneficent institution", indeed, the old solution of the great problem of "the relation of capital to labor", and cynically proclaimed property in man "the cornerstone of the new edifice" — then the working classes of Europe understood at once, even before the fanatic partisanship of the upper classes for the Confederate gentry had given its dismal warning, that the slaveholders' rebellion was to sound the tocsin for a general holy crusade of property against labor, and that for the men of labor, with their hopes for the future, even their past conquests were at stake in that tremendous conflict on the other side of the Atlantic. Everywhere they bore therefore patiently the hardships imposed upon them by the cotton crisis, opposed enthusiastically the proslavery intervention of their betters — and, from most parts of Europe, contributed their quota of blood to the good cause.

While the workingmen, the true political powers of the North, allowed slavery to defile their own republic, while before the Negro, mastered and sold without his concurrence, they boasted it the highest prerogative of the white-skinned laborer to sell himself and choose his own master, they were unable to attain the true freedom of labor, or to support their European brethren in their struggle for emancipation; but this barrier to progress has been swept off by the red sea of civil war.

The workingmen of Europe feel sure that, as the American War of Independence initiated a new era of ascendancy for the middle class, so the American Antislavery War will do for the working classes. They consider it an earnest of the epoch to come that it fell to the lot of Abraham Lincoln, the single-minded son of the working class, to lead his country through the matchless struggle for the rescue of an enchained race and the reconstruction of a social world.

Signed on behalf of the International Workingmen's Association, the Central Council. (Presented to U.S. Ambassador Charles Francis Adams January 28, 1865)